Praise for

The Politically Incorrect Guide® to
Jihad

"The Islamic jihad is advancing worldwide with greater impunity and aggressiveness than it has displayed for centuries; meanwhile, Western political leaders deny and downplay its nature and magnitude, and aid and abet its advance with short-sighted and ultimately suicidal policies regarding Muslim immigration and a host of other issues. In contrast to their denial and dissimulation, *The Politically Incorrect Guide® to Jihad* is a bracing dose of the truth. We have to know the reality of the present situation in order to formulate realistic policies to meet the jihadist challenge; for that, this book is an indispensable guide."

> —Robert Spencer, author of the *New York Times* bestsellers *The Politically Incorrect Guide® to Islam (and the Crusades)* and *The Truth About Muhammad*

"*The Politically Incorrect Guide® to Jihad* brings us face to face with truths concealed by the politically correct falsehoods that are standing in the way of defeating jihad."

> —Nonie Darwish, author of *Now They Call Me Infidel* and *Wholly Different: Islamic Values vs. Biblical Values*

"The very language we use to discuss the jihad directed against America and the West is a lie that is structured to keep us from being able to accurately define it. You cannot defeat an enemy you will not define. William Kilpatrick's *Politically Incorrect Guide® to Jihad* not only accurately defines the jihad threat, but also shows how to defeat it. As such, the *Politically*

Incorrect Guide® to Jihad is a highly recommended read for those looking to come to grips with one of the greatest threats of our time."

—Major Stephen Coughlin, author of *Catastrophic Failure: Blindfolding America in the Face of Jihad*

"Articulate and insightful as always, William Kilpatrick has documented the resurgence of Islamic jihad in our times; why it is being denied or ignored by many in the West; and—most importantly—the military, economic, and ideological steps that need to be taken to counter it. Get and read this critically timely book, and spread its message."

—Raymond Ibrahim, author of *Crucified Again: Exposing Islam's New War on Christians*

The Politically Incorrect Guide® to Jihad

Be sure to check out

The Politically Incorrect Guides® to...

American History
Thomas Woods
9780895260475

The Bible
Robert J. Hutchinson
9781596985209

The British Empire
H. W. Crocker III
9781596986299

Capitalism
Robert P. Murphy
9781596985049

Catholicism
John Zmirak
9781621575863

The Civil War
H. W. Crocker III
9781596985490

The Constitution
Kevin R. C. Gutzman
9781596985056

**Darwinism and
Intelligent Design**
Jonathan Wells
9781596980136

**English and
American Literature**
Elizabeth Kantor
9781596980112

The Founding Fathers
Brion McClanahan
9781596980921

Global Warming
Christopher C. Horner
9781596985018

**The Great Depression
and the New Deal**
Robert Murphy
9781596980969

Hunting
Frank Miniter
9781596985216

Islam (And the Crusades)
Robert Spencer
9780895260130

The Middle East
Martin Sieff
9781596980518

The Presidents, Part 1
Larry Schweikart
9781621575245

The Presidents, Part 2
Steven F. Hayward
9781621575795

Real American Heroes
Brion McClanahan
9781596983205

Science
Tom Bethell
9780895260314

The Sixties
Jonathan Leaf
9781596985728

Socialism
Kevin D. Williamson
9781596986497

**The South
(And Why It Will Rise Again)**
Clint Johnson
9781596985001

The Vietnam War
Phillip Jennings
9781596985674

Western Civilization
Anthony Esolen
9781596980594

Women, Sex, and Feminism
Carrie L. Lukas
9781596980037

The Politically Incorrect Guide® to
Jihad

William Kilpatrick

REGNERY
PUBLISHING
A Division of Salem Media Group

Material in this book was adapted from articles that originally appeared in *Crisis Magazine*, *Catholic World Report*, *National Catholic Register*, *FrontPage Magazine*, and *Legatus*, and is reprinted here with permission.

Regnery® and Politically Incorrect Guide® are registered trademarks of Salem Communications Holding Corporation

Cataloging-in-Publication data on file with the Library of Congress

ISBN 978-1-62157-577-1

Published in the United States by
Regnery Publishing
A Division of Salem Media Group
300 New Jersey Ave NW
Washington, DC 20001
www.Regnery.com

Manufactured in the United States of America

10 9 8 7 6 5 4 3 2 1

Books are available in quantity for promotional or premium use. For information on discounts and terms, please visit our website: www.Regnery.com.

Distributed to the trade by
Perseus Distribution
250 West 57th Street
New York, NY 10107

To the victims of jihad and to the brave souls who resist it

Contents

Introduction   The Untold Story of Our Time   **1**

PART I
Jihad Is Back

CHAPTER 1   The Resurgence of Jihad in the Twenty-First Century   **11**

     Welcome Back to the Past   11

     The Jihad Is Closer than You Think   14

     Don't Know Much about History   16

     Europe Will Go First   17

     Islamophobia-phobia   19

     George Orwell's England   20

     If You See Something, Keep Your Mouth Shut   21

     The Body Count   23

     Living in the Muslim World—and in Fear   24

CHAPTER 2   Are ISIS and Boko Haram Un-Islamic?   **27**

     Pretext or Motivating Principle?   30

     Un-Islamic Acts?   35

CHAPTER 3   The Roots of Jihad   **39**

     Muhammad: The Perfect Man Models Jihad   39

     The Koran: Allah Commands Jihad   44

     One Weird Trick   46

     A Religious Obligation   54

     Why Most Muslims Are Peaceful   56

CHAPTER 4   What's in a Name? What Jihad Really Means   **61**

     Is Jihad Really about Poverty and Discrimination?   62

     But They Were Provoked!   65

     Do I Have to Draw You a Picture?   66

     What Jihad Is For   71

     Europe's Waterslide into Dhimmitude   75

     A Dangerous Ally?   79

PART II
Jihad Without Bombs

CHAPTER 5	**The Quiet Kind of Jihad**	**89**
	Jihad in Sheep's Clothing	89
	Stealth Jihad Meets PC America	94
	It's in the Army Now	104
	Blindfolded America	109
CHAPTER 6	**Immigration and the "Baby Jihad"**	**115**
	Immigration or Invasion?	117
	No-Go Zones of the Mind	122
	Anti-Semitism Makes a Comeback	126
	The "Baby Jihad"	130
	Believe in Nothing and You'll Fall for Anything	135
CHAPTER 7	**Western Enablers of Jihad**	**139**
	It's All Relative	140
	Western Governments: Enforcing Appeasement	143
	The Police: Taking the Wrong Side in the Clash of Civilizations	148
	Even in America: Go to Jail, Go Directly to Jail	151
	Attack of the Pod People	153
CHAPTER 8	**Information Wars**	**159**
	Political Correctness in La La Land	166
	The Media: Hiding the Real Threat	169
CHAPTER 9	**Christian Enablers of Jihad**	**177**
	Preemptive Surrender	178
	The Mosque of Jesus, Son of Mary	181
	Are Muslims the "Natural Allies" of Christians?	184
	Not the Same Jesus	187
	Is There Such a Thing as a Bad Religion?	193
	Was Muhammad a False Prophet?	195
	Who You Gonna Believe, Me or Your Lying Eyes?	199

PART III
Defeating Jihad

CHAPTER 10   Strategies for Victory   **205**

The "Vast Majority" Myth   206

"Not Currently Killing Others" Is a Poor

Gauge of Moderation   210

Want to Win the Propaganda War? Win the Shooting War   213

Crushing Their Dreams   215

Strategies to Defeat Jihad   217

CHAPTER 11   Psychological, Spiritual, and Ideological Warfare   **229**

The Information Wars   231

An Ideological House of Cards   236

The Real Jesus   239

Beating Them at Their Own Game   241

Acknowledgments   **249**

Notes   **251**

Index   **297**

The Untold Story
of Our Time

The resurgence of Islam is the biggest story of our time. And the primary means by which Islam expands is *jihad*. Yet few people understand jihad because a politically correct fog has shrouded the topic from honest discussion. That makes the story of Islamic jihad not only a big story, but also one that's never fully been told.

Thus, many in the West still labor under the delusion that jihad is an interior spiritual struggle. Many more have swallowed the establishment line that jihad violence has nothing to do with Islam. Still others cling to the notion that our real enemy is not Islamic jihad but a mysterious global outbreak of "violent extremism."

The politically correct portrayal of jihad has lulled the Western world into complacency and left it unprepared for the rapid advance of militant Islamic groups such as ISIS, Boko Haram, and Al-Shabaab. Poorly informed Western citizens were likewise unprepared for the sudden proliferation of lone wolf jihadists.

Equally important, few are aware that another form of jihad—stealth jihad—can disable our cultural defenses from within while simultaneously providing an environment in which homegrown terrorists can flourish.

Jihad today is particularly insidious because much of it is being fought as a culture war. While focusing on the hot war of battlefield jihad, we tend to ignore the cold war of stealth, or cultural jihad. Yet, at least in the West, it is the main front. And, ironically, the stealth jihadists have built on the victories of the secular and leftist culture warriors. For example, they benefit from the rules of political correctness laid down by their counterparts on the left. Thus, any attempt at analyzing or explaining Islam from a non-Islamic perspective is met with cries of "bigotry" and "Islamophobia."

Jihad is not just hooded terrorists brandishing AK-47s, ready to kill and die for Allah. True, rampant persecution of Christians and other minorities in the Middle East and parts of Africa has reached a level of butchery seldom seen in history. But if you're only paying attention to the headlines about beheadings and sex slavery in Iraq and Syria, you may be missing the larger picture. Sometimes, major changes are best captured in stories that don't make waves. It's a good bet you haven't heard that Sweden now has the second highest incidence of rape in the world, behind only Lesotho—after accepting more than a hundred thousand Muslim immigrants into its population of less than ten million. To be fair, most Swedes won't find that item in their newspapers either. They know what's happening through word of mouth, but the media don't want to acknowledge that Sweden's experiment in multiculturalism has failed.[1]

In other words, the problem we face is much greater than ISIS. The Islamic State and similar groups are only the sharp tip of a very large iceberg called Islam. We're not supposed to say that, of course. We are told that Islam is a religion of peace.[2] And everyone from prime ministers to prime time journalists assures us that violent jihad has nothing to do with Islam.

One of the chief aims of the Islamist culture warriors is to convince us that we must not draw any connection between violent jihad and Islam, and they have been remarkably successful in doing so. It now appears that the Bush administration was the victim of just such an influence operation by the Saudis and the Muslim Brotherhood.[3] The "tiny minority of extremists," we were assured, had nothing to do with Islam, because, as President Bush took pains to instruct us on numerous occasions, "Islam" means "peace."[4] And if President Bush was taken in, the Obama administration seems to have been all in from the start. Cultural jihadists have been appointed to important government positions, and stealth jihad organizations such as the Council on American-Islamic Relations (CAIR), the Islamic Society of North America (ISNA), and the Muslim American Society (MAS) have been given virtual veto power over national security initiatives.[5]

In response to the black flag of jihad, the government and media elites of the Western world have raised the white flag of political correctness and appeasement. Although the history of Islam and the history of jihad are intertwined, the mainstream opinion-makers have decided it's better that you don't know. Their hope is that by making soothing sounds about Islam we can appease angry Muslims and convince the others to adopt a more moderate form of Islam.

But Islam is not inherently a moderate religion. ISIS, al-Qaeda, and Boko Haram are heirs of a tradition that goes all the way back to Muhammad. That's not to say that every Muslim is a terrorist-in-waiting. Fortunately, a great many Muslims ignore the harsher mandates of their faith. Islam itself, however, was founded in militancy and spread by violence. The jihad is on the rise again, but that's only because traditional Islam—the Islam of Muhammad—is undergoing a resurgence.

The politically correct crowd likes to say that ISIS and similar groups are un-Islamic.[6] But if jihad, sex slavery, and beheadings are un-Islamic, then Muhammad himself was un-Islamic. The *sira (Life of Muhammad)* is mostly devoted to descriptions of raids, battles, distribution of booty, slave trading—and, yes, beheadings. One suspects that Muhammad would have felt quite at home among today's jihad warriors.

The black flag that ISIS and other jihadis fly is itself a testimony to the Islamic nature of the terrorist organizations. One might expect that the white inscription on it says something to the effect of "Kill all you meet." But what it actually says is, "There is no God but God, and Muhammad is the messenger of God." If you're a Muslim, that's non-controversial. Those are the words of the *shahada*—the Islamic profession of faith. Recitation of the shahada is the first of the "Five Pillars of Islam," and it is the main component of the five-times-daily call to prayer. Typically the words of the shahada are the first words a newborn Muslim child hears whispered into his ears. As for the now-familiar phrase "Allahu akbar," that too is part of the daily routine. A devout Muslim who says his prayers faithfully will repeat the words twenty-five times per day, every day. "Allahu akbar" means "God is greater" (or "greatest"). Translated into the language of youth it means, "My God can beat up your God." This is the appeal of Islam to young men and it helps to explain why groups such as ISIS have no trouble finding recruits. Young men like to be on the winning side. They decidedly do not like being losers. Interestingly, the Koran describes those who end up in hell precisely as "losers" (10:45, 16:109, 29:52).[7]

The big picture is that Islam is a militant political religion. It's meant to be spread—and by force if necessary. Very often, however, force is not necessary. Stealth jihad—the slow, steady incremental spread of Islam through infiltration of social and cultural institutions such as media, schools, courts, local and state governments, and even churches—is perhaps even more effective in advancing Islam.

When the local school board installs an Islam-friendly curriculum rather than argue with Muslim parents or irate imams, that's a victory for the stealth jihad. When the local beach requires Islamically appropriate clothes, it's a good bet that the stealth jihadists—most likely dressed in business suits—have paid a visit. More insidiously, when Muslim Brotherhood sympathizers are appointed to high positions in the State Department,[8] the

Pentagon,[9] and the Department of Homeland Security,[10] you know you're in trouble. Except that you probably don't know about it. And even if you did, you'd realize that talking about it would bring charges of racism and "Islamophobia."[11] Best not to notice.

The stealth activists have the same goals as the armed jihadists, but they use different methods. What makes stealth jihad particularly difficult to criticize is that it sails under the flag of religion. Islam's culture warriors claim to represent authentic, peaceful Islam, and, because they know it will make you happy, they are happy to condemn armed jihadists as misunderstanders of the faith.[12]

The terrorists understand their faith well enough, but the stealth jihadists can count on most Americans not to understand it. They realize that the average American is uncertain about even the most basic questions concerning Islam. Thus, it is still commonly believed that a religion founded by a warlord (who remained a warlord till his dying day) is a religion of peace.

Moreover, both the Muslim brothers in the trenches and the Brooks Brothers jihadists in their offices are protected by the rules of political correctness. You can say that the former are a brutal bunch, but you can't say that their activities have anything to do with their religion. As for the latter, if you criticize them, you are guilty of "intolerance" and "insensitivity" toward their faith. Or perhaps you have caught the dreaded disease "Islamophobia," in which case you may be put on the extremist watch list maintained by the Southern Poverty Law Center.[13] You may think this very silly, but the people who matter in society—who can fire you, haul you into court, and tarnish your reputation—take it very seriously.

So also, ironically, do the churches. Many Christian leaders—who should understand Islam best—are caught in the same PC bind as the social and media elites. In their case, the rules of multicultural politeness require that they think well of all religions. They're primed to do that anyway. Since Islam shares common elements with the Jewish and Christian faiths, many assume that it must be a basically peaceful faith. Of course, everyone can see that ISIS is not peaceful, but they are quite willing to accept the propaganda that ISIS doesn't represent Islam.

Our leaders have failed to come to grips with the reality of Islam. Many of them are guilty of wishful thinking. They want to believe that the Islamic faith is just like ours. And if Muslim terrorists occasionally blow up a church or a marketplace, well, that is easily explained. For the optimistically inclined, it only proves that every religion has its own extremists and fundamentalists. As a result of this Pollyanna-ish outlook, many of us are badly informed about Islam and thus ill-prepared to cope with what is coming at us with increasing speed. And many have a bad case of "Islamophobia-phobia"—a word I coined to describe those whose greatest fear is to be thought intolerant of Islam.

Christians, in particular—all Christians—are threatened by the rise of Islam. Christians in the Middle East and Africa are being slaughtered in the name of Allah. Yet many in the West seem to think that the proper response to this genocide is to invite Muslims (usually representatives of stealth jihad organizations) to dialogue in genteel fashion about "shared beliefs." Others think that the answer to the Islamic threat is to double down on the boycott of Israel which, they have convinced themselves, is the cause of every global problem. Still others have yet to understand the magnitude of the threat, preferring instead to concentrate on global warming or other hypothetical calamities. To paraphrase Canadian author Mark Steyn, they are fiddling with the climate change thermostat while Christians are burning.[14]

He, in turn, was paraphrasing "fiddling while Rome burns." Apropos of that, in January 2015 the Islamic State issued an e-book entitled *Black Flags from Rome*—one of a series detailing their plans for world conquest, region by region.[15] That same month I published an essay entitled "Will a Future Pope Be Forced to Flee Rome?"[16] That may have been a bit optimistic on my part. The way things are looking now, it could very well be the present pope who will need to relocate.

Too alarmist? If you think of attacking armies, that may be so. But the Islamic State's plan for conquering Rome (and all of Europe) relies heavily on infiltration and immigration. In their estimate, demographics will do the job that past Muslim armies were unable to accomplish. Not too long ago, a representative of the Islamic State in Libya said that they would flood Europe with 500,000 refugees.[17] In fact that has already happened—in the space of about twelve weeks. True, the majority of them are economic migrants. But they will join the tens of millions of Muslim immigrants who have already moved to Europe, and, if recent history is any guide, they will not bother to assimilate. European optimists say that the newcomers will contribute much to the culture of Europe. Whether or not that's so, they will contribute disproportionately to its population growth.[18]

The most popular name for baby boys in England and many European cities is "Muhammad."[19] In Vienna, Birmingham, and other major cities, there are already more Muslim children than Christian children.[20] In other words, things are happening fast—things that practically no one envisioned a mere ten years ago.

In a book by Ernest Hemingway, one character asks another how he went bankrupt. The answer? "Two ways, gradually and then suddenly."[21] Where are we on the gradually-suddenly continuum? To ask the question is to realize that it's not really a continuum at all. First, you're going gradually downhill and then suddenly you find yourself dropping off the cliff. The problems that now beset Europe, the Middle East, Africa, and parts of Asia and North America have been building for years. It appears that these areas are now entering the "suddenly" time zone.

If there's one thing I hope you take away from this book, it's a sense of urgency. Jihad can be defeated, but time is short. If we don't, we'll find ourselves living in dhimmitude.

If you don't know what *that* is, don't worry. It's not a difficult concept to grasp. It is, however, a hard system under which to live, as we'll see in chapter four. The best reason to know about dhimmitude is to ensure that it never happens to you or your family.

Misinterpreting jihad can turn out to be a fatal mistake. *The Politically Incorrect Guide to Jihad* aims to dispel the disinformation and provide the accurate knowledge about jihad that is necessary to confront it and defeat it. The book will explore a range of timely issues. What are the Islamic roots of jihad? Is jihad caused by poverty and oppression? What is the "baby jihad"? Will jihadists gain access to nuclear weapons?

In addition to discussing the full range of jihad threats, the *PIG to Jihad* will provide an in-depth look at the steps that need to be taken to eliminate jihad. Because the jihad threat is multi-faceted, it needs to be fought on several different fronts—military, economic, and ideological. Jihad can be defeated, but only if we are willing to move beyond the politically correct falsehoods that currently handicap us.

The biggest story never told—the story about the magnitude of Islamic jihad and the motivation behind it—needs to be told. And soon. Islam has endured long periods of quiescence. But when it moves, it can move with surprising speed—as it did in the middle of the seventh century, when jihad warriors overran the Middle East and conquered much of North Africa. Given the relative lack of resistance to armed jihad and, especially, to cultural jihad, followers of the prophet have good reason to believe that this may be one of those times. And those of us who don't want our children and grandchildren to be followers of the prophet had better arm ourselves for the fight.

PART I

Jihad Is Back

CHAPTER 1

The Resurgence of Jihad in the Twenty-First Century

I once saw a trailer for a new *RoboCop* movie. "Meet the Future," said the accompanying caption. If the trailer was to be believed, the future will be a high-tech world where police don futuristic armor and ride futuristic motorcycles.

The idea that the future will be like nothing we've ever experienced before is a staple of science fiction. But here in the non-fiction world, it's beginning to look like "meet the past" is the more likely scenario for our future.

Welcome Back to the Past

In large swaths of the world, the past has already arrived. Take the recent interview on Egyptian TV in which a thoughtful, bespectacled, white-bearded cleric explained the proper way to beat your wife. According to the cleric, who looks for all the world like a wizard from the set of *The Lord of the Rings*, there is a "beating etiquette": "don't break her teeth, don't poke her in the eye," and beat her "no more than ten times" (whether monthly, weekly, or daily was not specified).[1]

Did you know?

★ More Americans were killed in the 9/11 attacks than at Pearl Harbor

★ Jihadis have been much more successful than the Nazis at infiltrating America

★ Turkey, formerly the model secular Islamic nation, is now run by a rabidly anti-Semitic Muslim Brotherhood true believer

Along with proper wife-beating, polio and pirates are also making a comeback. Polio is reappearing because the health workers in Pakistan and Nigeria who administer the vaccine are being killed off by strict constructionists of Islamic sharia law, who believe that vaccinations are un-Islamic (or else an American plot to sterilize Muslim children).[2] This is not simply a Third World problem. In Scotland last year, a large-scale public vaccination campaign was shut down following complaints from Muslim families.[3]

Piracy, which most of us had assumed was safely confined to Davy Jones's Locker, has also resurfaced. If you live near the coast of Somalia, it's a profitable way to make a living, or was, anyway, until the shipping companies began to institute stringent anti-piracy measures. In the heyday of Somali piracy (that is to say, about four years ago), the pirates were capturing cargo ships and oil tankers of a size which would have made Blackbeard turn green with envy.[4]

More ominous signs of the past's re-emergence are everywhere. According to numerous reports, the World Cup stadium in Qatar and its surrounding infrastructure are being built by what amounts to slave labor.[5] Nine hundred migrant laborers have already died from being forced to work in the 122-degree heat. Meanwhile, stories of sex slavery have become a feature of the daily news.[6] Again, this is not just a Third World phenomenon. A recent comprehensive study in the UK reveals that Muslim gangs have been sexually exploiting British children on a large scale for more than two decades. By one estimate, at least ten thousand girls, most of them between the ages of eleven and sixteen, are kept as virtual sex slaves at any one time.[7]

Stoning for adultery? Amputation for theft? Death for apostasy? All these supposed relics of the past have arisen from their graves like Dracula at twilight. Perhaps the most disturbing intrusion of the past into the present is the revival of decapitation. After taking the city of Mosul, ISIS fighters proceeded to behead captured soldiers and policemen on a mass scale.[8] The Internet, that iconic modern invention, now carries photos of Islamic warriors posing with their severed-head trophies.

The future is beginning to look like the distant past. But how did we let ourselves get blindsided by the return of ancient barbarism?

To understand that, you have to step back and take a look at the big picture, which can get lost in the news cycle. It's hard to keep up with the stories about Islamic violence. One week, the focus is on Boko Haram kidnapping girls in Nigeria, then on ISIS atrocities, then on Palestinians stabbing Israelis. Major terror attacks occur every year or so—9/11; train bombings in London, Madrid, and Mumbai; the mall massacre in Nairobi; the Boston Marathon bombing; murders of cartoonists and then concert-goers in Paris and of travelers at an airport in Brussels. But the overarching trend is the resurgence of jihad.

Never mind the daily slaughter of Christians by Islamic jihadists in Africa and the Middle East, let's just list just some of the more conspicuous examples of jihadist attacks on transportation systems in recent years:

- On March 1, 2014, a group of knife-wielding Islamic terrorists burst into the Kunming train station in Southern China, killing thirty people and injuring more than one hundred[9]
- In December 2013, an Islamic jihadist group claimed responsibility for twin suicide bombing attacks in Volgograd—one at a railroad station, the other aboard a trolley—which resulted in at least thirty-four deaths[10]
- On March 29, 2010, two stations of the Moscow Metro System were bombed by Islamic terrorists, leaving thirty-nine dead[11]
- More than 180 people were killed and 700 injured in Mumbai in July 2006, when Muslim terrorists attacked the train system[12]
- On July 7, 2005, fifty-two were killed and over 700 injured in coordinated attacks by Islamic jihadists against London's public transport system[13]

- A 2004 attack on Madrid's train system by Muslim terrorists left nearly 200 dead and 1,800 wounded[14]
- On September 11, 2001, Muslim terrorists hijacked four separate jet liners in a suicide mission that killed nearly 3,000 American citizens[15]

The past is catching up with the present. Even modern transportation can't escape the advance of barbarism. Other signs of re-primitivization are everywhere. Up until recently, the colloquialism "heads will roll" referred to a threat to fire employees. Nowadays, however, that phrase is more likely to evoke its original literal meaning—as in the beheadings that have become a common feature of the daily news cycle. The streets of ISIS-controlled cities are reportedly lined with the severed heads of police and soldiers—victims of the ISIS jihadists.[16] Those who thought that decapitation went out with the French Revolution have come in for a rude awakening.

It's disturbing to realize that such things can happen in this day and age, but we in America tend to console ourselves with the reassuring thought that, thank God, it can't happen here. Or can it?

★ ★ ★
Back-to-the-Past Alert

In October 2015, the terrorist bombing of a Russian jet over the Sinai killed all 224 passengers on board. If such attacks continue, air travel will become a risky proposition—about as unpredictable as a sea voyage in the sixteenth century. If jihadists continue to extend their reach, the concept of "friendly skies" will someday be a distant memory.

The Jihad Is Closer than You Think

To most Americans, jihad still seems far away—something for Syrians and Iraqis to worry about, but not us. Although the jihadists have a good supply of captured tanks, rocket launchers, and even anti-aircraft systems, they have nothing to match the military might that Nazis and Japanese possessed in World War II. So why worry?

Well, for starters, the jihadists have shown an ability to infiltrate and attack the American homeland that our former enemies never acquired. More Americans were killed in the 9/11 attacks than at Pearl Harbor. Since then, we have been witnesses to a long string of attacks, including the Beltway sniper shootings, the Fort Hood massacre, the Boston Marathon bombing, the attack on the Marine recruitment center in Chattanooga, and the San Bernardino mass shooting. That's not to mention the many bungled attacks—such as the failed attempts to explode airliners by "underwear bomber" Umar Farouk Abdul-mutallab and "shoe bomber" Richard Reid, and the car bomb that fizzled out in Times Square.

What's more, the Nazis and the Japanese never possessed nuclear weapons, but the Pakistanis do, the Iranians soon will, and al-Qaeda and ISIS are busy trying to acquire nukes of the portable variety on the black market.[17] Difficult as it may be to imagine, the next 9/11 could be a nuclear event.

Even if we manage to avoid a nuclear holocaust, the threat to Western civilization and Christianity remains. The jihadists' genocide against Christians and other non-Muslims in the Middle East is proceeding apace, and they have frequently expressed a desire to conquer both Rome[18] and America.

While many are now willing to admit that jihadists can damage our society through terrorist attacks, few can imagine the possibility of an actually Islamized America. The threatened jihadi conquest of Europe, let alone America, may seem ridiculously remote. But, then, major historical events are rarely anticipated. Americans didn't foresee the attack on Pearl Harbor

Something to Look Forward To

"Very soon, Allah willing, Rome will be conquered, just like Constantinople was, as was prophesized by our Prophet Muhammad."

—Yunis al-Astal, a Palestinian MP and an imam, in a Friday sermon in 2008

in 1941 or the attacks on New York and Washington in 2001 (even though Islamists had attempted to topple the World Trade Center only eight years before). Major shifts in historical trends are even harder to discern, and they are very rarely recognized as such by those who live through them. It is only in looking back that we understand that an old age has ended and a new one begun. Historical turning points are more like arcs than hairpin curves. The current arc of history seems to be drawing us back into a very dark past—a time when Islam ruled half the civilized world and threatened the rest of it. The Iranian Revolution of 1979, 9/11, and the Arab Spring are points along the curve.

The Muslim nations are rapidly changing. One reason that the West was so unprepared for the reappearance of traditional Islam as a world force is that, up until relatively recent times, most of the major Muslim nations were under the control of secular-minded strongmen who made a point of suppressing the full expression of Islam. The 1979 Iranian Revolution changed all that, and over time most of the Westernized secular strongmen were replaced by leaders who answered only to Allah. For example, Turkey, which for years was touted by Westerners as a model moderate Muslim society, is now run by a rabidly anti-Semitic Muslim Brotherhood true believer who seems intent on making Turkey the world's foremost Islamic power[19]—as it was as recently as one hundred short years ago.

Don't Know Much about History

Thanks to pressure from our politically correct media and government elites, however, the majority of Western citizens seem unable or unwilling to connect the dots and see the pattern. Moreover, the ability to recognize a great historical shift requires a certain familiarity with history, something that has fallen out of favor in our schools—particularly the unpleasant bits about the Islamic conquests of the past.

Absent historical knowledge, and thus absent the ability to make sense of current events, it is quite possible that our civilization will slip silently into a new Dark Ages. As Mark Steyn puts it, "Much of what we loosely call the Western world will not survive the twenty-first century, and much of it will effectively disappear within our lifetimes."[20]

What he predicts is not inevitable. But, given the fifth column that already exists in the West, it is quite possible. The signs are everywhere. Particularly in Europe.

> ★ ★ ★
> ## Doomed to Repeat It
> When the history of the West's encounters with Islam is dealt with at all in our schools today, it is presented largely from the Islamic point of view. According to the textbooks, Islam didn't conquer neighboring lands, it merely *spread* into them. And Islamic Spain was a multicultural paradise. The reason Johnny can't read the writing on the wall is that it's been covered over with whitewash.

Europe Will Go First

There are major signposts, such as the recent murders in Paris and Brussels. But numerous smaller signs may, cumulatively, be much more significant— the Muslim rape epidemics (enabled by government neglect, collusion, and cover-ups) sweeping England[21] and Sweden;[22] the no-go zones in Paris, London,[23] and Brussels;[24] and the 10,000-strong Muslim prayer-protest rally outside the Cathedral of Milan.[25]

In *The Force of Reason*, the courageous Italian journalist Oriana Fallaci wrote, "Europe becomes more and more a province of Islam, a colony of Islam.... In each of our cities there is a second city...a Muslim city, a city ruled by the Qu'ran."[26] In a telling sign of which way the wind is blowing, Fallaci voluntarily chose exile from Europe in 2005 rather than face a prison term for the crime of insulting Islam.[27]

Which brings us to the threat within. The jihadists could never have come as close as they are to accomplishing their goals without significant acquiescence on the part of many Westerners. Besides Fallaci, a number of

★ ★ ★

Where Will the Pope Live When Rome Falls to Islam?

It's not an idle question. For one thing, there is historical precedent. Popes have been forced from Rome in the past. For another thing, numerous Islamic authorities have explicitly targeted Rome for conquest.[28]

Rome may be the Eternal City, but it has seen rough times. In 846, for instance, Pope Leo IV had to briefly flee Rome when it was attacked by an Arab fleet. The following year, he ordered the construction of a great wall around the Vatican to protect it from marauding Muslims. Even as recently as the 1940s, Rome was occupied by a foreign army. Although the Nazis left the pope alone, there is no guarantee that that situation would have continued had the Germans been able to keep the Allied forces at bay.

If Rome falls to Islam, the pope—whoever he may be at that time—may choose to remain in Rome and suffer the almost certain martyrdom that would follow. That is up to him and the Holy Spirit. However, in light of the escalating Islamization of Europe, it would seem prudent for Vatican officials to draw up some contingency plans. If the pope chooses exile, it would probably have to be in North or South America, since it's unlikely there will be any safe havens in Europe. In fact, Italy is currently a safer place than many other European nations. Although many Muslim immigrants pass through Italy, it is not their first choice of residence. Other European countries offer much more generous welfare incentives than does Italy. Countries such as England, Belgium, France, Sweden, and Germany are likely to succumb to the jihad first.

other Western citizens have been hauled into courts in an attempt to silence their criticisms of Islam. These include Geert Wilders, a member of the Dutch Parliament, Lars Hedegaard, the president of the Danish Free Speech Society, and Mark Steyn, a syndicated Canadian columnist. Who needs sharia courts when European and Canadian courts will do the job for them? And what need is there for stealth jihadists when the media will gladly slant the news to fit the Islamist narrative? Whether through naiveté or out of hatred of the Western and Christian traditions, many Europeans and Americans seem willing to cooperate in the undoing of their own societies.

Aided and abetted by those fifth columnists, Islamization is already occurring in Europe. And many of the same conditions that make it possible there make it possible here, as well.

Islamophobia-phobia

One of the conditions enabling the jihadists' takeover attempts is what I call "Islamophobia-phobia"—fear of criticizing anything Islamic. From State Department officials, to op-ed writers, to Christian clerics terrified of anything that might cause the "interfaith dialogue" to break down, opinion-makers in Western countries exhibit a pathological refusal to see the jihad threat for what it is.

Fear of being thought Islamophobic has resulted in a kind of societal paralysis in the face of evil. An appalling example of this paralysis is the fact that, over the course of fifteen years, 1,400 girls in the English city of Rotherham were "groomed," drugged, raped, and traded by Pakistani gangs while police, city authorities, and child protection agencies looked the other way.[29]

Why did they turn a blind eye? In a word, "Islamophobia-phobia." They were afraid of being thought Islamophobic. The authorities certainly knew what was happening. The rape gang members would drive up to the children's homes run by the child protection agencies, select the ones they wanted, and drive off with them. According to the official inquiry report, police, council officers, and child protection officers feared they would be accused of "racism" and "Islamophobia" if they focused on crimes committed by Pakistanis.[30]

★ ★ ★

Islamophobia-phobia Kills

After forty-nine Americans died in the Orlando shooting on June 12, 2016, it emerged that the shooter's coworkers had alerted the authorities to his suspicious behavior. But, the FBI told reporters, they closed the investigation after he blamed the coworkers for "marginaliz[ing]" him "because of his Muslim faith."[31] As John Schindler, an expert on terrorism who served as an analyst for the National Security Administration, explained, "In 2009, the administration banned politically loaded words like 'jihad' even in classified Intelligence Community assessments discussing terrorism—a message that was received loud and clear in the counterterrorism community. Missing the next 9/11 could be survived, career-wise, while accusations of Islamophobia would not be…."[32]

George Orwell's England

Isn't the protection of children a more important value than the protection of an abstraction such as "diversity" or "multiculturalism"? Apparently not when your livelihood and reputation are on the line. The people who knew about the crimes were fully aware that in today's Orwellian England, an accusation of racism or Islamophobia could bring ostracism and an end to their careers.

It wasn't fear of Islam that ruined the lives of 1,400 children in Rotherham, it was fear of offending the guardians of political correctness and multicultural etiquette. As Islam expert Robert Spencer points out, an alliance of British leftists and Islamic supremacists had created a true climate of fear in the UK: "The Muslim rape gangs went unreported, unprosecuted, and in general unstopped because of far-left organizations like Hope Not Hate, Faith Matters, and Tell Mama, which raged relentless war against anyone and everyone who spoke about these issues. They demonized as 'Islamophobic,' 'hateful,' and 'bigoted' anyone who said that there were Muslim rape gangs at all, and that they had to be stopped."[33]

If You See Something, Keep Your Mouth Shut

The climate of fear that made the Rotherham tragedy possible also exists here. American law enforcement agents already know that they must tread lightly around the sensibilities of Muslims. The average citizen knows it as well. The people who do speak out about appeasement of Islamist demands soon find themselves the targets of well-organized smear campaigns. The Southern Poverty Law Center automatically labels all counter-jihad organizations as "hate" groups,[35] and the leftist Center for American Progress, which is funded by George Soros, has "exposed" Islamist critics in a 130-page report entitled *Fear Inc. The Roots of the Islamophobia Network in America.* Those who worry excessively about Islamophobia will be relieved to know that the well-funded Soros group is already on the case. Their booklet lists the individuals and organizations that are "amplifying fear and misinformation in this Islamophobic echo chamber."[36]

> ★ ★ ★
> ## Blaming the Messenger
> A researcher who tried to blow the whistle on the scandal to the Rotherham Council in 2001 revealed that she was warned she "must never refer to Asian men" and was sent to "a two-day ethnicity and diversity course to raise my awareness of ethnic issues."[34]

The leftist-Islamist campaign to silence critics of Islam has been a spectacular success.

Our intelligence agencies have been hamstrung by fear of offending Muslims,[37] investigations into possible Muslim Brotherhood penetration of the government have been blocked for fear of offending Muslims,[38] and the New York Police Department's surveillance of radical mosques has been suspended for fear of offending Muslims.[39]

After 9/11, the watchword was "If you see something, say something." But fear of Islamophobia has created a climate in which people are tempted to look the other way if they see a Muslim acting suspiciously. Here's a case in point. In 2008, five Muslims were convicted of a jihad plot to enter Fort Dix Army Base and kill as many as they could. How did the feds find out about the plot? A clerk in a Circuit City store told them that two men had asked him to convert a videotape to DVD. On the tape were images of men firing automatic weapons and shouting "Allahu akbar." The clerk hesitated to do anything at first, but after mulling it over, he finally asked a coworker, "Dude, I just saw some really weird s—. I don't know what to do. Should I call someone or is that being racist?"[40]

★ ★ ★

The Irony of Islamophobia-phobia

Although the "hateful" critics of Islam are supposed to have created a climate of fear, ironically it's the "Islamophobes" on the *Fear Inc.* list—people like Robert Spencer[41] and Pamela Geller[42]—who regularly receive hate mail and death threats and have been forced to hire bodyguards.

That clerk took the risk, but unfortunately no one did the same in the case of Major Nidal Hasan, the U.S. Army officer who massacred fourteen people at Fort Hood in 2009. Several of his fellow officers and superior officers were aware of his jihadist sympathies—he gave a Power Point presentation virtually confessing to his divided loyalties as a Muslim in the U.S. armed forces—but none of them spoke up for fear of being thought bigoted.[43] Given his bizarre behavior, it would have been perfectly rational for the Army to dismiss Major Nidal Hasan from service and deny him access to Army bases. On the other hand, whatever justified fears they had about Hasan, his fellow officers also had entirely rational fears about being accused of "racism" and "Islamophobia" had they reported him.

The word "phobia" refers to an irrational fear. The claustrophobic may feel that the walls of the elevator are closing in on him, but in reality he is perfectly safe. The premise of the Islamophobia campaign is that society has nothing to fear from the spread of Islam. Thus, people who express fears about Muslim immigration or even jihadist activity are victims of a delusion; if they understood Islam better, they would see that it is just like any other religion or culture.

The ostensible point of condemning "Islamophobia" is to counter irrational fears about Islam, but it's beginning to look as though the real purpose is to prevent ordinary people from entertaining rational and well-founded fears. At one time, training materials used by the FBI and the Defense Department drew a connection between jihad and Islamic doctrine. That was perfectly rational because such a connection does, in fact, exist. In compliance with the demands of Islamic groups, however, the materials—thousands of pages' worth—were purged lest Muslims be offended.[44] The Army is now safe from the threat of "Islamophobia," but is our country any safer now that the Army and other security agencies have willingly blindfolded themselves?

There is little evidence that Islamophobia—the supposed irrational fear of Islam—is on the rise.[45] But our government officials and opinion-makers alike are so afraid lest any of us fall into it that that they are eager to gloss over real threats.

The Body Count

Consider an article that appeared in the *Angelus*, the Los Angeles archdiocesan newspaper, after a married Muslim couple in San Bernardino, California, carried out the bloodiest jihad attack in the U.S. since 9/11. The piece by Father Ronald Rolheiser, calling for "greater solidarity with Islam," is a particularly egregious example of the kind of nonsense that passes for wisdom in the age of Islamophobia-phobia.

The author starts off by observing that "this is not a good time to be a Muslim in the Western world." Well, maybe not. Muslims in the West are probably getting a lot of suspicious stares these days. On the other hand, you could say that it's not a good time to be a non-Muslim, either. Just before Father Rolheiser wrote his piece, fourteen Californians were mowed down in cold blood by angry Muslims. That, in fact, was the occasion for his spectacularly wrong-headed article.[46]

Judging by the body count, it's non-Muslims that have the greater cause for concern. Muslims killed 130 Europeans during the Paris massacre and wounded another 370.[47] Muslims killed twelve in the Charlie Hebdo massacre[48] and four more at the Hyper-Cache food market.[49] The Madrid train bombings left 191 dead and 2,000 wounded.[50] In the attack on the London transit system, 52 people were killed and 700 were wounded.[51] Several hundred were wounded, and three killed, in the Boston Marathon bombing.[52] "Soldier of Allah"—as he called himself on his business cards—Major Nidal Hasan killed fourteen and injured more than thirty others at Fort Hood.[53] On September 11, 2001, a group of nineteen Muslims managed to kill nearly three thousand Americans.[54]

And that's just the short list. Moreover, it doesn't include other types of violent crimes perpetrated by Muslims on Western citizens, including the more than 600 victims of the New Year's Eve sexual assaults in Cologne;[55] the 1,400 rape victims in Rotherham, England;[56] and the numerous victims of rape in Sweden which—thanks to Muslim immigration—is the rape capital of the Northern Hemisphere.[57]

Living in the Muslim World—and in Fear

And consider the even greater threat under which non-Muslims in Muslim societies live, as a result of the resurgent jihad.

Near the end of his article, Father Rolheiser offers his own version of Shylock's "Hath not a Jew eyes?" speech: "We are both [Muslims and Christians] part of the same family: we have the same God, suffer the same anxieties, are subject to the same mortality, and will share the same heaven."[58]

Do we all really "suffer the same anxieties"? Well, yes. Everybody worries about money and health and family problems. But Christians who live in Muslim lands have some added anxieties, which are largely caused by Muslims: Will our church be firebombed? Will I be beheaded in the morning? Will my children be sold into slavery?

Jihad is a real and growing threat—both in the Middle East and in the West. Christians and other non-Muslims living under the rule of ISIS or Boko Haram already feel the brunt of it. They are being subjected to barbarities—from open slave markets to crucifixion—that not too long ago seemed forever consigned to the past. Meanwhile, we in the United States and the rest of the Western world find ourselves under attack from Muslims who want to spread the same regime to our countries. The Europeans will fall to the jihad before we do. And by "fall," I don't mean that the countries of Europe will be conquered by Muslim armies. That won't be necessary. What we will see, what we are in fact already witnessing, is a slow, steady process of submission. Well, slow and steady up to a point—and then, a rapid acceleration.

CHAPTER 2

Are ISIS and Boko Haram Un-Islamic?

When Muslims commit acts of terror, it is standard operating procedure for some authority or other to assure the populace that "this has nothing to do with Islam." This is said so frequently as to induce a boy-who-cried-wolf reaction in anyone with an ounce of contrariness. So it was refreshing to finally hear a world leader (in this case, a former world leader) admit that global Islamic terror actually does have something to do with Islam.

In an address at Bloomberg Headquarters in London in April of 2014, more than a dozen years after 9/11, former British Prime Minister Tony Blair finally described radical Islam as the single biggest threat facing the world today. He went on to criticize Western commentators who "go to extraordinary lengths" to avoid linking terrorism with Islam. "It is bizarre," he said, "to ignore the fact that the principal actors in all situations express themselves through the medium of religious identity."

Although Blair suggested that radical Islamic ideology "distorts and warps Islam's true message," he nevertheless emphasized that this extremist movement is based in religious belief. He added that we in the West can gain a better understanding of the Islamist ideology by remembering "the

Did you know?

★ Islam doesn't mean "peace"; it means "submission"

★ When two Muslim converts hacked a British soldier to death in London, the prime minister called it "a betrayal of Islam"

★ Bin Laden wanted to punish America for the Gulf War— but also to liberate us from immorality

★ A Muslim state that we're allied with has virtue police patrols and regular beheadings

experience of revolutionary communism and fascism." His main message? That the "defeating of this ideology" should be at the top of the global agenda. In short, Blair is calling for ideological warfare against "Islamism" (his term for radical Islam).[1]

During the Second World War and during the Cold War that followed, we didn't hesitate to engage in ideological warfare, first with Nazism, and then with communism. It was considered perfectly legitimate to go after the ideas that lay at the base of these totalitarian systems as a way of weakening belief in them. And we didn't particularly worry about who might take offense. But what if the ideology that threatens you comes wrapped in the cloak of religion? Blair calls for the defeat of the "Islamist" ideology, but how can you engage in ideological warfare if criticism of the enemy ideology is off-limits?

In our multicultural times, it is considered extremely bad manners to criticize a religion other than one's own. Respect for other people's deeply held convictions—no matter how different from our own—is considered to be the hallmark of civility and tolerance. Thus, while we feel free to talk about the evils of Nazism, communism, secularism, and capitalism, very few would even consider talking about the evils of Islam. It is taboo. As a result, when bad things are done in the name of Islam, our "commentators" (as Blair calls them) are quick to absolve Islam itself. The formula "this has nothing to do with Islam" is just one way of ignoring the religious dimension of terror.

Yet when jihadists explain their motivations, they almost invariably cite the words and example of Muhammad as found in the Koran and hadith—two sources with which they appear to be quite familiar.[2] That the average jihadist knows the Koran better than the average Christian knows the New Testament should tell us something, but apparently it hasn't. In general, we refuse to acknowledge what our Islamist enemies consider to be the most salient fact about themselves. This reluctance to identify the enemy's major motivation puts us at a considerable disadvantage—one that we didn't labor under in previous wars. Consider that our involvement in the Iraqi War lasted roughly twice as long as our war with Nazi Germany even though we were fighting a much less powerful opponent. Our ongoing engagement with tribal warriors in Afghanistan has lasted longer still.

Advice We're Ignoring

"Know the enemy."

—Sun Tzu, *The Art of War*

Still and all, the West would probably prevail if the struggle with Islam were confined to armed combat. But our civilizational struggle with Islam goes far beyond that. For example, the gradual Islamic takeover of Europe is being accomplished by stealthy cultural jihad rather than armed jihad. In Europe, the spread of Islam doesn't require fighting in the streets; it only requires that Europeans get used to burqas in the shopping malls, streets closed for prayer, cancellation of talks critical of Islam, naked anti-Semitism, and the establishment of religious and cultural ghettos in major cities.

Like many Americans, I didn't know much about Islam before the 2001 attack on the World Trade Center. And, to tell the truth, even after 9/11 I wasn't inclined to look too deeply into the matter. The events of 9/11, disturbing as they were, were not quite enough to overcome a certain inertia in me. Neither was the widespread jubilation in parts of the Muslim world that followed the attack, nor the knowledge that Islamic terrorists had carried out similar attacks before—the first World Trade Center bombing in 1993, the simultaneous truck bomb attacks on U.S. embassies in Nairobi and Dar es Salaam in 1998, and the suicide attack on the USS *Cole* on October 12, 2000.

Was there something about Islam that prompted such violence? Or were the terrorists distorting and misinterpreting their religion? The consensus seemed to favor the latter view, and for a long while I was inclined to go along with it. One of the benefits of taking the consensus view was that it

A Book You're Not Supposed to Read

The Politically Incorrect Guide to Islam and the Crusades by Robert Spencer (Washington, DC: Regnery, 2005).

absolved me from having to read the Koran and other Islamic source materials—texts that I somehow intuited would not make for enjoyable reading.

There were also other factors that prevented me from looking further. President Bush and other world leaders reassured us that Islam was a religion of peace.[3] I didn't know much about Islam, but I assumed that they and their expert advisors did, and so, for a while, I accepted their assessment. The prevailing notion was that terror attacks had nothing to do with Islam, but rather were the work of people who had thoroughly misunderstood the peaceful nature of their religion.

We were assured that "Islam means peace." In fact, as I eventually learned, Islam means *submission*—submission to the will of Allah, which, as we shall see, is not only the posture of devout Muslims but also the end goal of violent jihad against infidels.[4]

Pretext or Motivating Principle?

Shortly before murdering an Israeli policewoman, Ahmad Zakarneh sent a text message to his parents: "Mother, I'm going to heaven. If you see me sizzling in my old blood, rejoice. Don't say, 'He died' and be saddened, for I'm living by candlelight, under the Lord's throne of honor. Forgive me, father. I yearned for a saint's death. My religion called upon me to uphold the ritual. I am a martyr, by Allah's assistance. Rejoice."[5]

Numerous world leaders have repeatedly said that Muslim terrorists use religion as a "pretext" for committing violence.[6] The notion that jihadists use religion to conceal other motives is widely accepted. People don't like to associate religion with terror, and the "pre-text" hypothesis provides a convenient way of absolving the religion of Islam from the crimes of Islamists.

But does Ahmad Zakarneh sound like someone who is using religion as a pretext? The man plainly expected to die for his actions. Why would he lie to his parents about his true motives at such a crucial time?

Zakarneh's testimony to his parents is not an anomaly. On the whole, terrorists and would-be terrorists seem to hold genuine religious convictions. Indeed, one of the common signs of radicalization is increased devotion. This was the case with the San Bernardino killers,[7] the elder of the two Boston Marathon bombers,[8] the Fort Hood shooter,[9] and numerous other jihadists.

While world leaders are still searching in Clouseau-like fashion for a motive that would explain Islamic terrorism, to most people the motive is fairly obvious. It doesn't take an Einstein to connect the dots between "Allahu akbar" and sudden jihad syndrome. After killing Drummer Lee Rigby, Mujaahid Abu Hamza (formerly Michael Adebolajo) explained on camera that "we are forced by...many ayah [verses] in the Qur'an, we must fight them as they fight us."[10]

The lone wolf terrorists seem quite sincere in their religious beliefs. But how about the leaders of terrorist organizations—the Osama bin Ladens and the Abu Bakr al-Baghdadis? Surely they have ulterior motives? Well, in his "Letter to America," Osama bin Laden did complain that "you attacked us and continue to attack us." But more than half of the nine-page letter is religious in nature. Here's a small sample:

Absolving Islam

"There is nothing in Islam that justifies this truly dreadful act."

—UK Prime Minister David Cameron, commenting on the jihad attack in which two converts to Islam ran down, knifed, and hacked a British soldier to death on a London street

> It is to this religion that we call you; the seal of all the previous religions. It is the religion of Unification of God, sincerity, the best manners, righteousness, mercy, honour, purity, and piety. It is the religion of showing kindness to others, establishing justice between them, granting them their rights, and defending the oppressed and the persecuted. It is the religion of enjoining the good and forbidding the evil with the hand, tongue and heart. It is the religion of Jihad in the way of Allah so that Allah's Word and religion reign Supreme. And it is the religion of unity and agreement on the obedience to Allah, and total equality between all people, without regarding their colour, sex, or language.[11]

Those don't sound like the words of someone who is faking his religious devotion. Moreover, bin Laden believed in Islam so strongly that he wanted to share it with us: "We call you to be a people of manners, principles, honour, and purity; to reject the immoral acts of fornication, homosexuality, intoxicants, gambling, and trading with interest. We call you to all this that you may be freed from that which you have become caught up in."[12]

So, bin Laden's aim was not only to punish us for the First Gulf War, but also to free us from immorality. Like a Puritan divine, he wanted to put the fear of God in us, but he also seems to have had a genuine concern with saving our souls. Whatever you may think of bin Laden, it's difficult to conclude that religion was just a pretext for him.

Abu Bakr al-Baghdadi, the leader of ISIS, struck a similar tone in his inaugural speech as caliph: "Truly all praise belongs to Allah. We praise Him and seek His help and forgiveness. We seek refuge with Allah from the evils of our souls and from the consequences of our deeds. Whomever Allah guides can never be led astray, and whomever Allah leads astray can never be guided."

This is followed with several quotations from the Koran and an exhortation to "support the religion of Allah through jihad in the path of Allah." But it's not all about fighting. Like bin Laden, al-Baghdadi seems concerned with the state of men's souls. He tells the soldiers of the Islamic State that he does not fear for them in battle, but rather "I fear for you your own sins. Stay away from sins. Expel from your ranks those who openly commit sin. Be wary of pride, haughtiness, and arrogance. Do not become proud on account of gaining some victories. Humble yourself before Allah."[16]

This, I submit, is not the language of someone who thinks of religion as merely a handy pretext to justify a land grab. If bin Laden and al-Baghdadi were faking it, they deserve some sort of "best actor" award for their convincing performances.

According to the principle known as Occam's razor, the best explanation for anything is usually the one that is simplest. So, instead of casting terrorist leaders as calculating deceivers, why not take what they say at face value? In short, why not acknowledge that they truly believe that this is what God wants them to do? That, after all, is the obvious explanation. And those who deny the obvious run the risk of discrediting themselves in the eyes of those who can see the obvious.

On that score, the "pretext" argument cuts both ways. One could as easily say that world leaders who persist in maintaining that violence has nothing to do with Islam are themselves engaged in a pretext. One could argue that since there is so much evidence to the contrary, they must have

Allah Made Me Do It

"May Allah accept this from me."[13]

"I'm doing it in the name of Allah."[14]

"I'm going to do good work for God."[15]

—statements made by would-be and successful jihadists to explain their motivations for planning or executing acts of terror in America. Jihadists in other parts of the world say much the same thing.

★ ★ ★

What Would They Know about Islam?

Grand Ayatollah Ruhollah Khomeini

- Leader of the Iranian Revolution
- Expert on Islamic Law
- Author of more than forty books
- Supreme religious leader of Iran

Abdullah Azzam

- Founder of MAK (later renamed al-Qaeda)
- Mentor to Osama bin Laden
- Scholar and author
- Doctorate in Islamic jurisprudence from Al Azhar University

Omar Abdel Rahman (The "Blind Sheik")

- Mastermind of first attack on World Trade Center
- Doctorate in Islamic jurisprudence from Al Azhar
- Globally renowned scholar

Mullah Mohammed Omar

- Founder of the Taliban ("The Scholars")
- Studied at Karachi's premier seminary

Anwar al-Awlaki

- Chief propagandist for al-Qaeda
- Mentor to numerous terrorists
- President of the Muslim Student Association at George Washington University while studying for a doctoral degree

Abu Bakr al-Baghdadi

- Founder of ISIS and caliph of the Islamic State
- Ph.D. in Islamic Studies from University of Baghdad

some other, concealed purpose for saying so. Perhaps their real object is to avoid offending Muslims, for fear of more violence at their hands. Perhaps they understand that Islam inclines toward violence, and they fear that the wrong word will suddenly catapult the moderates into the radical camp. But if violence really does have something to do with Islam, don't the potential victims of Islamic violence have a right to know before they find themselves on the wrong end of a machete (if they're Christians in Nigeria),[17] an assault rifle (if they attend an office Christmas party in San Bernardino, California),[18] or a pressure cooker bomb (if they're at the Boston Marathon)?[19]

Un-Islamic Acts?

Even if we take our leaders at their word, we still have to ask, who's right? The jihadists themselves, or the world leaders who are constantly telling us that Islamic terrorism has nothing to do with the religion of Islam? After Drummer Lee Rigby's gruesome murder—the British soldier was nearly beheaded—Prime Minister David Cameron opined, "This was not just an attack on Britain and on the British way of life, it was also a betrayal of Islam and of the Muslim communities who give so much to our country."[20]

Of course, many Islamic leaders would agree with Cameron. In fact, prominent Muslims in the UK have asked the prime minister to start calling ISIS "the Un-Islamic State."[21] Likewise, other world leaders have insisted that there is a strict wall of separation between Islam and violence. In an interview with CNN's Fareed Zakaria, President Obama claimed that "99.9% of Muslims" reject radical Islam.[22] The implication was that, to understand what Islam teaches, we should look to the vast majority of peaceful Muslims rather than the handful of terrorists.

This might seem to be a compelling argument, but in fact it's full of holes. The issue is not what individual Muslims believe, but what Islam teaches.

We all know that what some (and even many) individual Catholics may believe about an article of faith or morals doesn't tell us what the Church actually teaches. According to various polls, a great many Catholics see nothing wrong with contraception and even abortion.[23] Yet we wouldn't conclude from this that the Church teaches that these practices are permissible. The Church has very clear teachings in these areas, as she does on the doctrine of the real presence of Christ in the Eucharist—another article of faith that many Catholics don't subscribe to.

The fact that some or many Muslims reject violent jihad and lead peaceful lives doesn't mean that Muslims have no religious duty to engage in jihad. In fact, although not all Muslims are expected to fight, all are expected to support jihad in some way. The specific rules and regulations surrounding jihad are laid out in *Reliance of the Traveller*, one of the most authoritative manuals of Islamic law (see section o9.0-15).[24] It's to their credit if Muslims ignore their obligation, but we shouldn't fool ourselves into thinking there is no such duty in Islamic law.

★ ★ ★
Sharia Law: Back by Popular Demand

The 2009 Pew "Global Attitudes Survey" of Pakistani public opinion found that 83 percent of Pakistanis favor stoning adulterers, 80 percent favor whipping or amputation for thieves, and 78 percent favor death for apostasy. A 2010 Pew survey of Egyptians showed similar results.[27]

Of course, the 99.9 percent figure that President Obama quoted is grossly inflated. Numerous polls have shown that a significant number of Muslims believe in violent jihad, and even greater numbers support the most brutal aspects of *sharia* law.[25] Nevertheless, Western leaders and even Muslim leaders (King Abdullah of Jordan comes to mind) continue to insist that terrorist behavior is un-Islamic.[26] Admittedly, it's confusing. Western leaders are no experts on Islam, but the leaders of Muslim nations know a lot about their own religion. Wouldn't they be able to tell if something is Islamic or

★ ★ ★ ★ ★ ★

Good Islam and Bad Islam

	Saudi Arabia (our ally)	Islamic State (our enemy)
Theocracy	✓	✓
Kills apostates	✓	✓
Regular beheadings	✓	✓
Amputation for theft	✓	✓
Women must be accompanied	✓	✓
Bans alcohol	✓	✓
Virtue Police patrols	✓	✓
Sharia is the law of the land	✓	✓

not? Yes, for the most part, they would. But, for reasons of state, it's not always prudent to say what they know.

Established Muslim nations, such as Jordan, Saudi Arabia, and Egypt, are highly vulnerable to external attacks from ISIS. Why is that? Because the Islamic State considers their leaders to be false Muslims who have betrayed the founding principles of Islam. With large percentages of their populations supporting jihad and strict sharia, these countries are also at risk of the growth of ISIS-type movements within their own borders. Thus it is in their best interests to condemn ISIS. And in the Muslim world, the best way to malign a movement is to call it un-Islamic. If Muslim leaders were to say—as Egypt's President Abdel Fatah el-Sissi has come close to saying[28]—that the problem of violence is rooted in Islam itself, they would risk losing their legitimacy, and possibly their lives.

That's not to say that the defense of the Islamic faith is all calculated hypocrisy. Most people have a filial attachment to the faith they were brought up in. Just as it's difficult to admit the faults of one's mother, it's difficult to entertain the thought that there is something intrinsically wrong with one's faith. In a sense, it's a matter of family loyalty. And this is even more the case in the Middle East, where family, tribal, and religious loyalties are all bound together.

So it's not surprising that many Muslims want to put as much distance as possible between their own religion and groups like ISIS. It's more of a mystery why Western leaders, Western media, and even Western churchmen persist in the fiction that Muslim terrorists who emulate the zeal and the deeds of their prophet are betrayers of Islam.

CHAPTER 3

The Roots of Jihad

Considering that the news brings daily reports of attacks by Islamic jihadists and lone wolves, it's surprising how little Americans know about Islam. For many, their knowledge of Islam doesn't go beyond a passing acquaintance with the "Five Pillars of Islam"—belief in one God, prayer, fasting, almsgiving, and pilgrimage. That all sounds fairly innocuous. Moreover, it's reassuring to find that the Koran contains many Old Testament stories and that Jesus is honored in Islam.

If you have only a surface acquaintance with Islam, then it's easy enough to believe that Islam is a peaceful religion that has been "hijacked" by a handful of "extremists" who "misunderstand" their own belief system.[1] But if you dig a little deeper, you'll find that there is good reason to worry.

Muhammad: The Perfect Man Models Jihad

Most non-Muslims, for example, don't understand the centrality of Muhammad to Islam. He is considered by Muslims to be the most perfect man who

Did you know?

★ "Peaceful Islam" is a holdover from the long-dead colonial era

★ Muhammad, the model for every Muslim, unfortunately modeled pedophilia, conquest, and torture

★ Jihad is a religious obligation that remains in force until the entire world submits to Islam

A Book You're Not Supposed to Read

The Truth about Muhammad: Founder of the World's Most Intolerant Religion by Robert Spencer (Washington, DC: Regnery, 2007).

ever lived—a man whose life is held up as a model for Muslims to imitate in every detail.[2] Yet most of his life was devoted to jihad warfare—which means that a faithful imitation of Muhammad is bound to result in unfortunate consequences.

If the atrocities committed by ISIS, al-Qaeda, Boko Haram, and other groups are thoroughly un-Islamic, then the very first misunderstander of Islam was Muhammad himself. He permitted rape and sex slavery, and he ordered that prisoners be beheaded.

Here are some of the prophet's exemplary deeds:

- He married a six-year-old girl and consummated the marriage when she was nine (Bukhari, 5.63.3896)[3]
- In violation of Arab moral standards he married his own daughter-in-law (Koran, 33:37)
- He ordered the beheading of all the men of the captured Banu Qurayza tribe and the enslavement of the women and children. According to some accounts, between eight and nine hundred men and adolescent boys were executed as Muhammad and his child bride looked on (Ishaq, 464)[4]
- He sanctioned the rape of women captured by his troops in battle (Muslim, vol. 4, no. 1438)[5]
- After the assault on the Jews of Khaybar, Muhammad ordered that a leader of the tribe, Kinana ibn al-Rabi, be tortured until he disclosed the location of the group's treasure. A fire was lit on Kinana's chest but, as he still refused to reveal the secret, Muhammad had him beheaded. Muhammad had promised Kinana's

young wife, Safiya, to another Muslim, but, after hearing of her beauty, he went back on his word and took her in "marriage" for himself. By some accounts, this occurred only hours after he dispatched her husband (Ishaq, p. 515; Bukhari, 1.8.367)[6]

Quite obviously, the prophet's life is hard to reconcile with the moderate modern view of things. So how do you solve a problem like Muhammad? To the Western mind the answer seems easy enough. Simply give Muhammad a downgrade. Deemphasize his importance. Recognize that all great men have feet of clay. Think of him as a very imperfect vessel through which Allah was trying to impart timeless truths. Above all, remember that he was a man of his time, and make allowances accordingly.

But if he was a man of his time—with all the brutality, blood lust, and narrow prejudices of those times—how can he be a model for our times? Because that's what he is for Muslims all over the world. In Islamic tradition he is considered to be the perfect human and therefore, as the Koran says, "a beautiful pattern" of behavior (33:21). This passage, by the way, comes just three pages before the passage in which Allah exonerates Muhammad for having married his daughter-in-law, Zaynab: "No blame shall be attached to the prophet for doing what is sanctioned for him by God" (33:38).

In Islamic law and tradition, Muhammad's example is considered paradigmatic. His behavior sets the standard for what is permissible and impermissible. With a few exceptions, the general rule of Islamic ethics is that if Muhammad did or sanctioned something, then it's okay for other Muslims

---

★ ★ ★

Following in His Footsteps

When ISIS burned a downed Jordanian pilot alive in a cage, some claimed that burning prisoners alive is un-Islamic. But ISIS had its answer ready: "the Prophet put out the eyes of the Uraynians with heated iron."[7] If Muhammad did it, it must be justified.

as well. (One of the exceptions is that whereas Muslim men are allowed to have only four wives at a time, Muhammad was permitted to have as many wives as he wished.)[8] Exceptions aside, Muhammad is the model for Muslims. The dominant Muslim belief is that he was without sin. Although no claim of divinity is made for him, he is a highly exalted person. Thus, the role Muhammad plays in the lives of Muslims is comparable to the role Christ plays in the lives of Christians. Just as Christians who are seeking direction ask, "What would Jesus do?" Muslims ask, "What would Muhammad do?"

If, as President Obama claimed, 99.9 percent of Muslims reject radical Islam, then, to be consistent, the same percentage would have to reject their own prophet. By twenty-first-century standards, Muhammad was a moral monster. We would expect a good person to reject much of his behavior. But if a Muslim rejects Muhammad, he is considered a bad Muslim and an apostate—and is therefore deserving of death.

Although Muhammad is not considered to be divine, he is considered to be the chief spokesman for the divinity. Almost every time Allah is mentioned in the Koran, Muhammad ("the Apostle") is mentioned in the same breath. Consider some sample passages:

- He that obeys God and his apostle shall dwell forever in gardens watered by running streams (4:13)
- Believers, obey God and obey the Apostle...Should you disagree about anything refer it to God and the Apostle (4:59)
- He that obeys God and the Apostle shall dwell with the prophets and the saints (4:69)

- He that leaves his dwelling to fight for God and his apostle...shall be recompensed by God (4:100)
- Believers, have faith in God and his Apostle (4:136)

And that's just from one sura (a chapter of the Koran). The God-and-his-apostle theme appears over and over in the pages of Islam's holy book. So on the one hand, Islam declares that God has no partners,[10] and on the other hand, Muhammad and God seem to have formed one of the great partnerships of all time—beside which Antony and Cleopatra, Lewis and Clark, and Rodgers and Hammerstein pale by comparison.

The religion of Islam was at one time widely known as "Mohammedanism." You can see why. Muhammad wrote the script, directed the play, and assigned the central role to himself. Since God is inaccessible and is known only through what Muhammad says of him, it's hard to escape the conclusion that when the Koran says "obey God and the Apostle" what is really meant is "obey the Apostle."

Muhammad is the cornerstone. The religion is built around him. He can't be left out of the story. And he can't be criticized.

Muhammad must be kept free of the stain of human imperfection because he is indispensable to Islam. The very authenticity of the Koran hangs on his word. Muhammad's claim to have received a revelation from God is not corroborated by any other source. No one else received any message from Gabriel, and no one witnessed any message being imparted to Muhammad (although he was on occasion

★ ★ ★
He May Be a Messenger, but He's No Messenger Boy

According to the authoritative *Reliance of the Traveller*, "Allah has favored him above all the other prophets and has made him the highest of mankind, rejecting anyone's attesting to the divine oneness by saying 'there is no God but Allah,' unless they also attest to the Prophet by saying "Muhammad is the Messenger of Allah.""[11] It's not good enough to declare your belief in the oneness of Allah, you also have to affirm the prophethood of Muhammad.

Guilt Tripped into Jihad by the Koran

"I don't understand how you can read the Qur'an and the sunnah of the Prophet and...not understand that jihad and the implementation of Sharia is absolutely demanded of all the Muslim [people]. I feel so guilt-ridden sometimes for knowing what's required of me but yet doing little or nothing to make it happen."

—Terry Lee Loewen, who planned a jihad attack on Wichita's Mid-Continent Airport in December 2013[12]

observed to sweat and go into a trancelike state). In the final analysis, Muslims have nothing to go on except his word. Consequently, they don't take kindly to any questioning of the prophet's trustworthiness.

The words and deeds of Muhammad make him incompatible with everything modern and moderate. But because Islam and Muhammad are conjoined at the hip, a lot of Muslims are going to choose Muhammad over modernity and moderation.

The Koran: Allah Commands Jihad

The Koran is Islam's holy book. It claims to contain God's clear revelations, but most non-Muslims have a difficult time in making any sense of it. So do many Muslims—which is why the Koran had to be supplemented early on with the hadith (the sayings of Muhammad) and the sira (the life of Muhammad).

Still, the Koran holds pride of place in Islam and its mere existence is considered to be a miracle. In fact, the beauty of the Koranic verses is considered to be the primary proof of the authenticity of Islam. Who else but God, ask Muslims, could have written such a book?

Unfortunately, it's from this purportedly beautiful book that a lot of jihadists get the idea that killing infidels is what Allah wants them to do. As we have seen, jihadists frequently cite the Koran as the source of their motivation.

So if we want to disabuse terrorists and potential terrorists of the notion that Allah wants them to kill infidels, the obvious place to start is the

Koran. We can't tell them, though, that there is absolutely no warrant in the Koran for killing unbelievers, because there patently is. "When the sacred months are over slay the idolaters wherever you find them" (9:5) is typical of many similar verses. According to a content analysis conducted by the Center for the Study of Political Islam, 24 percent of the Medinan chapters of the Koran—the violent

> ## A Book You're Not Supposed to Read
>
> *The Complete Infidel's Guide to the Koran* by Robert Spencer (Washington, DC: Regnery, 2009).

later chapters that Muslims believe "abrogate" the earlier more peaceful Meccan chapters—are devoted to jihad.[13] Or, as Taliban leader Baitullah Mehsud once declared, "Allah on 480 occasions in the Holy Koran extols Muslims to wage jihad."[14]

It is often suggested that if only critics of the Muslim faith would actually read the Koran, they would find in Islam's holy book the peaceful religion that has been misunderstood and distorted by the terrorists. True, there are peaceful-sounding verses in the Koran. For example, "There shall be no compulsion in religion" (2:256). The problem is, this verse—and much of the more peaceful-sounding language in the Koran—is cancelled out by the doctrine of abrogation, which is also found in the Koran (2:106). If later verses contradict earlier verses, the earlier revelations are considered abrogated. (The non-compulsion clause also doesn't square with Islamic apostasy laws. The prospect of being killed if you leave Islam provides a rather compelling reason for staying with your faith. For the exact citation, see *Reliance of the Traveller* 0.8.1 and 0.8.2.)[15]

Another Koranic verse that is frequently used to reassure Koranic illiterates is this one: "We laid it down for the Israelites that whoever killed a human being...shall be regarded as having killed all mankind" (5:32). That sounds fine unless you happen to be familiar with the very next verse: "Those that make war against God and His apostle and spread disorder in the land shall be slain or crucified or have their hands and feet cut off on opposite sides" (5:33).

The you-should-read-the-Koran tactic won't work with those who actually have read the Koran—including the jihadists. What might work on them? One tactic is to try and convince would-be jihadists that they are misinterpreting the Koran—that it should be interpreted in a more spiritual and peaceful way. But here again we run into a problem. Since the eleventh century, a consensus has existed among Islamic scholars that the "gates of *ijtihad*" (interpretation) are closed.[16] Calling for new interpretations is tantamount to rejecting centuries of Islamic tradition.

Some small sects, such as the Ahmadiyya community, do interpret the Koran in a symbolic rather than literal way, but they are considered heretics by mainstream Muslims and they are often the target of persecution.[17] More important, Muhammad, whose example is considered definitive by Muslim authorities, did not interpret the command to wage jihad in a figurative way, and his victims did not die figurative deaths. The Center for the Study of Political Islam's content analysis of the sira shows that approximately two-thirds of it has to do with fighting. Part Three, which covers the Medinan period of Muhammad's life, is particularly instructive in this respect. Its 500 pages are taken up almost entirely with descriptions of battles and raids.[18]

In short, the jihadist interpretation of the Koran is strongly supported both by the text and by the example of Muhammad. Why should they give it up when they have so much evidence on their side? Jihadists have been highly successful in recruiting Muslims to the cause precisely because they can demonstrate that warfare against unbelievers is a scriptural duty.

One Weird Trick

Trying to convince current and potential jihadists that the Koran should be interpreted in a peaceful way is an uphill jihad. Is there another way of addressing the issue? Well, yes, there is. More-over, to paraphrase the ubiquitous ad copy, this one weird trick can save you hundreds of fruit-less arguments. The other—largely untried—alternative for disabusing jihadists of jihadist notions is to discredit the Koran entirely. If the whole thing is a man-made fabrication, what does it matter what verse such-and-such says? If Muhammad made it all up, why waste your time in weighing the peaceful suras against the violent ones?

This argument is not often made because if you make it you will be attacked not only by Muslims but by non-Muslims as well. The latter will go after you with charges of divisiveness, insensitivity, bigotry, hatred, and whatnot. The former may go after you in more vigorous ways. That doesn't diminish the strength of the argu-ment, though. The Islamic edifice rests on the belief that God wrote the Koran and transmitted it via the Angel Gabriel to Muhammad, who merely recited it to his followers. If that's not true, then only a fool would rush into battle for the sake of Allah and the promised paradise. Take away the divine mandate to subjugate unbelievers, and you take away the rationale for Islam's war against the world.

> ★ ★ ★
> ## Religion of Peace?
>
> From the table of contents of *The Life of Muhammad*:
>
> | | |
> |---|---|
> | **The first raid on Waddan** | **281** |
> | **Hamza's raid to the coast** | **283** |
> | **Raid on Buwat** | **285** |
> | **Raid on al-Ushayra** | **285** |
> | **Raid on al-Kharrar** | **286** |
> | **Raid on Safawan** | **286** |
>
> —Ibn Ishaq, *The Life of Muhammad*
>
> Of the chapters that follow, the great majority—sixty-seven in all—are devoted to raids, battles, odes on battles, spoils of war, and assassinations ordered by Muhammad.

Although it's difficult to get a hearing for it, the argument itself is surpris-ingly easy to make. That's because Muslim apologists have set themselves up for a takedown by establishing an impossibly high standard of evidence. What proof is there that God wrote the Koran? Well, there's the circular argument: we know that God wrote the Koran because that's what the Koran says and we know the Koran is truthful because God wrote it. For many Muslims, that settles the matter. Islamic scholars, however, long ago realized that something more was needed. And the main argument they developed is that the Koran is such a piece of perfect, nonpareil prose that no one except God could have written it.[19] As I say, it's a hard case to make because, although there are some arresting passages in the Koran, there are also plenty like this: "Prophet, We have made lawful for you the wives to whom you have granted dowries and the slave-girls whom God has given you as booty; the daughters of your paternal and maternal uncles and of your paternal and maternal aunts who fled with you; and any believing woman who gives herself to the Prophet and whom the Prophet wishes to take in marriage" (33:50).

Maybe it sounds better in the original, but one suspects that even in Arabic this piece of legalese is still going to read like a passage from a text-book on contract law. Christians and Jews should be able to sympathize with the plight of the Muslim apologist. How would you like to be stuck with the task of defending those so-and-so-begat-so-and-so passages in the Bible as examples of incomparable style?

Furthermore, the literary shortcomings of the Koran are not limited to pedestrian prose. The author, whoever he was, also had little sense of composition, continuity, character, dialogue, or drama. Don't take my word for it. Here are some scholarly observations:

> His characters are all alike, and they utter the same platitudes. He is fond of dramatic dialogue, but has very little sense of dramatic scene or action. The logical connections between successive episodes is often loose, sometimes wanting; and points of importance, necessary for the clear understanding of the story, are likely to be left out. —C. C. Torrey, *The Jewish Foundation of Islam* (New York: Jewish Institute of Religion Press, 1933), 108.

The book aesthetically considered is by no means a first-rate performance...indispensable links, both in expression and in the sequence of events, are often omitted...and nowhere do we find a steady advance in the narration...and even the syntax betrays great awkwardness.... —Theodor Noldeke, *Encyclopedia Britannica*, 11th ed., vol. 15, 898–906.

The Koran is strikingly lacking in overall structure, frequently obscure and inconsequential in both language and content.... —P. Crone and M. Cook, *Hagarism: The Making of the Muslim World* (Cambridge: Cambridge University Press, 1977), 9.

But Tell Us What You Really Think

"A wearisome, confused jumble, crude, incondite; endless iterations, long-windedness, entanglement...insupportable stupidity, in short."

—Thomas Carlyle's famous verdict on the Koran, from *On Heroes and Hero Worship*

The Muslim comeback to such quibbling is that people who can't read classical Arabic can't possibly appreciate the Koran.[20] The soaring style and lilting language of it are simply lost on the Arabic-challenged. In short, if you don't speak Arabic, then who are you to judge?

When I first came across this argument, it seemed to make sense—for a few minutes, anyway. Then I remembered that I don't read Greek either, but when I read Homer in translation I can usually distinguish the parts where he is telling a ripping good story from the parts where he is merely nodding. For that matter, I don't read Russian, but when I read Tolstoy in translation I can appreciate the beauty of his descriptions while noticing at the same time that he occasionally goes on too long about peasants cutting hay in the fields. You don't have to read French to appreciate Balzac or Italian to appreciate Manzoni. Why is Arabic the only language that doesn't translate?

There are tedious passages in the Bible, too. But this does not present a serious problem for Christians since most of them do not consider the Bible to be a word-for-word dictation from God. Likewise, the fact that parts of the Bible are problematic from a scientific point of view doesn't vitiate the authenticity of the scriptures. The human writers of the Bible were limited by the scientific knowledge of their times. However, when the Koran says that the earth is flat and is composed of seven layers, Muslims are faced with a problem. On the one hand, Allah, the author of the Koran, would have unlimited scientific knowledge; on the other hand, he is uttering obvious scientific falsehoods.

As I explained in *Christianity, Islam, and Atheism*, "If you believe that the Koran is dictated by God, you are faced with the difficulty of explaining why the Author of Creation seems to lack the literary touch—that is, the knack for storytelling, sequence, composition, and drama that we expect in accomplished human authors. Yes, there are beautiful passages in the Koran, but as an exercise in composition, it would not pass muster in most freshmen writing courses."[21]

What's more, the Koran could never withstand the kind of scholarly examination that the Christian Bible has been subject to. Unlike the Bible, it is a primitive patchwork of borrowed ideas, half-told stories, and endlessly repeated curses. It's arranged arbitrarily by length of chapter because, as one of its translators admitted, "a strictly chronological arrangement is impossible."[22] The world is full of poorly written books, but this particular one is supposed to have been written by God himself. One would think that God could have done a better job. The point is that anyone who has read the Koran and has even a passing knowledge of scripture studies will realize that Islam's "holy book" would not meet the tests of critical and historical evidence we apply to the Christian revelation. Such tests constitute potent weapons in our ideological arsenal—if we are willing to use them.

The purely human origin of the Koran is further suggested by the very human defensiveness displayed by its author. He never tires of reminding his audience that the Koran is a genuine revelation, not a fake one. This obsessive concern with the Koran's authenticity is exhibited on almost every page. Here is a small sampling:

"This Koran could not have been devised by any but God" (10:37).

"This is no invented tale, but a confirmation of previous scriptures..." (12:112).

"This Book is beyond all doubt revealed by the Lord of the Universe...Do they say: 'He has invented it himself'?" (32:1–2).

"When our clear revelations are recited to them they say...'this is nothing but an invented falsehood'" (34:43).

As I say, these assertions about the authenticity of the revelation appear over and over. Far more space is allotted to vouching for the genuine nature of the revelation than to telling what the revelation is. But what sort of author feels compelled to tell us *ad nauseum* that his word is not a human invention? It's not likely that the Author of all Creation would be so insecure about what he had written. On the other hand, a man who *had* invented it all himself would have good reason to be defensive. Muhammad, however, also realized that the best defense is a good offense. Thus, as the Koran repeatedly reminds its readers, the surest path to hell is to doubt "Our revelations."

The net effect of all these self-referential attestations to the authenticity of the Koran is to cast doubt on its authenticity. It's as though your neighbor is telling you a fish story and feels compelled to assure you at regular intervals that "It's the honest truth. I swear!" The more he protests the truth of his account, the more you doubt it.

Because they insist that the Koran is the verbatim word of God, Muslims are stuck with the task of defending a second-rate literary production as though it were Shakespeare, Homer, and Dante all rolled into one. If they have been largely successful in so defending it, it is because not many want to challenge them on the point.

Even in the days before we all became aware that an attack on the Koran might result in a shortened life span, scholars of Islam, particularly Christian scholars, were often reluctant to criticize Islam. Islam, after all, was an Abrahamic faith, and it would be bad manners to question the foundations of a fellow religion. Thus, Christian scholars of Islam such as Montgomery Watt (1909–2006) and Louis Massignon (1883–1962) tended to put the best possible face on Islam while minimizing its faults.

Some, like the atheist Muslim apostate Ibn Warraq, have attributed this uncritical attitude to a fear that the kind of critical analysis that would prove fatal to Islam would also inflict a death blow to Christianity. According to Warraq, "They recognized that Islam was a sister religion, heavily influenced by Judeo-Christian ideas; and Christianity and Islam stood or fell together."[23]

There is probably some truth to this. One does sometimes detect a "We-religions-have-to-stick-together" mentality among professional dialoguers. However, at this point, the hands-off-the-Koran attitude probably has more to do with twenty-first-century concerns over sensitivity than with fears that if you start digging around the foundations of Islam, the whole Christian structure will come tumbling down too. Though Christianity has been hurt by various modernist assaults, it has withstood the critical-historical investigation in admirable fashion. In fact, it has successfully used the tools of textual analysis and historical evidence to its own advantage.

Islam would not fare so well in the face of a similar examination. Which once again brings up the question: why not subject it to the same rigorous standards? Dialoguers and scholars currently spend a lot of time ferreting out little nuggets of compatibility between the Koran and the Bible. But what's the point of establishing the common ground between a real revelation and a fake one? There are many commonalities between the *Book of Mormon* and the Bible as well, but Catholic scholars don't show much interest in trying to reconcile the two books— and wisely so.

If Islam weren't such a militant faith, it would probably be best to take an attitude of live and let live. Unfortunately, live and let live is not what the Koran is all about. Although a great many Muslims manage to ignore its harsher mandates, the violent injunctions are still there, beckoning to those who seek to devote themselves fully to Allah's commands.

★ ★ ★
Ending Islam's Diplomatic Immunity

Up to now, Islam's status as a religion has provided it with a sort of diplomatic immunity under which it has literally gotten away with murder. Thomas Jefferson said, "It does me no injury for my neighbor to say there are twenty gods, or no god. It neither picks my pocket nor breaks my leg."[24] But when your neighbor's religion tells him it's okay to break your neck and enslave your children, it might be prudent to expose that religion and its holy book to the light of serious examination.

Consequently, it's not just Islamic terrorists that need to be feared, but also Islamic theorists and theologians. They provide the ideological fuel which powers the terror machine. It's important to take out the terrorist, but in the long run, it's more important to take down the terrorist's ideology. And that, by necessity, involves a deconstruction of the Koran. If that measure seems much too drastic, consider the alternatives—a slow-motion capitulation such as is now happening in Europe, or a bloody war, once it finally dawns on the civilized world that it must resist.

We can excuse ourselves from criticizing the holy book of Islam and pointing out the moral failings of its prophet on the grounds that we value our lives. That seems like the soul of pragmatism, but it's a very short-sighted kind of pragmatism. The larger question is whether we value the lives of our children and the future of our society. If the Koran, Muhammad, and Islam in general remain unchallenged, the jihad will continue to spread, and there will come a day when we will wish we had contested the Koran while we still had the freedom to do so.

The official statements of ISIS, Boko Haram, and suchlike groups are replete with quotations from the Koran and the hadith—all backing up their belief that Muslims are required to wage jihad war on unbelievers. Like evangelical Christians spreading the Good Word, the jihadists say that they are only delivering the message that they have received. *Read it for yourself,* they urge fence-sitting Muslims, *and come join us.* And they do.

A Religious Obligation

The fact is, the obligation to engage in jihad warfare is a main pillar of Islam. If it's not included in the well-known five pillars of Islam, that's because it's considered a communal obligation, not an individual one.[25] But it is, nevertheless, of the essence of Islam.

The foundation of jihad doctrine is the distinction between Muslim and non-Muslim, more precisely between the "house of Islam" (dar al-Islam) and the "house of war" (dar al-harb). The purpose of jihad is to bring the "house of war"—non-Muslim territories—under the control of the "house of Islam." Thus, jihad is a perpetual obligation that remains in force until the non-Muslim world submits to the Muslim world.[26]

This is not ancient history, it's modern mainstream Islam. For instance, the influential scholar and popular television personality Sheik Yusuf al-Qaradawi, speaking at a 2003 Islamic conference in Sweden, said, "It has been determined by Islamic law that the blood and property of people of dar-al-harb...is not protected."[27]

This means that anyone living in the war zone—in other words, everybody outside the Muslim world—no matter how peaceful he may be, can be killed. For what? For the crime of being an unbeliever. Islamic war doctrine in its simplest form boils down to this: the Islamic community is obliged to make war on non-believers. With minor variations, that is the wording that appears in numerous Islamic law books and in the most authoritative commentaries on the law.[28]

There are, however, a number of exceptions and qualifications. For instance, if the unbeliever converts to Islam or if he submits to the authority of the Islamic ruler and agrees to pay the *jizya* tax, his life will be spared. Indeed there are many "ifs," "ands," and "buts" surrounding the rules of jihad warfare. And these qualifications often serve to provide comfort to potential victims of jihad, even if it's only a false comfort. Islamic apologists often say that jihad can only be defensive, that it can never be directed toward civilians, and that Islam forbids the taking of innocent life. That's all very reassuring—until you realize that the terms "defensive," "civilians," and "innocent" are understood differently in Islamic and Western societies. A close reading of Islamic law books reveals that only Muslims are innocent.

Whereas the term "innocent" is defined rather narrowly by Muslim jurists, the term "defensive" is construed in a broad sense. Indeed, the term is so elastic that it includes its opposite. Thus, offensive operations are often deemed to be defensive. For example, most of the many battles fought by Muhammad were battles that he initiated. Yet in the looking-glass world of Islamic jurisprudence, Muhammad was merely defending himself and Allah. Against whom? Against anyone who failed to acknowledge that Allah is the one God and Muhammad is his prophet.

In other words, anyone who fails to accept Islam is *ipso facto* an aggressor. Perhaps the most frequently repeated phrase in the Koran is "woe to the unbeliever" (or some variation thereof), followed by a warning that said

I Don't Think That Word Means What You Think It Means

"When we say 'innocent people,' we mean Muslims. As far as non-Muslims are concerned, they have not accepted Islam. As far as we are concerned, that is a crime against God."

—Anjem Choudary, a UK lawyer and Islamic activist, following the 2005 train and bus bombings in London[29]

unbeliever will be punished both in the next world and in this one. Difficult as it may be for the Western mind to grasp, in Islam mere unbelief is considered to be an act of aggression.

But how about Muslim-on-Muslim violence? None of the above seems to justify the frequent aggressions committed by Muslims against other Muslims. Muslims know that they are not supposed to wage war against other Muslims, but they do have a way around the prohibition. By the simple expedient of pronouncing your opponent a non-Muslim, you can presto-change-o transform him into an unbeliever and proceed with his execution. This is known as "pronouncing *takfir*"—an accusation of unbelief that can be roughly translated as "excommunication." ISIS, for example, has pronounced *takfir* on other Muslim groups, and various Islamic authorities have, in turn, pronounced *takfir* on ISIS.[30]

Even though Muslims may find it expedient to call other Muslims "un-Islamic," the main thing to understand is that there is a remarkable consensus among Islamic scholars and jurists about the importance of putting non-Muslims in their place.

Why Most Muslims Are Peaceful

Despite Muhammad's example, Allah's exhortations in the Koran, and the clear teachings of Islamic law on the obligation to engage in jihad, most Muslims today are not actively trying to blow up or behead us. If jihad is a religious duty in Islam, what explains the undoubted fact that the jihadists are in the minority?

First of all, the majority of the members of any religion are drawn to the more moderate practice of their faith. Few are willing to give up everything to act on their beliefs. That's why Francis of Assisi and Mother Teresa are known as "saints," and the rest of the faithful are just Christians.

But there's also a particular historical reason why most Muslims don't act on Islamic teachings about jihad—and why Islamic violence was in remission for decades until its sudden resurgence in the late twentieth century. Peaceful Islam, which Western leaders are counting on to win out over the more violent version touted by the terrorists, is a holdover from the long-dead colonial era.

Ever since 9/11 there has been much talk about reforming Islam so that the religion of Muhammad can be more in step with the modern world. But the Islamic reformation has already come and gone. It reached its high point in the middle of the last century. Unlike the Protestant Reformation, there was no dramatic moment of rebellion—no Ninety-Five Theses nailed to the door of the Grand Mosque in Cairo. Rather, the Muslim world experienced a gradual dilution of the faith as educated Muslims, enamored of the West and disillusioned by the failure of Muslim societies, drifted away from Islam.

In other words, the reformation that created "peaceful Islam" was marked not by a new flowering of Islam but by a neglect of Islam. Secular strongmen such as Nasser in Egypt, Hussein in Iraq, Gaddafi in Libya, and the Shah in Iran put strict limits on the power of the clergy. Hollywood films became popular and so did Western fashions. Beards and caftans went out of style, especially in the cities, and young women abandoned the hijab and ankle-length chadors in favor of Western style dress—including miniskirts.

Unfortunately, this "reformation" in the direction of moderation was only temporary. What looked like a change for the better from the Western point

The Politically Incorrect Guide to Jihad

Reminiscences of a More Peaceful Islam

"I was born into a mildly observant Muslim family in Iraq. At that time, the 1950s, secularism was ascendant among the political, cultural, and intellectual elites of the Middle East. It appeared to be only a matter of time before Islam would lose whatever hold it still had on the Muslim world. Even that term—'Muslim world'—was unusual, as Muslims were more likely to identify themselves by their national, ethnic, or ideological affinities than by their religion."

—Ali A. Allawi, a former Iraqi cabinet minister, reminiscing about his childhood and a more secular Islam[31]

of view looked like a loss of faith from the point of view of the true believer. For some devout Muslims, it looked like a capitulation to Satan. Thus, the original reformation—or rather neglect—of Islam was followed by a much more radical reformation. This time it was a reformation in the generally accepted sense of the word—an attempt to return to the original form of the religion. Moreover, it was a highly successful reformation that brought sweeping changes to Muslim nations that had been on the path to secularization.

The seeds of radical reform were planted by twentieth-century figures such as Sayyid Qutb, who rejected Western immorality and became the chief theorist of the Muslim Brotherhood in Egypt,[32] and Sheikh Fazlollah Nouri, whose theocratic ideals inspired the Ayatollah Khomeini.[33] Anti-colonialism added momentum to the reformation. Its first great victory was the Islamic Revolution that toppled the Shah of Iran in 1979. But it wasn't until the 9/11 jihadi attacks that most Americans' lives were touched by that reformed and newly resurgent Islam. Osama bin Laden, ISIS, and other jihadist groups are its twenty-first-century proponents.

Unfortunately, the conditions that made possible the mellowing of Islam during the last two centuries no longer exist. Islam then had been on the skids ever since the Battle of Vienna in 1683. Islam now is both feared and respected. The West then was strong and confident. The West now is still militarily strong, but in cultural and political terms it is perceived to be weak and indecisive.

Something else has changed as well. Islam's transition to a more moderate mode occurred before the era of mass communications—before television, before the Internet, before smartphones and iPads. It was somewhat easier to ignore the prophet then because he existed largely as a folktale figure—a semi-mythical personage who seemed almost as distant as a character in the *Arabian Nights*. It's a little more difficult to ignore him now, seeing that there are hundreds of websites devoted to telling you exactly what he did and said (with source references) and what he expects of you. The Internet has also made possible the re-creation of the sense of belonging to the *umma*—the worldwide community of Muslim believers.

Naturally, the West is hoping for still another reformation—one that would return the Muslim world to the sleepy-time Islam that existed under the rule of monarchs such as King Farouk and the Shah. But it's easy to underestimate the difficulty of the task. It wouldn't be just a matter of a tweak here, a modification there, and a little less literalism elsewhere. A reformed Islam—reformed, that is, to suit Western tastes—would require a radical reduction of the faith. Huge chunks of the Koran would have to be excised, ignored, or explained away. Sharia law would have to be abolished or else sharply curtailed. Most difficult of all, modernization would require a complete re-evaluation of Muhammad. However hard it would be to make that third reform a reality, it's easy to see why Westerners keep hoping for it: because Muhammad, the Koran, and sharia law are dangerous to our health. But the reformation of Islam will be a difficult task indeed. Muhammad, the *umma*, *jihad*, *jizya* and sex slavery are more present now than they were a hundred years ago. Those genies will be hard to put back into the bottle.

CHAPTER 4

What's in a Name? What Jihad Really Means

Tamerlan and Dzhokhar Tsarnaev, the Boston Marathon bombers, felt obliged by their religion to wage jihad. A song on their YouTube playlist is titled "I will dedicate my life to jihad."[1] Had they misunderstood or perverted the meaning of jihad? Many of Islam's official representatives in America would like us to think so. They tell us that jihad is simply an interior spiritual struggle or a quest for self-betterment.

For example, the Council on American-Islamic Relations (better known as CAIR) in Chicago has sponsored a bus ad campaign presenting a benign interpretation of jihad. In one ad, a picture of a young Muslim woman wearing a gym outfit and a hijab is captioned, "My jihad is to keep fit despite my busy schedule. What's yours?"[2]

But is that really what jihad means to Muslims—that they ought to make the effort to get to the gym more often?

Not according to activist and author Nonie Darwish, who grew up Muslim in Egypt: "This 'inner struggle' business is hogwash. In the Arab world there is only one meaning for jihad, and that is: a religious holy war against infidels.... I have never heard of any discussion of inner struggle in my

Did you know?

★ The idea that jihad is an interior struggle is "hogwash"

★ Wealth and education, not poverty and ignorance, are the risk factors for terrorism

★ The aim of Islamic holy war is not to convert the conquered—at least not immediately

thirty years living in the Middle East. Such nonsense is a PR ploy for Western consumption only....".[3]

In fact, there is very little sense of "interior struggle" in Islam. When the Koran, the hadith, the sira, and the Islamic law manuals refer to jihad, they are almost always referring to the jihad of the sword. In Islam, the most commonly agreed-on definition of jihad is "war against non-Muslims."[4] The purpose of jihad is to establish, spread, and defend the religion of Islam. Although jihad is obligatory, admittedly not everyone is obliged to engage in battle. One can fulfill the obligation through financial support, moral support and, nowadays, through political activism, propaganda, and lawfare. The Koran, however, makes it quite clear that actual fighting is the preferred form of jihad—certainly preferable to prayer and charitable works: "Do you pretend that he who gives a drink to the pilgrims and pays a visit to the Sacred Mosque is as worthy as the man who believes in God and the Last Day, and fights for God's cause? These are not held equal by God.... Those that have embraced the Faith, and left their homes, and fought for God's cause with their wealth and with their persons are held in higher regard by God" (9:19–20).

Those bringing holy war to the infidels are still "held in higher regard" by many Muslims today, as evidenced by the jubilation in the Muslim world following the 9/11 attack,[5] the celebrations in Gaza after the Boston Marathon bombings,[6] the widespread mourning after the death of a jihadist assassin in Pakistan,[7] and the applause for the Brussels attack by Muslim students in Belgium.[8]

Is Jihad Really about Poverty and Discrimination?

But wait just a minute. Can we really blame the poor, uneducated Muslims in the Third World and the slums of Europe for cheering on their team? Even as we deplore the violence, surely we must address the conditions that foster it. Isn't enthusiasm for violent jihad really a result of the terrible disadvantages these populations labor under? Even if jihad doesn't actually mean "interior struggle," isn't the violence an unfortunate side effect of a very real struggle that Muslims have to cope with—against poverty and discrimination?

That seems to be the consensus among Western analysts of Islamic terrorism. Take a recent address to the UN Security Council by Cardinal Pietro Parolin, Vatican Secretary of State. In encouraging the Security Council to address the "root causes" of terrorism, he observed, "Young people traveling abroad to join the ranks of terrorist organizations often come from poor immigrant families, disillusioned by what they feel as a situation of exclusion and by the lack of integration and values in certain societies."[9] In other words, the violent jihad is really about the usual suspects—poverty and discrimination. The argument here is that young men without any realistic prospects for success at home are forced to seek success and glory on foreign battlefields.

In fact, studies have shown that jihadists come from more prosperous backgrounds and are better educated than the average Muslim.[10] Osama bin Laden was born to wealth and privilege in Saudi Arabia. Muslim doctors have been the plotters in a number of terror attacks, and an honors grad of Northeastern University, the son of a prominent Boston endocrinologist, left America to run ISIS's social media campaigns.[11] As National Bureau of Economics researcher Alan Krueger and coauthor Jitka Malechova note, "Any connection between poverty, education, and terrorism is indirect, complicated, and probably quite weak," and there is "little reason for optimism that a reduction in poverty or an increase in educational attainment, by themselves, would meaningfully reduce international terrorism." A public opinion poll of Palestinians "indicates that support for violent attacks against Israeli targets does not decrease among those with higher education and higher living standards," and terrorists who died fighting for Hezbollah

★ ★ ★

Another Prosperous Jihadi

Mohamed Atta, the leader of the 9/11 terrorists, had degrees in architecture and urban planning from Cairo University and the Technical University of Hamburg.[14]

were "at least as likely to come from economically advantaged families and have a relatively high level of education."[12] *Medical News Today* actually named "wealth and education" as risk factors for terrorism.[13]

In any case—going back to Occam's razor—why look for a complicated cause when a simple explanation will do? Poverty may have something to do with why young men go off to foreign lands and risk being blown to kingdom come. But you don't really need to look beyond "kingdom come" itself to explain their willingness to be blown there.

For many a young man, the certainty that there are seventy-two high-bosomed maidens waiting for him on the other side is reason enough to risk the sacrifice of life and limb. And according to most interpretations of the Koran, the only sure way of securing paradise is through martyrdom.[15] Thus, Islam's promise of paradise via jihad creates a very real temptation for young men to take the shortcut to get there. As Professor Louis René Beres points out in an article for Gatestone Institute, "The jihadi terrorist claims to 'love death,' but in his or her mind, that 'suicide' is anything but final: The would-be killer has been promised that death will represent just a trivial and momentary inconvenience, a minor detour on just one more glorious 'martyr's' fiery trajectory toward a life everlasting, in Paradise."[16]

It's a hard combination to beat: life everlasting plus the kind of afterlife that a young man can readily appreciate. One advantage of the Islamic conception of paradise is that it's considerably easier to understand than the Christian idea of heaven as union with God through the Beatific Vision. That may be why most Christians prefer to die in their beds rather than on the battlefield. As I said in *Christianity, Islam, and Atheism,* "Most Christians are not sure if they are quite ready for union with God, but most young men, of whatever religion, are pretty sure they are ready for the rewards offered in the Islamic paradise."[17]

As retired Georgetown professor Father James Schall has pointed out, "When we try to explain this religion [Islam] in economic, political, psychological, or other terms, we simply fail to see what is going on...we are in fact dealing with a religion that claims to be true...."[18] The aforementioned Cardinal Parolin would surely admit that getting to heaven is a major motivational force for Christians. Why is it difficult to understand that devout Muslims have similar motivations?

★ ★ ★

...and a True Believer

Among the items Mohamed Atta packed for his final journey were a wedding suit, a bottle of cologne, and a letter addressed to his brides-to-be in paradise. (An airport error caused his luggage to be left behind on the day of the 9/11 flight.)[19]

The Muslims who join ISIS are true believers who know their Koran and take it seriously. A former Islamic State member described the catechetical process: "We were promised women in heaven and on earth too based on IS jihadist teaching of the verses of some Suras of the holy book of Quran and hadiths by prophet Muhammad, all of which were explained through the Tafsir (explanation) by Islamic scholars like Ibn Majah, Bukhari and Ibn Kathir."[20] In fact, there are not just "some Suras" of the Koran that describe the heavenly garden of delights, but dozens of them. It's a promise whose appeal is not confined to people with few prospects in this world. And it's a promise that looms large in the minds of jihadists.

But They Were Provoked!

So jihad terror can't be blamed on poverty and discrimination. Still, aren't at least some of the violent attacks the fault of people in the prosperous West? If "Islamophobes" and other irresponsible actors would just quit provoking Muslim violence, wouldn't we have a lot less of it?

That was the assumption behind the predictable response to the jihad attack on a Muhammad cartoon exhibit in Garland, Texas, in 2015. To wit: it's not nice to attack people with AK-47s, but, then, it's not nice to draw offensive cartoons of Muhammad either. Or as Alisyn Camerota of CNN put it, "there's a fine line between freedom of speech and being intentionally incendiary and provocative."[21]

This was said in the course of an interview with Pamela Geller, one of the organizers of the Muhammad Art Exhibit and Cartoon Contest that was interrupted by the Islamist attackers. The cartoon contest itself was a response to a Muslim-sponsored "Stand With the Prophet" event that had been held in the same venue four months earlier, calling for restrictions on speech insulting to Islam.[22]

The draw-Muhammad contest upset a lot of people. As is well known, drawing pictures of Muhammad—not just semi-obscene pictures in the style of *Charlie Hebdo*, but any depiction—is offensive to many Muslims.

What's more difficult to understand, though, is why non-Muslims also rushed to call it "blasphemous." That was the description of the contest artwork in a front-page headline in *L'Osservatore Romano*, the Vatican newspaper. The article also criticized the exhibit's "provocative intent, almost wanting to throw gasoline on the fire."[23] But why should Catholics take up the Muslim complaint about blasphemy? The last time I checked, Muhammad was not one of the prophets recognized by the Catholic Church. And has it occurred to Vatican officials that much of the artwork in their own "exhibit"—the Vatican Museum—would be considered scandalous, if not blasphemous, from a Muslim perspective?

Do I Have to Draw You a Picture?

But what about the "provocative intent" criticism? That, at first glance, seems legitimate. Everyone knows by now that drawings of the prophet attract trouble. Why can't Geller and other critics of Islam raise their objections in a nice, non-provocative way?

It seems like a reasonable question until you stop and consider that the reasoned-criticism approach has been tried, with very little effect—except to inspire violence from Muslim mobs to whom even moderate critiques are offensive. Witness the reaction when Pope Benedict merely quoted a fourteenth-century Byzantine emperor in the middle of a scholarly address to a group of academics at the University of Regensburg.

The reaction to Pope Benedict's Regensburg talk was rioting and murder. When, several years later, he spoke out about Pakistan's blasphemy laws—which were being used to justify persecution of Christians—Muslims in Pakistan staged huge rallies to condemn the pope. Six weeks later, Shabaz Bhatti, a prominent Catholic critic of the blasphemy laws, was shot down by gunmen.[24] When, following the bombing of a church in Alexandria, Pope Benedict urged the Egyptian government to do more to protect Christians, he was told to stop interfering in the affairs of Egypt.[25] The Grand Imam of Al-Azhar—Islam's most important university—broke off relations with the Vatican as punishment.

These examples might give the impression that Benedict took an aggressive stand toward Islam, but this is not the case. His many statements about his respect for Muslims and Islam and his affirmations about the common ground shared by Christians and Muslims far outweigh any negative criticisms he made. For the most part, Benedict, along with other recent popes, has refrained from criticizing Islam. In fact, it's hard to imagine a more careful, respectful, and nuanced critic of Islam than Pope Benedict; far from being deliberately provocative, his remarks were made in the interests of dialogue, mutual understanding, and mutual respect for human rights. Yet Muslims responded with fury and violence.

It's not just Muslims who object to any criticism of Islam. Defenders of Islam Inc. is a worldwide conglomerate. The cosponsor of the Muhammad

Art Exhibit was Robert Spencer, the author of several books on Islam and the director of Jihad Watch. Spencer's writings on Islam are well-informed and based almost entirely on Islamic sources. His talks are well-reasoned and are, for the most part, defenses of free speech and of the rights of victims of Islamic oppression. He has never called for violence or lawlessness. Yet he and Geller were barred from entering the UK on the grounds that their presence would be a threat to community security.[26] Here in the U.S., the Southern Poverty Law Center has designated Spencer as the head of a hate group.[27]

The featured speaker at the Garland event was Geert Wilders, a member of the Dutch Parliament. Wilders is in some ways not unlike the Churchill of the pre-war years to whom he has often been compared: he devotes most of his energies to warning complacent Europeans about the gathering storm that threatens to engulf them. Despite the Churchillian resemblance, it's a safe bet that most Americans have never heard of Wilders. Even in Europe, every effort has been made to deny him a platform. When he produced a short documentary film about Islamic violence, he was hit not only with death threats but also with a lawsuit charging him with religious defamation.[28] Although he is the most popular politician in the Netherlands, the European media dismiss him as "far-right."[29]

Like Spencer and Geller, Wilders was also barred from entering the UK, where he was to speak to members of Parliament (although two years later he was re-invited). In hopes of preventing his appearances in Garland and on Capitol Hill, two Muslim congressmen requested that he be denied entry to the U.S.[30]

If you haven't heard of Wilders, you may have heard of Ayaan Hirsi Ali. She also was a member of the Dutch Parliament and, coincidentally, she coproduced a short film about violence against Muslim women. As a result, she received numerous death threats and was eventually forced to move to America.

America is, of course, a bastion of free speech. Unless, that is, you're speaking of Islam—in which case you might not be allowed to speak. Two years ago Hirsi Ali was scheduled to receive an honorary degree at Brandeis University and to speak to students at a diploma ceremony, but the invitation was rescinded when Muslims complained.

Undoubtedly, many wish that Pamela Geller and her ilk would stop annoying Muslims. To many, cartoons and caricatures seem an overly robust way of expressing criticism of Islam. But it appears that we hearken to no other kind. Since 9/11, there have been hundreds of books, thousands of articles, and thousands more news reports all attesting to the existence

> ★ ★ ★
> # The Sinkable Molly Norris
> Molly Norris was a cartoonist for the *Seattle Weekly* who ran afoul of angry Muslims five years ago when she proposed an "Everybody Draw Muhammad Day" contest. A fatwa was duly issued, and Norris was forced to change her identity and go into hiding. She hasn't been heard from since.[31] And, to my knowledge, no newspaper holds an annual Molly Norris day in honor of her commitment to free expression. Unlike the unsinkable Molly Brown, Molly Norris sank out of sight without a trace.

of a violent component in Islamic ideology. Yet a significant proportion of our citizenry still cling to the illusion that Islam is a religion of peace. When no one pays attention to the quiet criticism, it may be time to take out the artist's brush and the cartoonist's pen.

"Do I have to draw you a picture?" is the age-old challenge to those who are slow to understand. The question seems particularly apt for our own times. The answer is, "Yes, you do," because ours is a particularly simple-minded generation. We are so deeply enmeshed in simplistic narratives that conflicting facts don't register unless they are spelled out for us—and preferably in blood-red letters.

The point of the Muhammad art exhibit was not to rile up Muslims, but to wake up non-Muslims who are paying no attention to the everyday evidence that something is seriously amiss in the Muslim world. Seeing that Muslims have rioted over far less, it was plonkingly predictable that there would be an overreaction on the part of some Muslims. But that's the problem. Western citizens only notice when the Muslim reaction is of a spectacular nature. They ignore the slow and steady erosion of our freedoms that occurs when the wish to be inoffensive becomes paramount. In some quarters, the Garland incident is already being cited as a reason to erode them a little more. For example, on the Monday after the attack, *McClatchy DC* news carried a story with the headline, "After Texas shooting: If free speech is provocative, should there be limits?"[32]

I think not. Not only because the freedom of speech is a right that we should never surrender in the face of violent threats, but also because the list of things that provoke Muslims to violence doesn't stop with free speech. In Saudi Arabia, Bibles and rosaries are considered provocative and no churches are allowed. In the "no-go" areas of many European cities, any woman with an uncovered head "provokes" a violent response from local Muslim men. In some Muslim countries, ringing church bells is considered provocative, and in other places it is provocative to rebuild a church that is falling down—so provocative that Christians have lost their lives for the offense. In Afghanistan, education for girls provokes murderous violence. In Pakistan, it's provocative to be a Christian, or an atheist, or a human rights activist—people in all those categories have suffered assassination at the hands of provoked Muslims.

A large part of the "provocative intent" of the Garland exhibit was to prevent such things from ever happening here. The event and its aftermath serve to remind us that it's not a good idea to let the most violent among us determine the limits of free speech. If the Muhammad Art Exhibit is dismissed as incendiary and needlessly provocative, it means that Muslim extremists get to call the shots about what is and is not a permissible form of expression in America. Today it will be Muhammad cartoons that offend. And tomorrow? Well, it could be anything, because Muslim radicals seem to have an unlimited capacity for being offended.

Some will say that Geller and Spencer are needlessly stirring up trouble. In reality, they are saving us from much greater trouble down the road by flushing out the danger we face while there is still time to face it down. If Americans don't wake up to wake-up calls of the drive-by-jihadist variety, they will wake up someday to find that the time for defending their freedoms has already passed.

What Jihad Is For

As we've seen, jihad is not an interior struggle, but a holy war against infidels. Jihadists are motivated not by poverty and discrimination, but by the promises and commands of their religion. And, unfortunately, we can't stop the jihad by refraining from provoking Muslims—unless we want to give Islam the final say over every aspect of our lives. That, in a nutshell, is the very purpose and goal of jihad, precisely the aim for which holy war against us is undertaken by devout Muslims.

The Koran commands, "Fight those who believe not in Allah nor the Last Day, nor hold that forbidden which hath been forbidden by Allah and His Messenger, nor acknowledge the religion of Truth, (even if they are) of the People of the Book, until they pay the Jizya [tax]with willing submission, and feel themselves subdued" (9:29).[33]

Islam means submission, and it demands that everyone submit to Allah's commands—not just willing Muslim believers, but infidels as well. Thus, the sharia ban on blasphemy is meant to apply not just in Iran and Arabia,

A Book You're Not Supposed to Read

The Legacy of Jihad: Islamic Holy War and the Fate of Non-Muslims by Andrew G. Bostom (New York: Prometheus Books, 2008).

but everywhere. The Garland event drew attention to Islam's universal ambitions. Its organizers insisted, in effect, that Americans are not bound by Islam's blasphemy laws and should not submit to them.

Non-Muslims sometimes make the mistake of thinking that Islamic holy war is waged to force people to convert to Islam, but it's more complicated than that. Conversion is the long game. But the immediate goal is submission. After the Islamic conquests of North Africa, for example, the population gradually shifted from about 90 percent Christian to 90 percent Muslim. But that took centuries. The Muslim conquerors didn't demand that the North African Christians immediately convert or die. Instead, they made them submit to conditions that would make it likely that they would convert in the long run.

Those conditions are the Islamic "dhimmi" system—a system of sharia-like rules for non-Muslim subjects. One of the rules required Christians and other subjects to pay a tax called the jizya. It was a heavy tax, and one of the reasons that Muslims were in no hurry for Christians to convert was that the jizya provided a steady income. The word "dhimmi" means "protected person," and the jizya was, in effect, a protection racket. In other words, "Pay us and we will protect you from what we will do to you if you don't comply."

The other purpose of the jizya was to emphasize who was in charge. When they paid it, Christians were often required to kneel before the local Muslim dignitary as a sign of submission, or to approach him on all fours. Sometimes the tax collector would deliver a slap to the face as an added humiliation. This was in accordance with the Koranic injunction that non-Muslims must not only pay the tax, but also "feel themselves subdued" in the process (9:29).

The conditions that govern the lives of dhimmis were elaborated in the Pact of Omar (named after the second caliph, Omar bin al-Khattab). The two dozen or so stipulations include a prohibition on building new churches and repairing old ones, a prohibition on displaying crosses, and a demand that dhimmis give up their seats "to honor the Muslims."[34]

Unfortunately, the dhimmi laws are not a thing of the past. Churches are prohibited in Saudi Arabia, and Christian visitors to the Kingdom are not allowed to bring Bibles with them. In Pakistan and other Muslim countries, Christians are looked upon by many as inferior beings, fit only for menial jobs. In Iraq and Syria, the Islamic State has re-imposed the jizya tax, and Islamic State scholars cite the Koran and the Pact of Omar as justification for doing so.

Islam is a very tolerant religion. It doesn't require that you convert as long as you submit to it. All they are asking for is a little groveling. Thus, if you are a Christian living in the Ottoman Empire you kneel while you pay the 80 percent tax, and if you're a sailor in the U.S. Navy whose boat mysteriously falls into Iranian hands, you kneel and then offer apologies for your behavior while thanking your captors for their "fantastic" hospitality. Oh, and if you're a female sailor, all you have to do is don a hijab as a sign of respect for—actually, submission to—Islamic law.

In the meantime, be assured that your secretary of state will back you up by offering his own profound appreciation for "the quick and appropriate response of the Iranian authorities."[35] At the same time, your president can be relied on not to mention the incident at all, he having made some sort of gentleman's

★ ★ ★

Vocabulary Review

What is the meaning of the word "Islam" again? "Peace"? Er, no. That was what the vast majority of Americans thought it meant circa 2001. But since then, most of us, with the exception of a couple of presidents and secretaries of state, have discovered that it actually means "submission."

★ ★ ★

The Problem with Multicultural Footwashing

During Holy Thursday Mass in 2016, Pope Francis washed the feet of migrants, three of whom were Muslims. Most Catholics understood this as a gesture of humility and brotherhood. That is how the Catholic press reported it—and that, undoubtedly, was the pope's intention.

Many Muslims, however, may see it differently—not as a gesture of brotherhood, but as one of submission and surrender. After all, submission is what Islam expects of other faiths. Muslims consider Islam to be the supreme religion. To the extent that it tolerates the "People of the Book" (Christians and Jews), Islam tolerates them on the condition that they acknowledge its supremacy.

When the pope kneels before a Muslim, these are the thoughts that will come into the minds of many followers of Islam. For them, the pope's gesture will serve as confirmation of the age-old Islamic conception of Christianity as a second-rate religion. Although some Muslims may be moved by the pope's gesture and some may even be converted, it's likely that a majority of Muslims will interpret it as a sign of weakness.

The Holy Thursday Mass came two days after the Brussels bombings, and at a time when Muslim persecution of Christians was escalating. If Christianity was anything other than a humiliated faith, Muslims would expect to see some kind of strong response or some gesture of resolve.

These unfortunate interpretations of the foot-washing ceremony could have been avoided if Pope Francis had not sought to give it a multi-religious flavor. Apparently, he was hoping to make a statement about the church's inclusivity. But the statement may have backfired. Muslims who see the pope's gesture as one of submission before Islam are not going to be convinced of the wisdom of Christian charity, they are going to be convinced of the prudence of sticking with the strong-horse religion. They will be more, not less likely to throw in their lot with the militants. If the Catholic Church appears to be submitting to Islam, they will reason that the only safe course of action is to do the same.

agreement with the Iranians which requires him to pretend that every-thing they do is both fantastic and appropriate.

About two weeks prior to the Persian Gulf naval incident, German citizens were subject to another form of humiliation. On New Year's Eve, a group of a thousand North African and Arab men sexually assaulted women outside the main train station in Cologne.[36] The total number of victims who were either robbed or sexually assaulted was about 600. Many of the women were forced to run through a gauntlet of their tormentors. Similar occurrences took place in numerous other major European cities that night.[37]

All these outrages—from the re-imposition of the jizya to the humiliation of U.S. sailors to the rapes of European women—have the same purpose: to persuade infidels to submit. And some of us seem all too ready to do so. To see a non-Muslim population sliding into dhimmi status in the twenty-first century, you just have to look at Europe.

Europe's Waterslide into Dhimmitude

During the Second World War, Americans naturally had a strong interest in events in Europe. The war in Europe was the stuff of daily headlines in the U.S., and this interest in European affairs continued for a long time afterwards. Americans recognized that their own fate was tied to that of their allies across the Atlantic.

Despite the fact that Europe is even closer now in terms of travel time, that interest has waned considerably. Whatever is happening in Europe—the ever-pending Greek default, the refugee crisis, the fate of the EU itself—seems to have little to do with us. Except for the occasional major headline, most Americans haven't the faintest idea what is happening in the UK and on the continent. Unless there's a war going on, we don't pay much attention to European affairs. Yet there is a war going on in Europe, and it's part of a wider global war, the outcome of which will profoundly affect the future of Americans. The reason we don't notice is that, although there are occasional bombings and shootings, Europe's war is primarily a culture war—a war to determine whether or not Islam will eventually be imposed on the people of Europe. How is that war progressing? Consider a couple of recent headlines:

- "UK waterpark bans bikinis, orders visitors to wear 'Islamically appropriate' clothes"[38]
- "Turn empty Catholic churches into mosques, French Muslim leader says"[39]

It's been announced that Waterworld in Stoke-on-Trent will hold women-only nights, where women will be expected to wear "full-length jogging bottoms and a dark-coloured t-shirt" in accordance with Islamic rules of modesty. Seeing as the Lord Mayor of Stoke-on-Trent is a chap named Majid Kahn, and that Mohammed Pervez is the head of the city council, one assumes that the city is located in a heavily Muslim area of England. Thus, many will accept the news as no big deal—as just a reasonable local concession to diversity, which, of course, is our strength and our salvation. Some of us might even be inclined to welcome the idea. After all, isn't it about time that somebody did something about the near-nudity one encounters in beaches and water parks?

That's one way of looking at it. On the other hand, as Conservative MP Philip Hollobone said, "Imagine...if the boot was on the other foot and swimmers were told they had to dress appropriately in respect of Christians." If you're familiar with the way things work in politically correct Britain, you'll realize that that's a non-starter. In explanation of the new policy, a Waterworld spokesman said, "We pride ourselves in having the adaptability and diversity to cater to demands of our guests."[40] But as Brits are coming to realize, the only diversity that counts in England today is Islam.

Over on the other side of the Channel, a top Muslim official has suggested turning empty or abandoned Catholic churches into mosques. There are presently about 2,500 mosques in France, but it's estimated that at least 5,000 are needed for France's growing Muslim population.

Again, at first glance, there seems to be no cause for alarm. After all, as Dali Boubakeur, rector of the Grand Mosque in Paris, said, "It's the same God, these are neighboring rites, fraternal, and I think that Muslims and Christians can coexist and live together." Christian leaders concurred. Monseigneur Ribadeau-Dumas, spokesperson for the Bishops' Conference of France, told radio station Europe 1 that "Muslims should, like Christians and Jews, be able to practice their religion."[41]

Oh, well, that's all right, then. Still, behind the headlines one detects some alarming shifts in population and in spirituality. Not only are Catholics unable to keep their churches full, they're unable to keep them open. The monseigneur says that Muslims should be able to practice their faith just like Christians. But what happens when Muslims practice their faith and Christians don't? Christian indifference has resulted in a population vacuum and a spiritual vacuum. And it's no secret who has been filling the empty space. Muslims are, so to speak, doing the jobs that Christians won't do—that is, the work of praying and propagating.

If these shifts continue apace, the real question will not be whether Muslims will be able to practice their religion but whether Christians and Jews will. Although "Islamophobia" is the buzzword of the day, statistically one is much more likely to fall victim to "Christophobia" at the hands of zealous Muslims. As is now dawning on the world, in those places where Islam is practiced to the fullest, non-Muslim worship is highly restricted. The Islamic system for subjugating infidels has been revived in its entirety in ISIS-ruled Iraq and Syria. But even in Pakistan and Iran, Christians had best confine their Christianity to the inside of a church. In Afghanistan, there are no churches left. Meanwhile, the question of freedom of religion for Jews living

Su Casa Es Mi Casa

"The main mosque in Dublin is a former Presbyterian church. In England, the St. Mark's Cathedral is now called the New Peckam Mosque, while in Manchester, the Mosque of Disbury was once a Methodist church. In Clitheroe, Lancashire, the authorities granted permission to have an Anglican church, Saint Peter's Church in Cobridge, transformed into the Madina Mosque. It is no longer taboo in the media to talk about 'the end of British Christianity.'"

—Giulio Meotti, "Europe: Allah Takes over Churches, Synagogues"[43]

in Muslim-majority lands is more or less an academic question, since there is only a remnant of Jews left in the Muslim world.

Jews in France who have taken note of the population shift and understand what it portends are leaving that European country in large numbers. Those who remain are still guaranteed freedom of religion—as long as they can hire enough security guards at the synagogue to ward off firebombers, armed assailants, and the occasional Muslim mob.[42]

As for Christians, the future also seems dim, or, to use the technical term, dhimmi—the system under which Christians are relegated to second-class status and expected to know their place, to practice their faith as quietly and unobtrusively as possible, and to avoid any word or action which might be perceived as an insult to Islam and its prophet.

If a future of dhimmitude seems difficult to imagine, take a tour of Europe's great and small cathedrals and note the shrunken size of the congregations. Will Europeans who have been unable to resist secularization be likely to resist Islamization? While the founders of secularist movements and ideologies tend to be of the radical-individualist sort, the rank-and-file tend to be of the trend-following sort. And it's rather amazing how quickly they pick up on the latest trends. In the blink of an eye, historically speaking, fringe behavior has become fashionable. But what's trendy today is often gone by tomorrow. The sudden acceptance of same-sex marriage and transgenderism may seem like signal victories for secularism, but they might better be seen as the prelude to the demise of secularism. Because the biggest trending trend in the Western world is not transgenderism, but Islam. And if the general citizenry can be so easily and rapidly converted to accept behavior that only yesterday was considered aberrant, they can just as easily be converted to a once-alien belief system. When push comes to shove, Europeans may discover that the switch from bikinis to burqa bathing wear is not so difficult after all.

It took North Africans centuries under the dhimmi system to convert to Islam, but then again, medieval Africans did not subscribe to a relativistic view of life. The conversion of modern-day Europe will likely be accomplished much more rapidly. Ten years ago few would have thought that transgenders would be the new heroes of our society. But Western societies now seem disposed to celebrate any change so long as it's perceived to be a rejection of Western mores. It doesn't take a Nostradamus to predict that mass conversions to Islam may well be the in-thing in a decade or less. But, whereas transgenderism is most probably a passing fad, Islam is not a flash in the pan. The next big fad may turn out to be the fad to end all fads.

Because of the pervasiveness of relativism in the UK and on the continent, Europe's "culture war" hardly qualifies as a war. A slow-motion capitulation might be a more accurate description. Whatever you wish to call it, Americans need to pay attention, because the relativist mindset which is enabling the Islamization of Europe is almost as firmly entrenched on this side of the Atlantic. Americans need to pay attention because, despite its strange appeal for some, living under sharia law is not something you would wish on your worst enemy—much less want for yourself.

A Dangerous Ally?

Relativism is clearing a path for the Islamization of the West, particularly in Europe. Moreover, there is a strong alliance between the Left and Muslims in

I, for One, Welcome Our New Muslim Overlords

"Islam is here to stay."

—French Prime Minister Manuel Valls[44]

Western countries. At the same time, ironically, conservative Christians who have been faring badly in the fight against militant secularism look to Muslims as possible allies to stand alongside them in the culture wars.

Some Catholic intellectuals, for example, seem to think that Muslims are our natural allies in this struggle because they supposedly share similar values and because, like Catholics, they are opposed to adultery, pornography, and homosexual behavior. Catholic philosopher Peter Kreeft, for example, has championed what he calls an "ecumenical jihad" against secularism,[45] while conservatives and Christians as diverse as Dinesh D'Souza,[46] E. Michael Jones,[47] and Timothy Cardinal Dolan[48] have emphasized the common moral ground shared by Catholics and Muslims.

As has conservative scholar Professor Robert George. In a piece for *First Things* entitled "Muslims, Our Natural Allies," he argues that Muslims are our natural confederates because they believe in "modesty, chastity, and piety."

The particular occasion for the piece was the celebration of World Hijab Day on February 1, 2014 and, in fact, the article is accompanied by a short video in which an attractive, articulate and, shall we say, "with it" young woman in a hijab makes the case for wearing the Islamic head covering as an expression of freedom and modesty. For example, "Does it bother you that I have control over what I choose to show and withhold from the world?" (A disclaimer may be in order here. One of the reasons that the young lady is so adept at promoting the hijab is that selling hijabs is her business. She is the founder and owner of Pearl-Daisy, an online hijab and clothing store in the UK.)

Even if they agree with him on the "allies" issue, regular readers of Professor George may be disappointed in this piece. In contrast to his usual lucid and cogent analysis of social and constitutional issues, this piece relies largely on emotional arguments. For example, much of the piece is taken up with praising George's many Muslim friends, all of whom seem to be model citizens: "I have met hundreds of religiously observant Muslims over the past several years and many are now my close friends.... They are among the finest people I know...they work, as we do, to inculcate in their children the virtues of honesty, integrity, self-respect, and respect for others, hard work, courage, modesty, chastity, and self-control.... They thank God for the freedom they enjoy in the United States...."[49]

This tells us a lot about the quality of the company Professor George keeps, but it doesn't tell us much about the Muslim faith. We are simply left with the impression that only a fine belief system could produce such fine people. But, of course, it's not always wise to judge a belief system according to the character of those who believe in it. Sometimes, people manage to rise above whatever belief system they embrace or have been born into. For example, one of our family friends when I was growing up was a member of the Communist Party U.S.A. (until he left it to join a still more radical communist organization). Yet he was the soul of kindness and gentleness. I doubt very much that he would ever have raised a hand against a fellow human being. But, for all that, he devoutly believed in an ideology that was responsible for the oppression of millions.

More to the point, if personal acquaintance is going to be the measure for deciding issues, I am also acquainted with a former Muslim who is a very fine person, but who felt compelled to leave Islam because of its cruel and oppressive nature. Her name is Nonie Darwish, and anyone who has read her book *Cruel and Usual Punishment* would not come away with the impression that Islamic morality is similar to Christian morality.[50]

Nevertheless, Professor George, along with Kreeft, D'Souza (now apparently an ex-Catholic), Jones, and others, holds that Catholics share a common morality with Muslims. One example of this, says George, is that both stand opposed to the objectification and de-personalization of women that we see in advertising, entertainment, and fashion. He asks, "Is there an actress in all of Hollywood who, when appearing at one of those absurd award shows dressed in a see-through gown...can compare with the beautiful young Muslim woman in the video I posted?"[51] Personally, I'd vote for the Muslim woman, but what does that have to do with the price of tea in China? Or, in this case, the reality of Islamic beliefs and practices? The question is not whether modest looks and dress are becoming, but whether or not the young woman's argument that the hijab represents freely adopted modesty is true in general.

She makes the case that wearing the hijab is a matter of choice. Sometimes it is, of course, but there is compelling evidence that the majority of Muslim women wear the hijab because they have to. In Iran, for instance, the wearing of the hijab in public is a legal requirement—as it is even in Aceh Province in supposedly moderate Indonesia. Where the hijab is not legally required it is often socially mandated. By "socially mandated," I don't mean that women wear it out of fear that someone's maiden aunt will cluck her tongue, but out of fear of physical harm. As Jane Kramer reported in a New Yorker piece, "More often those girls were under orders from their fathers and uncles and brothers, and even their male classmates.... Girls who did not conform were excoriated, or chased, or beaten by fanatical young men meting out Islamic justice. Sometimes girls were gang raped."[52]

That's not a description of some tribal village in the hinterlands of Afghanistan. It's an account of conditions in the Muslim suburbs surrounding Paris. According to Serge Trifkovic, "Many French-born Arab girls in the ghetto resort to wearing *hijab* as the only protection against face-slashing and gang-rapes."[53] Is wearing the hijab a matter of personal choice? In some places, yes. But according to a survey conducted in 2003, 77 percent of French girls who wore the hijab said they did so because of physical threats.[54] Given those facts, it's hard to argue that the hijab represents freedom.

Of course, people eventually become accustomed to whatever reality they have to live with. Under such intense social pressure, it is understandable that many Muslim girls and women will come to accept the hijab, or even the burqa, as just part of life. It can become psychologically intolerable to constantly chafe about conditions over which one has no control and about which one must not complain. Indeed, it is a common observation that people often feel the need to justify the situations they must endure. No doubt, many Muslim women have convinced themselves that wearing the hijab is the good and proper thing to do, but this is not quite the same as the Christian ideal, which is that modesty and chastity are freely chosen virtues that reflect an interior disposition rather than a socially enforced requirement.

George also makes a point of contrasting Muslim modesty with Western cultural pressure to objectify and even "pornify" women. In doing so, however, he tends to gloss over the much greater objectification of women that occurs in traditional Muslim cultures. It may be true, as he says, that the typical American male looking at the sexy Hollywood actress will be tempted to de-personalize her so that "who she actually is as a person is utterly submerged," but what of the women in the niqab or burqa?[55] The niqab has openings for the eyes only. The burqa completely hides a woman's features. Isn't that also a situation in which the personality of the woman is utterly submerged?

And it's not just a matter of clothing. The objectification runs much deeper than that. Anyone who has read Nonie Darwish's account of growing up in Egypt, or Wafa Sultan's remembrance of her life in Syria, or Ayaan Hirsi Ali's description of her childhood in Somalia will realize that the objectification of women in Muslim societies is several orders of magnitude

★ ★ ★

The Status of Women in Islam

The widely consulted Islamic law manual *Reliance of the Traveller* stipulates that women must stand behind men and boys in prayer (f 12. 32), that the testimony of a man is equal to the testimony of two women (o 24. 10), and that the indemnity to be paid for the death or injury of a woman is one-half the indemnity paid for a man (o 4. 9). Moreover, although a man can divorce his wife at will, a woman cannot divorce without her husband's permission (n 1.1, n 3.2, n 3.3). [58]

greater than it is in the U.S. or Europe. In fact, it is written into sharia law that women are second-class citizens with second-class rights.

For a personal account of how this Islamic law for women works in practice, read Darwish's remembrance of first seeing a church wedding in an old Hollywood movie and her amazement at "the way a Christian woman was honored and elevated by her husband and society."[56] Or read Sultan's account of how her grandfather in Syria forced her grandmother to solicit a young woman to be his new bride.[57] And no, it hasn't gotten better for women since then. In much of the Muslim world, the situation for women has worsened.

Professor George is also concerned—as we all should be—about "the sexualization of children at younger and younger ages" in our culture.[59] However, this sexualization of children, bad as it is, takes place in our culture largely on the level of advertising, entertainment, and grade-school sex education. In Iran, Yemen, Saudi Arabia, Bangladesh, and Northern Nigeria, it manifests itself in the soul-destroying institution of child marriage. In Iran, for example, lawmakers are trying to lower the marriageable age for girls from thirteen back to nine[60] (where it stood during the rule of the Ayatollah Khomeini). Mohammad Ali Isfenani, chairman of the Iranian Parliament's Legal Affairs Committee, has called the current minimum age of thirteen "un-Islamic." Moreover, the Iranian Parliament recently passed a bill that would allow a man to marry his adopted daughter.[61] In his essay, Professor George contrasts the "upright life" esteemed by Muslims with the debased ethics of Hollywood. But in some respects, Islamic ethics more closely resemble the ethics of Woody Allen and Roman Polanski than those espoused by the Catholic Church.

Although George does acknowledge that in some Muslim cultures, "the covering of women is taken to an extreme and reflects a very real subjugation," he does not seem to realize just how widespread this subjugation is. His perspective is what is generally taken to be the broad, cosmopolitan view, but it seems to reflect an acquaintance with only a very narrow subset of the Muslim world. It is highly likely that the "religiously observant" Muslims in his circle are ignoring many of the rules they are supposed to follow as good Muslims.

The notion that "the piety and moral convictions" of traditional Muslims "make them natural allies of social conservatives" is a stretch. To bolster his point about social conservatism among Muslims, George points to the fact that a majority of American Muslims voted for George W. Bush in the 2000 election.[62] He neglects to mention, though, that according to a poll conducted by the American-Muslim Task Force, 89 percent of Muslims voted for Barack Obama, the pro-abortion candidate in 2008.[63]

Moreover, according to a 2012 poll conducted by Wenzel Strategies, many American Muslims are not champions of religious liberty and free speech. Fifty-eight percent of the Muslim-American respondents believed that criticism of Islam or Muhammad should not be allowed under the U.S. Constitution. Forty-six percent said that Americans who criticize or parody Islam should face criminal charges, while one in eight respondents felt that such crimes merit the death penalty.[64]

Someone whose goal is absolute supremacy is a dangerous ally. And Islamic supremacism is the raison d'etre of Islam—expressed not only in the Koran, in sharia law, and in the system of dhimmitude, but also occasionally by prominent American Muslims. For example, Omar Ahmad, the cofounder of CAIR (Council on American-Islamic Relations) told a Muslim audience in California in 1998, "Islam isn't in America to be equal to any other faith, but to become dominant. The Koran should be the highest authority in America, and Islam the only accepted religion on earth."[65] That's the kind of statement we might expect from an ayatollah in Iran or a mufti in Arabia. It ought to raise questions about whether conservatives and Christians can profitably ally themselves with Muslims—and, if so, with which Muslim groups.

Catholics and Muslims have worked together toward common goals in the past, most notably at the World Population Conference in 1994. But a lot has transpired since then in the Muslim world. The Muslim Brotherhood and other Islamist groups have considerably more influence now, and moderate Muslims have considerably less. Perhaps conservatives in the Western world can still work together with Muslims against militant secularism, but they need to find a more reliable principle to guide them than "the enemy of my enemy is my friend."

PART II

Jihad Without Bombs

CHAPTER 5

The Quiet Kind of Jihad

The bloody jihad attacks in Europe have undoubtedly pushed European populations and their governments in the direction of submission to Islam. After all, who wants to risk violent death? In the short term it can seem prudent to appease armed aggressors, even though in the long run it's the most foolish thing you can do. With angry Muslim mobs threatening violence whenever they're "offended," it's easy to think that whatever is upsetting them this time—bikinis at the waterpark, bacon for breakfast at the local pub, or pictures of pigs in children's books—is not really the hill you want to die on.

But it's not violent jihad alone that is conquering Europe for Islam. In his 2014 speech blaming Islamic terrorism on "Islamism," former UK Prime Minister Tony Blair alluded to the recently uncovered "Trojan Horse" plot by Muslims to take over more than twenty schools in the Birmingham area of England.[1] Which brings us to the quiet kind of jihad.

Jihad in Sheep's Clothing

All jihad has the same goal: putting the reins of power into hands of Muslims, and ultimately the complete submission of Western society to Islam. But the

Did you know?

★ Ahmed "the clock boy" seems to have deliberately provoked a confrontation

★ A top expert on Islamic law was let go by the U.S. military for pointing out that Muslims have a religious obligation to wage jihad

★ A manual for U.S. troops in Afghanistan directed them to avoid "any criticism of pedophilia" so as not to upset the locals

★ ★ ★

Winnie-the-Pooh: An Endangered Species in the Land of His Birth

"Guidance from leading educational publisher the Oxford University Press prohibits authors from including anything that could be perceived as pork-related in their books."

—*Daily Mail*, January 13, 2015[2]

A spokeswoman for the Oxford University Press explained that while they now avoid publishing pictures of pigs and pork on account of "cultural sensitivities," they "wouldn't dream of editing out a 'pig' character from an historic work of fiction."[3] So Winnie-the-Pooh may be safe for now. But the use of the word "historic" in that disclaimer is ominous; if you have a great idea for a *new* children's book with a pig in it, no point in pitching it to Oxford University Press.

threat comes in two forms: armed or violent jihad, and stealth or cultural jihad. Since armed jihad is more conspicuous, it gets most of our attention.

Stealth jihad, which, as the name implies, is the less noticeable type, is an attempt to turn a culture in an Islamic direction by infiltrating and influencing key institutions such as schools, courts, churches, media, government, and the entertainment industry. It's the incremental spread of Islamic law and culture in a society by means of activism, propaganda and lawfare. Think of it as an influence operation. It's the long march through the institutions that the Italian Marxist Antonio Gramsci recommended to European communists. Leftists have already co-opted many of society's institutions. What's to prevent jihadists from doing the same?

Armed jihad is the sudden descent of the scimitar on the neck of the unprepared. Stealth jihad is the slow process by which citizens are lulled into a state of unpreparedness. It's the gradual softening-up routine that conditions the unsuspecting "mark" to eventually accept sharia law.

If all goes smoothly, the scimitar may be unnecessary. The stealth jihadists have made enormous inroads in Britain and in Europe.

And currently, there are at least a dozen well-financed and well-connected stealth jihad organizations operating in the United States. If they play their cards right, resistance to their agenda will be minimal. Their influence is amplified by the willingness of legions of educators, business-men, church leaders, and politicians—all eager to display their open-mind-edness—to lend a hand.

While they slowly build up power and influence, the stealth jihadists count on the rest of us to mistake the wolf at the door for a sheep. They can't afford to speak openly about their aims—at least, not initially. But once the stealth jihad is past a certain point, it's the average citizen who will be forced to hold his tongue.

That's the way the process works. If it happens slowly enough and if the authorities pretend it's nothing out of the ordinary, you can get used to the ubiquitous headscarves in the streets, the demands for halal food on every menu, and the Muslim majority on the local school board.

Stealth jihad need not be particularly stealthy. In fact, Muslim groups can be quite vocal about their demands. But in comparison to suicide bomb-ings and beheadings on London streets, demands for halal menus, special toilet facilities in public places, and sharia courts for resolving family mat-ters seem minor in nature.

What's more, there's an implicit understanding that granting these con-cessions will serve to keep the violent kind of jihad at bay. It's the latest twist on the old mafia extortion ploy. This time around, it goes something like this: "You and I are reasonable men, but my friend here is hard to con-trol. He can get very excitable if his son is forced to sit next to pork-eaters at the school cafeteria." It's all unspoken, of course, but those who are attuned to cultural change will find it easy to convince themselves that their own sons and daughters can only benefit from eating a more multi-culturally sensitive diet.

The trouble is, such concessions are more, not less, likely to bring the other, violent kind of jihad closer.

In significant ways, stealth jihad paves the way for armed jihad. In its early stages, it can create localized environments where homegrown jihadists can grow and flourish. In its later stages? Let's hope we don't find out.

Remember that the purpose of every kind of jihad is to coerce submission to Islam. The stealth jihadists have succeeded in carving out significant areas of European cities in which Islamic law is now enforced. Many of the "sensitive urban zones" that ring Paris, for example, are effectively controlled by Muslims. They are places where pork, alcohol, uncovered women—and official representatives of the non-Muslim state, such as the French police—are not welcomed by the locals. Many Muslims in Europe would prefer to integrate with the host culture. But stealth jihadists have succeeded in creating parallel Muslim societies that can operate under Islamic rules with very little outside interference. European authorities have been reluctant to challenge the distinctly un-European customs, many of them illegal, that have developed in the "no-go" areas.

The Europeans were hoping that what happened in the sensitive zones would stay in the sensitive zones, but that hasn't been the case. The Muslim enclaves that stealth jihad helps to create eventually become breeding grounds for terror. In addition to the occasional synagogue firebombing, European cities have been treated to a steady stream of riots, violent demonstrations, refusals to abide by public health regulations, car-burnings, and "virtue police" patrols that ensure that the locals comply with Islamic codes of dress and behavior.

And now these areas are breeding major terrorist attacks on people and places outside the zones. The perpetrators of the *Charlie Hebdo* massacre didn't pop up out of nowhere. Cherif Kouachi, one of the two assailants, was part of the 19th Arrondissement Network, a terrorist group that operates out of a Paris neighborhood with a large Muslim population.[4] Their friend Amed Coulibaly, who killed four hostages at a kosher market, grew up in Grigny, another suburb of Paris with a heavy concentration of Muslims.[5]

The Molenbeek area of Brussels, Belgium, where Salah Abdeslam was arrested for the Paris attacks, is yet another such area, and another breeding ground for terror attacks.[6] These increasingly sharia-compliant neighborhoods provide environments where terrorists and would-be terrorists can find like-minded collaborators and supporters.

But that's Europe, with its large, unassimilated Muslim populations and sharia-compliant no-go suburbs. What about America?

Stealth jihad in the U.S. is more advanced than you might think.

Its influence can be seen in textbooks and on college campuses, in the media, and even in the movies. There are numerous American activist groups dedicated to stealth jihad. Nearly all of them are offshoots of the Muslim Brotherhood, the organization that over the past several decades, lest we forget, has played a key role in the second "reform" of Islam—in the direction of closer adherence to the Koran, revival of sharia law, and violent jihad. Today the Brotherhood is the group most responsible for the recent widespread persecution of Christians in Egypt. Although disguised as civil rights groups, the Muslim Brotherhood–offshoot organizations in the United States would like nothing better than to see sharia become the law of the land. And their litigators are as adept at lawfare as ISIS is at warfare.

The most prominent of these groups is CAIR, the Council on American-Islamic Relations. After every violent jihad attack, you can count on a CAIR spokesman to show up on your TV screen to perfunctorily condemn the violence and then to warn about the "real" threat—the supposed backlash against the Muslim community. CAIR has long been accepted by the media and the government as the face of moderate Islam in America, but the evidence suggests it is anything but. In fact, it is considered by some to be the premier

A Book You're Not Supposed to Read

Muslim Mafia: Inside the Secret Underworld That's Conspiring to Islamize America by David Gaubatz and Paul Sperry (Washington, DC: WND Books, 2009).

stealth jihad organization in the U.S. It has close ties with the Muslim Brotherhood, and in a 2008 court decision it was designated as an unindicted co-conspirator in a large-scale terrorist funding operation.[7] And, although the U.S. government acts as if CAIR were a model of moderation, the government of the United Arab Emirates includes it on its list of worldwide terrorist organizations.[8] According to David Gaubatz and Paul Sperry's *Muslim Mafia*, CAIR operates more like a criminal underworld conspiracy than a civil rights organization. Likewise, numerous other "moderate Muslim" organizations have equally questionable connections. Most of the groups that purport to represent American Muslims—the Islamic Society of North America (ISNA), the Islamic Circle of North America (ICNA), the Fiqh Council of North America, the Muslim Student Association, and so forth—are also closely linked to the Muslim Brotherhood. These links were established in the landmark Holy Land Foundation Trial in 2008, the largest terrorist-funding trial in U.S. history, in which a number of Muslim Brotherhood front organizations were named as unindicted co-conspirators.[9]

Stealth Jihad Meets PC America

Surprisingly, the stealth jihadists meet with little resistance. That lack of pushback can be explained by one other factor in the overall mix—political correctness.

To many, political correctness means nothing more than that a bunch of busybodies may get to rename your favorite sports team because the current name deeply offends them. It's annoying, but it's not the end of the world. Better to go along to get along, we reason.

The trouble is, political correctness might well spell the end of the world as we know it. Over the years, the PC codes have hardened into something like prison bars. In fact, you can go to jail for violating them. In Europe, it's not uncommon for critics of Islam to face fines and jail time.

Speech codes were originally intended to protect the fragile egos of college students. But now, they are increasingly used to protect the "right" of Muslims not to be offended. Again, not everyone sees this as a big deal. Some may argue that it's worth stifling yourself in order to keep the peace—that there's no sense in exciting excitable people.

No doubt there's something to be said for the quiet life. But unless we want an extraordinarily quiet life—the kind where citizens are afraid to speak their minds for fear of ending in prison or worse—it's time to put political correctness in its place.

Without the PC climate that protects it from examination, it's doubtful that Islam in the West could have advanced so far, so fast. It's ironic that a system intended to protect against intolerant speech is helping to usher in a reign of intolerance that threatens to silence us all. If you want to see where political correctness leads, take a trip to Saudi Arabia. They've been practicing the art of appropriate speech for far longer than we have, and they've honed it to a sharp edge.

Hint: when you pack, remember to leave your Bible at home.

It's lucky for the stealth jihadists that the resurgence of militant Islam happened to coincide with the emergence of political correctness. Political correctness greases the skids for stealth jihad; stealth jihad feeds on political correctness just as bacteria feeds on sugar. Political correctness is the "open sesame" password that allows the stealth jihadists in America to go just about anywhere they please. The long march through the institutions needn't take that long when the institutions are putting out the multicultural welcome mat.

Political correctness dictates that we don't have a right to intrude on the cultural space of the "other." PC thinking requires an excessive respect for

★ ★ ★

One Small Win for the Stealth Jihad

As just one example among hundreds of others, consider how a bistro in Winooski, Vermont, removed a window sign advertising its delicious bacon because a Muslim woman claimed it was offensive.[11]

and deference to other cultures. Multiculturalism, after all, does not mean that different cultures should mix together in the great American melting pot, but that each subculture should retain its distinct identity. According to PC multicultural dogma, the preservation of the other's culture in its undiluted form is such a high priority that to expect the newcomers to conform to the native culture is tantamount to an act of imperialism. The confluence of political correctness and cultural jihad has already brought Europe to a perilous state. Some observers of the European scene feel that civil wars are just over the horizon. The situation is not nearly so bad in America, but it could quickly deteriorate if our assorted opinion-makers continue to self-censor. One effect of the self-censorship is that the American public has no idea of how bad the situation has become in Europe, and thus no inkling that the same sort of thing could someday happen here.

Right now, most Americans are more afraid of violating the rules of PC than they are of another 9/11 occurrence. They're afraid, in other words, of being thought bigoted, racist, or—God forbid—Islamophobic. "Jihad" is not the kind of thing one mentions in polite society. There's little resistance to stealth jihad in America, because the few who do resist are reliably cast by the PC enforcers as anti-Muslim haters. Most people don't want that to happen to them. So they don't make a fuss when Muslims make demands. They go along to get along.

We have very little defense against the Trojan-horse type of jihad. First, because we are hindered by a PC multicultural ideology that demands that we be tolerant unto death. And, second, because the cultural jihadists are well aware of this weakness in our armor. They know that we dare not criticize a non-Christian religion, and they know how to take advantage of our reluctance. Criticize anything Muslim or Islamic, and charges of racism, religious bigotry, and Islamophobia will soon come your way, and maybe a lawsuit as well.

To see how stealth jihad—helped along by the background threat of armed jihad—regularly achieves victories in politically correct twenty-first-century America, consider the following scenarios.

- Suppose that you are an editor at a mid-sized publishing house, and suppose you are considering a proposal for a book on Islamic terrorism. The sample chapters are thoroughly researched and well-written, but you notice that the author links Islamic jihad to Islam itself. It's the kind of book that, in ordinary times, you might be inclined to publish. But these are not ordinary times. With all the talk about "Islamophobia" and "hate speech" against Muslims, you know the New York sophisticates in your world will look askance upon the publication of any book that criticizes Islam. You don't want your company to be associated with cultural imperialism, or even racism. The massacre of the editorial staff at *Charlie Hebdo* magazine is also fresh in your mind. Of course, nothing like that is likely to happen in America, but you're not sure if you have the right to put your company's employees at any risk, no matter how slight. Besides, you're sure the author won't have any trouble finding another publisher.

- Suppose you are the pastor of a large suburban parish and suppose further that several members of your parish want to invite a well-known speaker to talk about the threat from militant Islam. You check the Internet and find that the speaker is listed by the Southern Poverty Law Center as the head of a hate group. Upon further checking, you find that this speaker has had speaking invitations rescinded by four different bishops. You doubt that the man is really a hater, and you're disposed to hear what he has to say. At the same time, you realize that an invitation would probably bring unwelcome pressure from local Muslim groups and unwelcome attention from the local media. If the story gets into the news, your own bishop will not thank you for throwing a wrench into the Muslim-Christian interfaith dialogue. And in the back of your mind, you recall that numerous churches in other parts of the world have been firebombed by Muslim terrorists. You tell yourself that it's highly unlikely that your own church would ever be a target but, still, why put your parishioners at even the slightest risk? Besides, you're sure that other parishes in other cities will provide a venue for the speaker. In the big scheme of things, it won't matter if one parish decides to pass up the opportunity.

- Suppose that you sit on a city commission that has to decide on a proposal for the construction of a mosque and Islamic center. Opponents of the plan point out that the city's Muslim population is too small to justify the building of the large and expensive project. Some of them angrily insist that mosques are used as recruiting centers for jihad, that 80 percent of American mosques teach an extremist ideology, and that the deeds to a quarter of American mosques are held by a Muslim Brotherhood trust. How, they want to know, can you possibly consent to such folly? On the other hand, you are a strong believer in religious freedom. You would not oppose a similar request for a new church or a synagogue. How can you deny Muslims the opportunity to worship in their own way? Your minister feels the same way. When you ask his advice on the matter, he reminds you that all Christians have a duty to welcome strangers. Your meetings with Imam Badawi, the leader of the Muslim community, have also been reassuring. He deplores the atrocities committed by ISIS, and assures you that they are betrayers of Islam. The true Islam, he maintains, is a religion of peace and justice. You have your doubts about the wisdom of the project, and you wonder what the long-term consequences will be. Still, it's your belief that the traditional American principles of religious liberty, tolerance, and impartiality should trump all other considerations. You decide to give the Islamic center project the go-ahead.

Is the hypothetical mosque project an example of stealth jihad at work? Or does it represent a legitimate desire to freely worship God? Or is it a little bit of both? That's the trouble with stealth jihad. It's difficult to resist it because it's difficult to say whether any particular demand or request is an example of cultural aggression or simply a desire for equal treatment. In most cases, those who have to make the decisions will be predisposed to accept the more benign interpretation. Otherwise they risk running afoul of the rules of political correctness, which—although unwritten—carry quite a sting for violators. Very few relish the prospect of being called racist, or bigoted, or Islamophobic.

Multiply the three scenarios above by a thousand, and you can see why Americans remain relatively complacent about the threat from Islam.

A Stealth Jihad Arsenal

"The mosques are our barracks, the domes our helmets, the minarets our bayonets, and the faithful our soldiers."

—Turkish president Recep Tayyip Erdogan[12]

When everyone in the information business decides that the prudent thing is to pass the buck, everyone else ends up with only a passing knowledge of Islam.

It's not as though Americans don't know about terrorist attacks in Tunisia, Nigeria, Paris, and Brussels. But because the media police their own thoughts so carefully, these events tend to be presented as discrete happenings with no connection to a larger pattern. More significantly, very little attention is paid to the phenomenon of stealth jihad—the quiet preparatory process that makes possible the more spectacular acts of jihad.

When Father Jim or Bishop Murphy decides to rescind a speaking invitation lest the local chapter of the Council on American-Islamic Relations take offense, it's partly because of pressures created by stealth jihadists. When a book publisher decides to pass on a book that might hurt the sensitivities of the Muslim community, it's because stealth jihad has magnified the clout of the Muslim community well beyond its actual numbers.

A new mosque on the block? Cancel the controversial speaker? Head coverings and halal meals in the middle school? Criminal penalties for those who insult a prophet?

Some of these issues are already with us, and some of them will be coming soon to a parish, court, or school board in your neighborhood. The success of stealth jihad depends on the willingness of those who decide these issues to take the easy way out—that is, to do the politically correct, non-offensive thing. Let's hope that the deciders understand that there are larger matters at stake than whether or not someone's feelings are injured.

★ ★ ★

Ahmed "the Clock Boy": A Case Study in Stealth Jihad

Courtesy of the Office of Congressman Mike Honda

You've no doubt heard about the "clock boy"—the fourteen-year-old Muslim student who brought a self-made clock to school to show to his teachers and was then detained by police on the suspicion that the clock might be a bomb.

The media pounced on the story as a classic case of Islamophobia, the president complimented Ahmed Mohamed on his "cool clock" and invited him to the White House,[13] and just about everyone agreed that the bespectacled young clock maker was a boy genius. Offers of scholarship money poured in from giant social media companies, and the Cambridge Public Library, which might have been expected to show more prudence (it stands next to Cambridge Rindge and Latin—the school attended by the Boston Marathon bombers), hosted a "Stand with Ahmed and Build Your Own Clock Day."[14]

And then the clock narrative began to unwind. It turns out that Ahmed didn't make the clock, but had merely taken out the innards of a Radio Shack digital clock and installed it in a pencil box.[15] What's more, it appears that the boy was not as innocent as portrayed. The first teacher he showed it to told him to put it in his locker and not show it around. Nevertheless, Ahmed continued to show it around until he found a teacher who reacted with the apparently desired response.[16]

When the Irving, Texas, police showed up, they found the boy to be uncooperative,[17] and, considering that two jihadists had recently attempted to machine-gun an art exhibition in nearby Garland, they decided it was prudent to detain Ahmed until they were sure of the situation.

★ ★ ★

The case that the teen was deliberately trying to provoke a confrontation was strengthened as more was learned about his family. His older sister, Eyman, was once suspended from her school for threatening to blow it up.[18] His uncle runs a trucking company called Twin Towers Transportation.[19] And his father, Mohamed Elhassan Mohamed, is a publicity-hungry activist who calls himself a sheik, wears flowing white robes, and is a 9/11 Truther. The elder Mohamed routinely returns to Sudan to run as a presidential candidate, and he once debated Pastor Terry Jones of Koran-burning fame.[20]

In one of his posts (in Arabic), Ahmed's father rails against Islamophobia and says that "Muslims...must exploit every opportunity to reveal the truth of Islam."[21] He has certainly done that. With the help of his lawyers, publicists from CAIR, and considerable assistance from the media, Mr. Mohamed has parlayed the incident into a whirlwind global publicity campaign. This included an appearance for his son on the Dr. Oz show, a photo-op with the Queen of Jordan at the UN, and a world tour for the family. The tour took the family to Mecca and to meetings with various world leaders, including the genocidal president of Sudan, Omar al-Bashir.[22] To top it all off, the media's favorite all-American family then decided to relocate to Qatar in response to an offer from the Qatar Foundation for Ahmed to study at its Young Innovators Program.[23]

"Muslims...must exploit every opportunity to reveal the truth of Islam"? In retrospect, it looks like Mr. Mohamed not only "exploits" opportunities, but also does his best to create them. The whole incident seems to be a preplanned family plot intended to reinforce the Islamophobia narrative and gain some publicity for the family in the bargain.

Instead of a classic case of Islamophobia, the clock boy affair might better be seen as a classic case of stealth jihad. It's reminiscent of the "flying imams" incident several years back in which a group of six imams praying loudly in Arabic and otherwise behaving in

★ ★ ★

unusual ways scared the daylights out of fellow passengers on a flight to Phoenix. After being ejected from the plane before take off, the imams turned around and sued not only the airline and the police, but also passengers who had reported their suspicious behavior to the flight crew. Eventually, U.S. Airways and the imams settled out of court for an undisclosed amount. Fearful that the incident would have a chilling effect on airport security, Congress passed a law to give immunity to citizens who report suspicious behavior.[24]

Will the Ahmed affair have a similar chilling effect? Will teachers be more likely to look the other way when Muslim students act suspiciously? We are continually reminded that if we see something we should say something. But what if the penalty for seeing and saying is to be held up for ridicule by everyone from the press to the president? By instantly granting celebrity status to the Muslim community's young Tom Edison, the social elites were implying that the teachers and police back in Irving were just paranoid rednecks. In fact, Ahmed himself said something to that effect. In an interview with Al-Jazeera, he stated that he was detained "because I'm a Muslim…this would not have happened to any of my classmates." As a reward for his battle against Islamophobia, CAIR presented Ahmed with the American Muslim of the Year Award at its Twenty-First annual "Champions for Justice" banquet.[25] By sheer coincidence, the ubiquitous CAIR was the group that provided legal counsel for the flying imams in their successful action against U.S. Airways.[26]

And by sheer coincidence, Ahmed's family, like the flying imams, brought suit. A potential charge of bigotry isn't the only thing that school officials will have to worry about if they notice suspicious behavior. Ahmed's family threatened a civil rights suit against the City of Irving and the school district unless they were paid $15 million. That's 15 million more reasons to say nothing when you see something. Stealth jihad doesn't hit you over the head with a club, it hits you with a lawsuit.

★ ★ ★

Of course, most people don't wait to be sued or fired, they already know what political correctness demands of them. Mark Steyn reminds us of an incident that occurred at the check-in desk of U.S. Airways in Portland on the morning of September 11, 2001. Ticket agent Michael Tuohey relates the encounter: "I got an instant chill when I looked at him [Mohammed Atta]. I got this grip in my stomach and then, of course, I gave myself a political correct slap…I thought, 'My God, Michael, these are just a couple of Arab businessmen.'"[27]

9/11 woke up America, but since then many Americans have fallen into a semi-comatose state, knocked slap-happy by repeated politically correct blows to the head. Thanks in part to the PR work of groups like CAIR and their boosters in media and government, a sizable number of citizens have gone back to sleep. The digital clock that Ahmed Mohamed brought to school was fully intact except for its casing. The clock-and-bull story manufactured by the social elites is also carefully put together—except for one detail. Someone removed the alarm.

It's in the Army Now

If the conquest of America ever comes—as Islamists say it will—it will come about through stealth jihad. Perhaps the most disturbing example of the quiet kind of jihad infiltrating an American institution is the inroads the stealth jihadists have made on the U.S. military. Here, once again, we see the confluence between stealth jihad and the armed variety. Both have the same aim—conquest of our society for Islam—and they aid and abet one another.

Although our armed forces can repel armed jihad, they're not very well-equipped to resist the other kind. After all, stealth jihad is much more difficult to detect and resist than the armed variety. It's simply not the type of aggression the Army is trained to deal with.

Take the case of Major Stephen Coughlin. He was an Army reservist and a top expert on Islamic law for the Joint Chiefs until he made the mistake of pointing out that Islamic law obliges Muslims to wage jihad. The Pentagon didn't cotton on to that idea, and Coughlin was dismissed from his Pentagon job as an intelligence contractor.[28]

The official attitude was nicely captured in a remark by an admiral who, upon hearing Coughlin's assessment, replied that he would first "have to check with my imam on that."[29]

You can see why the military has to contract out for its intelligence. Why would a high-ranking U.S. Navy officer have to consult his imam? Well, for reasons of political correctness, of course. It would be offensive not to bring the imam into the loop. For similar reasons, General Petraeus used to visit provincial leaders in Afghanistan dressed up as Lawrence of Arabia,[30] and, also for similar reasons, a manual for U.S. troops in the region directed them to avoid "making derogatory comments about the Taliban," "any criticism of pedophilia," or "anything related to Islam."[31]

And for having the temerity to bring up the subject of Islam in connection with jihad terror attacks, Major Coughlin lost his contract. He was terminated at the behest of one Hesham Islam, a special assistant to the deputy secretary of defense.[32]

"Islam"? In the Pentagon? Well, never mind. Better not go there. Apparently Mr. Islam was in charge of outreach to the Muslim community. He outreached to the Islamic Society of North America and to other Muslim Brotherhood-linked groups and invited them to luncheons in the Pentagon. In this, he was carrying on a long tradition of Pentagon outreach. For example, shortly after 9/11, future terrorist leader Anwar al-Awlaki was invited to attend a luncheon at the Pentagon because the secretary of the Army was anxious to diversify his dinners with some moderate members of the Muslim community.[33]

At that time, the FBI was already aware that al-Awlaki was tied to the 9/11 hijackers, but apparently the Army was not aware (presumably its intelligence contractors were on vacation).[34] This state of unawareness seems to have persisted for a long time. At about the same time that Major Coughlin's superiors were checking with their imams, Army psychiatrist Major Nidal Hasan was checking with his own imam about the fine points of jihad, and whether or not killing U.S. soldiers would qualify one for martyr status.[35]

Who was his imam? It was none other than the ubiquitous Imam Anwar al-Awlaki. The FBI knew about the communications between Major Hasan and al-Awlaki (there were eighteen of them in all), but decided that no action was warranted. Many of Hasan's own colleagues in the Army thought of him, in the words of one, as "a ticking time bomb," but they also took no action. Hasan's stealth jihad was not particularly stealthy.[36] In fact, as we have seen, he wore his jihadist sympathies on his sleeve. But the etiquette of political correctness required that his fellow officers look the other way lest they be accused of Islamophobia.

All of this brings up an interesting question. If the Army isn't particularly effective at spotting stealth jihad, who is? Or to put it another way, "Who's going to stop 'em?" Although the FBI has a better record in this regard, it's clear from Major Hasan's case that it too is hampered by PC protocols. Indeed, as we shall see in a few pages, FBI trainers are prohibited by protocol from drawing any connection between Islam and terrorism. Perhaps this is why the FBI failed to heed the warning from their Russian counterparts that Boston Marathon bomber Tamerlan Tsarnaev's connection with radical mosques made him a potential threat.[37]

Who, then, can we look to? The CIA? Four years ago a *Washington Post* article revealed, without naming names, that the then-current chief of the CIA's Counterterrorism Center had converted to Islam six years before. The lengthy piece treated the conversion as a mere point of interest—the kind of minor detail that would not be of any real concern to the *Post's* sophisti-cated readers. Although converts to Islam have a higher incidence of radical activity than the general Muslim population,[38] the *Washington Post* reporter gave no indication that anything could possibly go wrong.[39] Looking on the bright side, maybe it's fortunate that somebody in the higher ranks of the CIA knows something about Islam, seeing that John Brennan, the CIA chief, seems to know so little. He has been in the habit of defining jihad as "a holy struggle...to purify oneself or one's community."[40] If that's so, then it must follow that a stealth jihadist is like a secret Santa who quietly goes around performing acts of purification without even waiting to be thanked.

If not the CIA, then maybe the police? The trouble is, the only police force with a highly effective counterterrorism program, the NYPD, recently bowed to pressure and shut down a major component of that program—its surveillance of certain mosques and Muslim student associations. Why? The surveillance operation was deemed offensive by the Muslim community.[41]

How about Congress? Congress is on guard, but not against stealth jihad. When, in the summer of 2012, five House members complained that they had good evidence of Muslim Brotherhood penetration of U.S. government agencies, they were treated to a resounding rebuke by fellow legislators for having offended the Muslim Community. The five were particularly con-cerned that the Department of State had been taking actions that "have been enormously favorable to the Muslim Brotherhood and its interests." Secre-tary of State Hillary Clinton's top aide, Huma Abedin, has close personal ties to the Muslim Brotherhood, and the five representatives thought some-one should look into the matter.[42]

Was there any merit to the concern over Abedin? We may never know. All we know is that the request was condemned by members of Congress for being ugly, vicious, hurtful, outrageous, and dangerous. In short, the investigation was never conducted. House and Senate members seemed

★ ★ ★

Welcome to New York

There's a story about Abu Bakr al-Baghdadi, who is now the leader of the ISIS terrorists in Iraq. Supposedly, when he was released from an American detention camp in Iraq in 2009, he told his captors, "I'll see you guys in New York."[43] Hint to Mr. Baghdadi: if anyone questions you when you come to New York to scout for targets, just tell them that their questions are deeply offensive to you and to the whole Muslim community. They'll give you the keys to the city.

more worried about the possibility that they could be accused of Islamophobia or McCarthyism than the possibility that Islamists could be infiltrating the government. Judging by their reaction, "infiltration," like "jihad," is no longer a suitable topic for polite company.

To sum up, neither the Army, the FBI, the CIA, the police, nor Congress seems up to the task of resisting stealth jihad. That leaves…the president. At about the same time that the five House members were making known their concerns about actions that "have been enormously favorable to the Muslim Brotherhood," the president was making plans to send F-16s and Abrams tanks to assist the Muslim Brotherhood government in Egypt.[44] In the president's mind, the real danger emanated not from the Muslim Brotherhood, but from "those who slander the Prophet of Islam."[45] (Later, once the Muslim Brotherhood was forced out of power by large popular demonstrations, President Obama declined to supply the new secular government of Egypt with arms for months, then closed the credit line that had allowed Egypt to buy U.S. weapons in a move the *National Interest* headlined as "Obama Wrecked U.S.-Egypt Ties.")[46]

Meanwhile, his Department of Justice was busy purging FBI training manuals of guidelines for spotting stealth jihadists. As DOJ spokesman Dwight Holton put it, "training materials that portray Islam as a religion of violence or with a tendency towards violence are wrong, they are offensive, and they are contrary to everything that this president, this attorney general and Department of Justice stands for. They will not be tolerated."[47] Henceforward, the Federal Bureau of Investigation would have to confine itself to inoffensive investigations.

Heads should have rolled (in the metaphorical sense) a long time ago in the Pentagon, the State Department, the CIA, the DOJ, and among the president's foreign policy advisors. Because that never happened, heads are rolling (in the literal sense) all over the world. Because our leaders have chosen to put their heads in the ground regarding the nature of jihad, a lot more heads may soon be on the block.

Blindfolded America

Remember Stephen Coughlin, the intelligence contractor the U.S. military let go over his embarrassing insistence on connecting jihad with Islam? He has quite a lot of interesting things to say about stealth jihad in *Catastrophic Failure*, his tightly argued and thoroughly documented book.

The confusion in U.S. policy with regard to terrorism is no accident, says Coughlin, but the result of a deliberate Muslim Brotherhood plan to influence decision-making at the highest levels of the government and the military.[48] Coughlin is an attorney, intelligence officer, and an expert on Islamic law and ideology. He is well known for his "Red Pill" briefings to the security and defense establishments and to members of Congress. The "Red Pill" is a reference to the pill that allowed the characters in *The Matrix* to see reality as it is and to leave behind the false virtual reality that had been constructed for them.[49]

Coughlin discusses the Muslim Brotherhood's penetration of the government, the military, the security establishment, transnational

> ## A Book You're Not Supposed to Read
>
> *Catastrophic Failure: Blindfolding America in the Face of Jihad* by Stephen Coughlin (Washington, DC: Center for Security Policy Press, 2015).

bodies, and even the interfaith community. Just as important, he explains the overall strategy that guides the Muslim Brotherhood's various influence operations. A major component of the strategy is deception. Thus, Muslim Brotherhood–linked groups in America—which are anything but moderate—present themselves as the moderate experts on Islam who possess the knowledge to counter the radicals.

Of course, they don't advertise themselves as the Muslim Brotherhood. But when American security agencies such as the Department of Homeland Security consult with the Council on American-Islamic Relations, the Islamic Society of North America, the Muslim American Society, or a dozen other such groups, they are in effect dealing with the Brotherhood.[50] As we have seen, the connections between these organizations and the Brotherhood are well established, but for various reasons our agencies ignore the evidence. One reason is that many in the government believe that the Muslim Brotherhood itself—the progenitor of almost all terrorist groups—is genuinely moderate. Another reason is that the Brotherhood-linked groups are practically the only game in town. They are well-organized and well-funded, and have been ingratiating themselves with successive administrations for decades.[51]

Whatever the reason, these are the groups our security leaders turn to for advice. And, according to Coughlin, it's not just input that is sought, but also direction. In effect, he says, we have outsourced our understanding of Islam to groups who do not have the best interests of America at heart. The other side of the coin is that the advice of other competent experts is ignored. When the advice of the Muslim experts contradicts the advice of non-Muslim experts, the Muslim advice is favored and the non-Muslim expert may well find himself out of a job.[52]

Why does Muslim expert advice consistently trump non-Muslim expert advice? According to Coughlin, the security-intelligence establishment is in thrall to the same multicultural and relativist dogmas that afflict the rest of us. One of these dogmas, elaborated in Edward Said's 1978 book *Orientalism*, is that no culture can ever explain another culture. Each culture is the final arbiter of its own meaning. For an outside culture to try to explain Islam is, therefore, tantamount to an act of cultural imperialism. Thus, says Coughlin, Muslim cultural experts are not even required to provide evidence for their assertions: "Often, all that is required to halt an inquiry or analysis are the words, 'Islam does not stand for this' from a cultural expert."

The upshot, says Coughlin, is that many of our critical decisions on homeland security and on military and foreign policy are guided by groups whose main objective is to turn all societies into Islamic societies.[53]

According to Coughlin, a prime instance of a Muslim Brotherhood influence operation was the 2012 purging of more than 1,000 documents and presentations from counterterror training programs for the FBI and other agencies, on orders from the White House. This was done in response to a letter to John Brennan, then assistant to the president for Homeland Security and Counterterrorism, now head of the CIA. The letter, which was signed by dozens of leaders of Muslim activist groups, complained about the "use of biased, false, and highly offensive training materials about Muslims and Islam."[54] "Offensive"? You know your nation's really in trouble when Muslims complain about "offensive" training materials used by the Department of Defense and the FBI, and the Department of Justice immediately complies by ordering a purge of all training manuals in all security agencies that contain even a hint of a link between terrorism and Islam.[55] And after the FBI training program was made Islam-compliant, the Department of Defense followed up with what Coughlin describes as a "Soviet-style purge of individuals along with disciplinary actions and re-education."[56]

Coughlin contends that similar kowtowing to Islamic interests has undermined our war efforts in Afghanistan and elsewhere. Rules of engagement that subordinate the safety of our troops to the overriding principle

★ ★ ★

Is Stealth Jihad Hollowing Out the Army?

A survey of West Point graduates found that nearly half of young officers think the current military leadership is weak, while 78 percent think that the high exit rate of good officers threatens national security.[58]

of respect for Islam have a profoundly demoralizing effect on soldiers and make good people think twice about a career in the Army.[57]

According to Coughlin, such demoralization is among the chief aims of Islamic strategists. "The Islamic way of war," he writes, "places substantial effort on the preparation stage, the object of which is to induce a collapse of faith in the cultural, political and religious institutions underpinning the target." As an example of this strategy, he cites a book by Pakistani Brigadier General S. K. Malik. Malik stressed that the chief effort prior to actual warfare should be to "dislocate" the enemies' faith: "To instill terror into the hearts of the enemy [it] is essential in the ultimate analysis to dislocate his faith. An invincible faith is immune to terror. A weak faith offers inroads to terror."[59] "Terror," observes Coughlin, "cannot be struck into the hearts of an army by merely cutting lines of communication or depriving it of its routes to withdraw. It is basically related to the strength or weakness of the human soul. It can be instilled only if the opponent's faith is destroyed."[60]

Coughlin observes that the object of jihad, of both the stealth and armed variety, is the destruction of faith. Therefore, "jihad is primarily understood in terms of spiritual war...a form of warfare that the Pentagon is not disposed to recognize."[61]

There is, however, one organization in America that should be disposed to recognize spiritual warfare. Unfortunately, the Christian church has proved no better at recognizing and resisting Islamic influence operations than the government and the military. Coughlin's book contains a sixty-three-page chapter titled "Interfaith Outreach." While Coughlin's main concern is the undermining of national security, he maintains that Islamic activist groups have taken the entire culture as their target. In "Interfaith Outreach," he discusses the Muslim Brotherhood's attempt to subvert non-Muslim religious communities—a process that parallels the penetration of the military and is likewise intended to result in a "dislocation of faith."

Coughlin focuses in particular on the interfaith dialogue between Muslims and Catholics. Like the security establishment's "dialogue" with Muslim representatives, the interfaith dialogue, he claims, is rigged to discourage any critical analysis of Islam. One of the principles that guides the dialogue process is that the participants "speak in a way that people of that religion can affirm as accurate."[62] This, of course, is simply an extension of Edward Said's contention that one culture has no business explaining another culture. It means that participants in talks with Muslims always have to defer to the Muslims' interpretation of Islam. Thus, if anyone has the temerity to bring up the subject of Islamic violence, it will be enough for his Muslim partner in dialogue to state that Islam has nothing to do with violence, and perhaps to recite a couple of verses from the Koran, and that will be that. What kind of a "dialogue" is that?

Full and frank discussion is further inhibited by an overarching emphasis on trust and friendship. The ground rules stipulate that "dialogue must take place in an atmosphere of mutual trust."[63] Moreover, dialogue partners must pledge "to remain committed to being friends when the world would separate us from one another." That sounds nice, but isn't there a danger that the bonds of friendship might actually undermine objectivity? Thus, writes Coughlin, "persons who undertake a reasonable effort...[of] performing a competent assessment of the 'other's' religion could be characterized as lacking the requisite trust..." In other words, too deep an inquiry might bring accusations that one is uncharitable, intolerant, or Islamophobic. So, in order "to remain committed to being friends," dialoguers tend to avoid the crucial questions in favor of discussing common ground.[64]

But maybe there's less common ground than appears. The lesson of stealth jihad is that however unfriendly, un-PC, or even "offensive" it may be to criticize Islam and stand up to those who are plotting our subjugation to it, it has to be done.

CHAPTER 6

Immigration and the "Baby Jihad"

In order to do the long march through the institutions, you have to have enough bodies to do the marching. That's where mass Muslim immigration and the "baby jihad" come in. Many critics look upon Muslim immigration into non-Muslim societies as a form of stealth jihad. For example, Sam Solomon and Elias Al-Maqdisi describe Muslim immigration as a "modern-day Trojan Horse." They're not saying that every single Muslim immigrant wants to subvert Western society, but rather that mass migration and Islamic conquest have been linked ever since Muhammad.[1]

And it's working again. Many places in Europe have changed almost beyond recognition because of mass immigration. As Canadian author Mark Steyn frequently reminds his readers, "The future belongs to those who show up for it."[2] Mass Muslim immigration, in combination with the collapsing European birthrate, is rapidly changing the culture of Europe. It's also changing the political makeup of the EU. Since Muslims in Europe and the UK tend to vote as a bloc, politicians have begun catering to them, thus magnifying their influence. It's widely thought, for instance, that the victory margin for French President Francois Hollande—a strong proponent of Muslim immigration—was provided by Muslim voters.[3] In 2016 a Muslim

Did you know?

★ At the beginning of the twentieth century, there were almost three times as many Christians as Muslims in the world; by the end of the twenty-first, there will be more Muslims than Christians

★ Polling shows 74 percent of people in the Middle East and North Africa are anti-Semites

★ The first Muslim mayor of London, elected in 2016, has called moderate Muslims "Uncle Toms"

A Book You're Not Supposed to Read

Modern-Day Trojan Horse: Al-Hijra, the Islamic Doctrine of Immigration, Accepting Freedom or Imposing Islam? by Sam Solomon and Elias Al Maqdisi (Afton: Advancing Native Missions, 2009).

who has called moderate Muslims "Uncle Toms" was elected mayor of London.[4]

If the history of Muslim migration teaches us anything, it's that Muslims do not assimilate to existing cultures and religions; instead, Islam becomes the culture and religion of the lands they migrate to. There's even an Islamic term for this slow-motion conquest by migration—the *hijra*. It's named after the relocation of Muhammad and his followers from Mecca to Medina in 622 AD. Muhammad didn't come to Medina in order to integrate, he came to dominate. In a relatively short time, he expelled or killed the Jews in Medina and established Islam as the only religion in the region.

Muhammad's use of migration as an instrument of Islamization became the model for subsequent *hijras*. It still is today. In a 1974 speech at the United Nations, Algerian president Houari Boumedienne proclaimed, "One day, millions of men will leave the Southern Hemisphere to go to the Northern Hemisphere. And they will not go there as friends. Because they will go there to conquer it."[5]

Four decades later, in the summer of 2015, Boumedienne's prediction appeared to be coming true, as Europe was overrun by refugees from the Middle East and North Africa. The massive relocation he predicted has already begun.

It used to be that anyone who warned about the Islamization of Europe was dismissed as an alarmist. After all, tourists can still stroll the Champs-Élysées or snap photos of the Coliseum in relative safety. Besides, the Muslim population of Europe is still under 10 percent. It seems a tad premature to worry about Islamization. On the other hand, if you walk a few blocks from the tourist sites, you may well find that the signs are in Arabic and the women wear veils. And it's not just a question of how many, but who. Who are the Muslims in Europe? Perhaps the most salient fact about them is that they are young.

Just a few years ago, Mark Steyn was regarded as a scaremongering crank for predicting the eventual Muslim takeover of the continent, and a rare article in Britain's *Daily Telegraph* acknowledging that migration from Islamic countries "will change the continent beyond recognition" noted that "almost no policy-makers are talking about it."[6] But plenty of Europeans are talking about it now—including European Muslims who proudly march with signs proclaiming their intention to dominate Europe.[7] The surprising thing is that everyone seems surprised. Why? Until recently, political correctness has ruled out any frank discussion of the consequences of mass Muslim immigration. To call attention to Europe's gradual transformation into Eurabia is to invite accusations of "racism" and "Islamophobia" from the stealth activists and their allies. Better not to mention it.

A Book You're Not Supposed to Read

America Alone: The End of the World as We Know It by Mark Steyn (Washington, DC: Regnery, 2008).

Immigration or Invasion?

But in 2015, the problem became too obvious to ignore, as refugees from the Muslim world poured into the continent, overran borders, and strained the Europeans' social services and their generous hospitality to "the other" to the breaking point. Still, the media managed to find an angle that would allow them to avoid confronting the drastic changes the migrants were bringing to the lands of their refuge. The news narrative was all about hungry women and children and barbed wire barriers. The level of the discourse was reduced to what British author Peter Hitchens called "an emotional spasm."[8]

That's not to say that the plight of refugees shouldn't call up emotions. The problem comes when news analysts, government officials, and church representatives present the situation as a Dickensian dilemma that leaves one with no choice other than to side with Scrooge or with Tiny Tim. Because those were the terms of the discourse, momentous issues were being decided on the basis of poster-child optics.

The clinching argument for many was the image of a drowned Syrian child that went viral. Of course there is no doubt about what to do if you spot a drowning boy in the water. But the photo tells us absolutely nothing about what sort of immigration policies governments should adopt. It could be argued that if immigration policy in Europe were less liberal, fewer people would risk their lives to get there—and fewer would die on the journey.

And what about the images we don't see—images of the European victims of ill-considered immigration programs? Right now I'm looking at a photo of an eighty-seven-year-old Dutch man lying in a hospital bed, his face beaten black and blue. He and his eighty-six-year-old wife, both of them Holocaust survivors, were attacked in their apartment by two men of Moroccan descent who threw them on the floor, kicked them repeatedly, and shouted, "Dirty Jews—from now on your property is ours." The husband and wife, who had been living independently, are now confined to wheelchairs at a rehabilitation center.[9]

Such photos aren't featured on the evening news—nor are the photos of bruised and bloody rape victims in Sweden and England. Likewise, you'd be hard pressed to find pictures or stories about the Muslim and Christian women and children who have been abused and assaulted in refugee camps.

A letter from a coalition of social work organizations about conditions in one German refugee camp reports "numerous rapes, sexual assaults," and "forced prostitution." Christians and other minorities are particularly at risk, with the result that authorities have had to set up separate facilities for them. But the victimizers don't confine themselves to the camps. Soeren Kern, a senior fellow at the Gatestone Institute, reports that the rape of German women by asylum seekers is "commonplace." That may be because under Islamic law, infidel women who live in the dar al-harb (house of war) are considered fair game. Kern details twenty-one cases, many of them involving teenaged girls and younger. He suggests that there are many more incidents that are covered up by police and public officials "because they do not want to give legitimacy to critics of mass immigration."[10]

A Book You're Not Supposed to Read

Submission: A Novel by Michel Houllebecq, translated by Lorin Stein (New York: Farrar, Straus, and Giroux, 2015).

Those stories don't fit the standard narrative about peaceful Muslims fleeing from war with ISIS in Syria and Iraq to seek a better life for themselves and their children. There are many such people, of course. But, as is now clear, many of the "refugees" are from countries far from the war, and some of the actual Syrians who did make the trek came to Europe not from Syria but from other places of refuge such as Turkey, where they had been living safely for years. The great majority of the current wave of migrant-refugees are young single men. The media still favors close-ups of Madonna-like women with children, but the wide-angle view presents quite a different picture.

The big picture is that we may be witnessing the beginning of the end of Europe. Though the media treated the 2015 immigration crisis as something from out of the blue, it has been building for years. A few Cassandras have been warning about the coming Islamization of Europe for some time now, but, as time goes by, the timeline keeps moving up. The original forecasts predicted that the Muslim takeover of the continent would happen sometime in this century; then, the day of reckoning was moved up to the mid-century mark; and then, as the picture became clearer, to circa 2030. Now, with the new flood of migrants, another revision may be in order. I see that Michel Houellebecq's new novel, *Submission*, forecasts the election of a Muslim president in France in 2022.

In light of the threat to European civilization, it is strange that so many commentators see the crisis mainly as an opportunity for welcoming the "other," overcoming irrational fears, and proving one's compassion. Take some comments by Father Matthew Gardzinski, who is in charge of the migrants' section for the Pontifical Council for the Pastoral Care of Migrants and Itinerant Peoples. In an interview with Catholic News Agency, Gardzinski expresses a rather rosy view of migrants. "While one country loses the persons who migrate," he notes, "the receiving country gains their ideas and creativity." He seems, however, to have a less sanguine view of Europeans. According to the article, he is concerned about "xenophobic, restrictive, or fearful attitudes." What stands behind the fear? "Is it really something objective," he asks, "or is it something more subjective, because I feel threatened, or challenged?"[11]

"Is it really something objective?" Father Gardzinski might try asking that to the girls of Rotherham or the rape victims in Sweden or Cologne.

From the European proponents of mass Muslim immigration, one gets the impression that indigenous Europeans are all comfortable, and somewhat selfish, upper-middle-class burghers with spare rooms to spare in their spacious chalets. Migrants and refugees, on the other hand, are portrayed as victims of forces beyond their control. But a great many Europeans feel the same way about their own lives. They have little or no say about the rules that are set for them in Brussels. And, as poll after poll has shown, a majority of Europeans see themselves as victims of EU immigration policies.[12]

Many of them, moreover, do not just think of themselves as "victims" in the broad sense of being inconvenienced by rules imposed by distant Eurocrats. Increasingly, Europeans are becoming victims in the more narrow sense of the word—that is, victims of violent crimes: rape, assault, and robbery. That kind of victimhood has been a problem for quite a while. For example, it's estimated that over the last two decades, approximately 1 million English women and girls have been raped, most of them by Muslim immigrants.[13] The new wave of Muslim immigrants—75 percent of whom are male[14]—seems likely to create many new rape victims. As Pat Condell, an acerbic YouTube commentator, puts it, "the European Union is importing a violent, misogynistic rape culture that directly threatens the safety of women."[15]

Father Gardzinski's concern, however, is not with existential realities, but with psychological states. He sees Europe's migration crisis as being more in the nature of an identity crisis: "the challenge to build your own identity" along multicultural lines. Presumably, that's to be done by overcoming one's irrational fears ("Islamophobia" in the lingo of psychology). The point he misses is that this is not a crisis of identity for Europe, it's a crisis of survival—a crisis that could very well result in the end of Europe as we know it.

Meanwhile, while Europeans are tying themselves into knots to accommodate the refugees, many Muslim nations are cool to them. Take Saudi Arabia. It has the capacity to take in many refugees, but, apparently, very little desire. It has, however, offered to help assist in the migrants' transition to life in Europe. The Saudis have offered to build 200 mosques for Syrian refugees in Germany.[16] Why, you may wonder, don't they build 200 mosques for Syrians in Arabia? They would be cheaper to build, and it would be much more convenient for the Syrians.

Except Saudi Arabia won't let in Syrian refugees. The reason that the Saudis don't want the Syrians is that they fear the instability that might ensue.[17] What if jihadists mixed in with the refugees and tried to undermine the government? Many Europeans have the same fears, but they have little say in what happens to them. What is happening to them, as the Saudis understand all too well, is a *hijra*—a slow-motion conquest by migration. And the Saudis are all too happy to give the hijra a helping hand.

No-Go Zones of the Mind

The migrant crisis is portrayed as a case of compassion versus intolerance. It's much more complicated than that. But just as it's difficult to ignore the image of the drowned boy, it's difficult to argue with pleas for compassion, many of them coming from religious leaders. We are reminded that the Holy Family were refugees in Egypt, that the Jews were admonished to love the foreigner "because you were foreigners in the land of Egypt," and that Christ told his disciples that in welcoming a stranger they were welcoming him.

But what if there are 44 million strangers in the land? That's the estimated number of Muslims who were living in Europe (including Russia) as of 2010[18]—half a decade before the "migrant crisis" year of 2015, when nearly 2 million more arrived in Germany alone.[19] Some of them are well-integrated into European society, but many others are not. They speak Arabic or Farsi or Turkish, their women wear burqas, and their first allegiance is not to Germany or France, but to the *umma* (the global Muslim community). Even after living in Europe for years, they are still, in effect, strangers. Many seem unacquainted with Western standards of right and wrong—like the Muslim man in the UK who, after raping a thirteen-year-old girl, was spared a prison sentence when he explained to the judge that he didn't know what he had done was illegal.[20]

You are likely aware of a gaffe that occurred on a segment of Fox News in January 2015 when terrorism expert Steven Emerson mistakenly described Birmingham as a "totally Muslim" city where non-Muslims "don't go."

Emerson apologized for his error, and Fox News apologized profusely.[21] But that wasn't good enough for the rest of the media, who quickly went to town on Emerson's uncharacteristic mistake. In fact, they ridiculed not only his mistake, but even the bare assertion, which had been made in a series of Fox News segments, that there are any such things as "no-go" zones in France and other European countries.[22] Adding fuel to the fire, Anne Hidalgo, the mayor of Paris, told CNN that she intended to sue Fox News for dishonoring the image of Paris.

A Book You're Not Supposed to Read

Eurabia: The Euro-Arab Axis by Bat Ye'or (Madison: Farleigh Dickinson University Press, 2010).

No-go zones in Paris? According to CNN, it's just another urban legend used to "perpetuate a fearful narrative about Muslims."[23] Except that it's true. The no-go zones aren't officially designated as such, and there is no law saying that non-Muslims can't enter them. But they do exist, and non-Muslims are well-advised to steer clear of them. Soeren Kern, who has done extensive research on the subject, defines no-go zones as "Muslim-dominated neighborhoods that are *de facto* off-limits to non-Muslims due to a number of factors including the lawlessness, insecurity, or religious intimidation that often pervades these areas."[24]

The official designation is "sensitive urban zones." A French government website lists 750 of these "zones urbaines sensibles," complete with satellite maps.[25] Not all of these self-segregated areas are entirely Muslim or entirely off-limits to police and firemen, but many of them are highly dangerous, and none of them are—as the media would have us believe—imaginary.

Kern has documented the no-go situation across Europe in a multi-part series for Gatestone Institute. He quotes from dozens of French newspaper articles and television documentaries that focus on the zones and that often do use the term "no-go zones"—along with such other terms as "lawless zones," "areas of lawlessness," "battlefields," and "lost territories." He also cites a 120-page research paper that documents dozens of French neighbor-hoods "where police and gendarmerie cannot enforce the Republican order." In addition, Kern refers to a 2,200-page report, "Banlieue de la Republique" (Suburbs of the Republic), which found that major Parisian suburbs are becoming "separate Islamic societies."[26]

Perhaps the mayor of Paris is unfamiliar with these areas. Or perhaps she is worried about what would happen to the tourism industry if the word got out. And it wouldn't help the tourism business if it were widely known that about 40,000 cars are burned each year in France by Muslim youth, that France has become a hotbed of anti-Semitism, or that Jews have been leaving France in droves.[27]

Of course, you can't help but notice some things. The American media wasn't able to avoid reporting the massacre at the *Charlie Hebdo* office or the killing of four Jews at a kosher market shortly after. And there has been some reporting of a spate of deliberate hit-and-run killings committed by Muslim motorists, along with stories of attacks on French police by knife-wielding individuals of the "Allahu akbar" persuasion. Still, the media declines to connect the dots. The point is that such incidents are intimately connected to the existence of the supposedly imaginary no-go zones. The zones provide the environment that produces and supports the terrorists. As Kern puts it, "Muslim enclaves in European cities are also breeding grounds for Islamic radicalism and pose a significant threat to Western society."[28]

Just as dangerous as the brick and mortar no-go zones are the no-go zones of the Western mind—topics that the media and the insulated ruling class don't dare to contemplate. The growing Islamization of Europe is one of those topics. Since the existence of sensitive urban zones confirms the Islamization process, their reality must be denied.

Steve Emerson was mistaken about the number of Muslims in Birming-ham, but it may turn out that he simply spoke too soon. Today there are already more Muslim than Christian children in that city.[29] Ludi Simpson, a Manchester University statistician, forecasts that within four years, native white Britons will be a minority in Birmingham—a decade earlier than the previous estimates.[30] That prospect doesn't seem to faze the Right Reverend David Urquhart, the Anglican bishop of Birmingham, who said, "I am delighted to live in a city of diverse faiths where all play their part." That's one way of looking at it. On the other hand, if present trends continue, the future of Birmingham may turn out to be much less diverse than the bishop can imagine.[31]

Peter Hitchens recently observed that many of Europe's "most influential people are set on committing a sentimental national suicide."[32] European and American elites seem to think that the only question at issue in the current crisis is, "Will Europeans be compassionate?" But other crucial questions need to be asked, such as "Will Europe survive?"

That might seem like an overly alarmist question. Yet it was a question that was ever present to Europeans in past centuries—particularly those who lived on the southern and eastern borders.

It's no coincidence that Eastern Europeans are more resistant to Islamic immigration than those living in the West. Poles, Slovaks, and

★ ★ ★

Remarks on Muslim Immigration to Europe by Hungarian President Viktor Orban:

"Today in Europe it is forbidden to speak the truth....

It is forbidden to say that those arriving are not refugees, but that Europe is threatened by migration.

It is forbidden to say that tens of millions are ready to set out in our direction.

It is forbidden to say that immigration brings crime and terror to our countries.

It is forbidden to point out that the masses arriving from other civilizations endanger our way of life, our culture, our customs and our Christian traditions.

It is forbidden to point out that those who arrived earlier have already built up their own new, separate world for themselves, with its own laws and ideals, which is forcing apart the thousand-year-old structure of Europe.

It is forbidden to point out that this is not an accidental and unintentional chain of consequences, but a preplanned and orchestrated operation; a mass of people directed towards us."[33]

Where Will the Europeans Find Refuge from the Refugees?

"These people do not escape the Middle East, they bring the Middle East with them."

—Middle East analyst Barry Shaw[35]

Hungarians have a long history of struggle with Muslim invaders.[34] It's estimated, for example, that Muslims enslaved a million persons from the Polish-Lithuanian Commonwealth between the fifteenth and eighteenth centuries.

If that seems like ancient history, consider that the Eastern Europeans have a more recent experience of invasion and occupation. After all, it was only twenty-five years ago that they broke free of communist rule. Having recently been enslaved by one totalitarian ideology, they are not anxious to repeat the experience with another oppressive system. Caliphs and commissars can be equally unpleasant. The Poles' and Hungarians' recent subjugation by Communist overlords has no doubt refreshed their memories about the earlier invaders.

Anti-Semitism Makes a Comeback

Europe's embrace of mass immigration can be explained in part by Europeans' massive guilt complex about the Nazi era. It's no coincidence that Germany, which has the most guilt to deal with, has pledged to take in the most refugees.

But other European nations are not free of guilt. Some of them collaborated with the Nazis, and even those who didn't, feel a need to expiate for the sin of European anti-Semitism.

The irony is that Europe's current welcoming policy toward immigrants and refugees seems destined to bring about the very fate it is intended to avoid. European governments have decided that the best way to expunge any trace of racism or xenophobia is to invite into their midst people who are as far removed from European culture and tradition as it is possible to be. The reasoning seems to go as follows: if Europeans persecuted the Jews for their "otherness," they can make up for it by accepting millions of "new Jews"—not actual Jews, but people who by reason of their otherness can stand in as proxies for the Jews.

The problem is that the "new Jews" are on the whole decidedly anti-Semitic. Europe's atonement for its past anti-Semitism is to invite into the continent the most anti-Semitic people on the planet. It's no secret that the majority of the refugees and immigrants now pouring into Europe are Muslims. What's more, many of these Muslims are from the Middle East and North Africa (MENA), the most anti-Semitic part of the Muslim world.

According to a 2014 poll conducted by the Anti-Defamation League, 74 percent of those polled in the MENA region had anti-Semitic attitudes. The top ten in the ADL Global Index are:

- West Bank and Gaza—93 percent of the adult population holds anti-Semitic views
- Yemen—88 percent
- Algeria—87 percent
- Libya—87 percent
- Tunisia—86 percent
- Kuwait—82 percent
- Bahrain—81 percent
- Jordan—81 percent
- Morocco—80 percent[37]

★ ★ ★
Come Back Hitler, All Is Forgiven

In a 2009 statement, Sheik Yusuf al-Qaradawi, one of the most popular and influential spiritual leaders in the Muslim world, called the Holocaust "a divine punishment" of Jews, and prayed that the "believers" would finish the job started by Hitler.[36]

In short, the "new Jews" are reminiscent of the old Nazis. As a matter of fact, Hitler is considered a hero in many of the MENA countries, and *Mein Kampf* is a popular book there.

It seems odd for a continent dedicated to the proposition that what happened to the Jews must "never again" happen to lay out the red carpet for people who are dedicated to finishing Hitler's work. Here it seems appropriate to add the obligatory qualifier and note that of course not every Muslim hates Jews. But, then, neither did every German in the Nazi period hate Jews. And certainly many of them never endorsed the final solution to the "Jewish problem." Still, as the German experience showed, a dedicated minority can wreak havoc if the majority is willing to stand by and look the other way. Given the results of the ADL poll, a large number of Muslims might be willing to avert their eyes. And in Germany, Muslims already outnumber Jews by about forty to one.

There might be less to worry about if Germany took pains to assimilate its growing Muslim population. But the guilt hangover from World War II mandates that the multicultural "other" be given special treatment. And one way of showing respect for the other is to absolve him of any duty to assimilate. To ask the other to assimilate implies that you think your culture is better than his—which, of course, would be a major social blunder. That helps explain why parallel Muslim cultures with separate rules and institutions have grown up alongside the native cultures in Germany and the rest of Europe.

What's happening is not a Germanization of Islam, but an Islamization of Germany. As Germany braced itself to receive some 800,000 refugees and migrants in 2015 (even that number would have been a four-fold increase over the previous year—and, as we have seen, the final count may have been as high as 2 million), very little was done to acquaint them with Western standards of behavior. Instead, the new Muslim immigrants are swelling the "no-go" zones where polygamy is commonplace, sharia courts operate, and churches are being turned into mosques. Moreover, rather than undertake the difficult task of integrating young people into Western society, Germany, according to one report, is "handing over the religious education of the next generation of German Muslims to Islamist radicals."

One could counter that it's not easy for the government to oversee what's being taught in the madrassas, but Vijeta Uniyal, the author of the report, isn't talking about madrassas; he's referring to the public schools. In a number of German states, the Islamic Studies program has been given over to the Turkish-Islamic Union for Religious Affairs (DITIB). That organization, which has close ties to Turkey's Islamist party, the AKP, oversees the writing of textbooks, the selection of teachers, and the content of the curriculum.[38] Given the anti-Semitic leanings of the AKP leadership, one wonders how their friends in the DITIB deal with such a sensitive topic as the Holocaust.

Or will they have to address the subject at all? In the state of Bavaria, it has been proposed that Muslim students should be exempt from mandatory visits to former concentration camps. The stated reason is that children from Muslim families have no connection to the German past.[39] Yet a chief architect of the final solution—a man who worked closely with Eichmann and Himmler—was Haj Amin al-Husseini, the Grand Mufti of Jerusalem, and one of the most prominent and influential Muslims of the time.[40] Moreover, as the ADL poll shows, anti-Semitism is still very much alive in the Middle East. In short, the students in Germany who are likely in most need of Holocaust education are the ones least likely to receive it.

Muslims are exempt from Holocaust education by reason of the excuse that they have no connection with the German past. But very little is being done to give them a connection with the German present. Consequently, a lot of German Muslims don't connect with propositions that most Germans take for granted—that all men are created equal, and that sort of thing. Thus, thanks to the twisted logic of multiculturalism, a new European holocaust may be in the making, with Germany once again at its center.

The target of the next holocaust, however, may not necessarily be Jews. That's for the simple reason that Jews are leaving Europe in large numbers. Having taken note of multiple attacks on Jewish synagogues, businesses, and individuals, many have decided not to wait around to see how Europe's experiment with Muslim immigration turns out.

In the absence of Jews, Muslim supremacists have always been able to find other targets for their enmity—pagans, Zoroastrians, Hindus, Buddhists, Amadiyyah, and Christians. One needn't consult the history books to notice. Boko Haram is waging war on Christians in Nigeria, and the Islamic State is conducting a holocaust against the Christians and Yazidis of Iraq and Syria. The Muslims trekking north into Europe not only carry the seeds of anti-Semitism; they also harbor animosity toward non-Muslims in general. A popular slogan in the Middle East is, "First comes Saturday, then comes Sunday." It means that after the Muslims have finished with the Jews, they will come after the Christians. But what if—as is increasingly the case in Europe—the Jews are no longer around? The secondary target will likely become the primary one.

The "Baby Jihad"

In 1974, when Algerian president Houari Boumedienne predicted mass migration from the Southern to the Northern hemisphere "to conquer it," he also made an additional threat: "And they will conquer it with their sons. The wombs of our women will give us victory."[41] It was another prescient insight. In fact, the stealth jihad in Europe today is being pushed along not by migration—the hijra—alone, but by migration combined with maternity. This war of the wombs that Boumedienne predicted has been dubbed the "baby jihad" by author Raymond Ibrahim.[42] It is a war that Europe is fast losing.

As I wrote four years ago, "As Europeans started to lose their faith, they stopped having babies. They stopped having babies because they had nothing meaningful to pass on to the next generation—and also because babies get in the way of self-gratification. The decline of Christianity in Europe created a population vacuum and a spiritual vacuum, both of which Islam soon began to fill. If Christian faith had been more robust in Europe, it is unlikely that radical Islam would have advanced so far, so fast."[43]

The population shift is already under way. Filled with faith, the Muslim population is growing rapidly—not just from immigration, but from high birth rates. Lacking faith, the indigenous population is growing older. Although the Muslim population of France is only about 10 percent, the latest survey finds that 25 percent of French teenagers are Muslims. Judging by that and various other population statistics, it is probable that Muslims make up over 50 percent of the population under age twenty in some major urban areas.[44] Indigenous Europeans are a majority, but they are an aging majority.

The decline of Christianity in Europe led to a loss of cultural confidence and a loss of will. This loss of faith also translated into a declining birth rate. If you think you have nothing meaningful to pass on to the next generation, then it's likely that the next generation will be raised by those who believe that "Europe is the cancer" and "Islam is the answer."

Muslims are a minority in Europe, but history provides many examples of small but dedicated minorities who have been able to impose their beliefs on the majority. Once past a certain population point, a minority of true believers can rapidly transform a culture. Where is the tipping point for Europe? Ten percent? Fifteen percent? Whatever the exact

★ ★ ★
Famous Last Words

Now that Muslims are turning Europe into Eurabia, Europeans will have one more excuse not to have children. "It wouldn't be right," they will say, "to bring children into such a difficult environment."

★ ★ ★

The Odds Are against the Europeans

Social-network researchers at Rensselaer Polytechnic Institute have concluded that "when just 10 percent of the population holds an unshakeable belief, their belief will always be adopted by the majority of the society."[46] France is already over 10 percent Muslim, and the majority of Frenchmen, like most Europeans, don't seem to have any strong convictions about anything outside of an unshakeable belief in long vacations and early retirement.

figure, that tipping point in time now seems likely to arrive much earlier than anyone had anticipated.

The replacement of dying native European populations by fast-growing Muslim immigrant populations[45] is taking place in the context of a huge worldwide Islamic population explosion. According to Raymond Ibrahim, there were almost three times as many Christians as Muslims in the world at the beginning of the twentieth century. By the end of the twenty-first, there will be more Muslims than Christians.[47]

We have already seen that there are now more Muslim than Christian children in Birmingham, England's second-largest city. The same is true in a number of other large and mid-size cities—Luton, Leicester, Bradford, and Slough. At least three boroughs in London have more Muslim than Christian children, including Tower Hamlets, which has an overall population of 273,000. What do demographic changes like this mean for cities like Birmingham? According to Mark Steyn, "absent any countervailing dynamic, its future is Muslim."[48]

In fact, you could argue that—thanks to the "baby jihad"—the *present* of a lot of British and European cities is Muslim. On first hearing about the Rotherham "grooming" scandal, an American might think that now that the rest of Britain knows the shocking story, all will be put to right and things will go back to the way they were before—in other words, back to normal. But in many parts of England, this is the new normal. Even that term—"new normal"—only makes sense to those who are old enough to remember the "old normal." What we call the new normal is for many young Westerners simply normal.

Beheadings, for example, have become almost a regular part of the daily news cycle. In 2013, there was the near-decapitation of a young soldier on a London street. In 2014, a grandmother was beheaded by a Muslim in North London.[49] Throughout the fall of that year, news stories carried videos of an English-speaking ISIS fighter beheading American and British captives.[50] In early November 2014, it was revealed that English police had foiled a plot by four Muslims to behead the Queen.[51] The idea of a beheading is shocking to the sensibilities of an older person. But if you were born twelve or thirteen years ago and are just now beginning to pay attention to the news, beheadings don't represent a new and gravely disturbing turn of events; they are just part of the background noise in the multicultural dystopia.

And even parents and grandparents can become accustomed to the new normal. As evidenced by the Rotherham rape scandal, mature adults in responsible positions can learn to adjust to the most outrageous crimes if the cultural pressure is strong enough. A Muslim population on its way to majority status can exercise quite a lot of pressure.

The combination of mass migration, high birth rates for Muslims, and collapsing birth rates for native Europeans spells a massive transformation of European culture. Or, some might argue, its replacement by a very different culture—one the Europeans would never have chosen to embrace if the matter had been put to an up-or-down vote.

This culture allows polygamy and temporary marriage for men, allows men to marry children, allows men to divorce their wives with ease, and, in general, looks upon wives and children as little more than property.

It is, according to former Muslims such as Nonie Darwish, Wafa Sultan, and Ayaan Hirsi Ali, a highly dysfunctional system that results in a tangle of family pathologies. As Darwish notes, the Muslim family system creates distrust not only between man and wife, but also between father and son, mother and daughter-in-law, and between the wife and her friends (who are potential rivals for her husband's affections). Darwish concludes that the dysfunctional and violent nature of Islamic societies is simply the Islamic family system writ large: "I truly believe that the anger that is pushing the wheels of Islamic terrorism can be traced to pent-up anger within the Muslim family."[52]

All of which tilts the odds against you if you were born in Tehran or Peshawar. Or, increasingly, in Birmingham, London, Paris, Brussels, or Berlin. Why? Because Europe's elites have been encouraging the importation of this family structure into Europe. Not intentionally, of course, but by embracing open immigration policies that will allow Muslim family values to take root in Europe.

The "rape culture" is, in turn, a product of the violent family patterns that Darwish describes: "physical abuse of women in Muslim culture is very common," "girls are physically beaten by their brothers and fathers," "boys are given messages of hostility toward a girl's uncovered head, arms, and legs," and are told that "those uncovered girls deserve to be disrespected."[53]

Of course, just about all European girls and women are uncovered and thus deserving of disrespect. As Pat Condell puts it, "Third World Muslim men are raised from the cradle to despise and fear women and to treat them as inferior."

A couple of years ago, the Afghan parliament rejected a measure that would have banned child marriage. The measure also would have banned the "practice of buying or selling women to settle disputes" and would have protected rape victims from criminal charges of fornication or adultery. Opponents of the measure said that it "violated Islamic principles."[54]

Believe in Nothing and You'll Fall for Anything

Europe is disturbingly far on its way to adopting those "Islamic principles" for its own. Not officially, of course, but in practice Europeans have already begun to adapt—to polygamy, forced marriage, female genital mutilation, and other diversities. In addition, Danish Jews are advised not to wear yarmulkes, Swedish blondes are dyeing their hair black, and Parisian women have taken to wearing head coverings so as to blend in with their surroundings.

Why, you might ask, don't they stand up for their beliefs? Well, possibly because they don't have too many—beliefs, that is. When it comes to the kinds of beliefs that sustain a culture—belief in God, family, church, and country—Europeans have become sadly deficient. And lacking those beliefs, many lack the resolve to defend themselves and their heritage.

A Book You're Not Supposed to Read

While Europe Slept: How Radical Islam Is Destroying the West from Within by Bruce Bawer (New York: Doubleday, 2006).

A recent *New York Times* article revealed that 90 percent of teens in the predominantly Muslim districts of Molenbeek and Schaerbeek, Belgium, think of the Brussels terrorists as heroes.[55] The main thing to notice here is not that these youth have warped values (which they do), but that their heroes are people who are willing to die for what they believe. Which means that some of these young people are likely willing to die for the same beliefs. Meanwhile, a question posed to thirteen-year-olds in an Italian middle school revealed that 90 percent of them would convert to Islam if the Islamic State showed up at their door.[56] Not much hero material there. A willingness to fight and die for one's beliefs is apparently an alien concept for many young Italians. If they've heard of the 800 martyrs of Otranto, they must wonder why they all didn't just convert. That would have been the sensible thing to do.

In a contest of wills, who seems more likely to prevail? The young Muslims in Brussels or the young "whatevers" in Italy? I use the term "whatevers" because so many young people in the West are conditioned to go in whatever direction the tide is flowing. The two students in the class of twenty-five who went against the tide—who refused to consider conversion—were from devout Catholic families.

The struggle with Islam is in large part a spiritual struggle. It will be won by those with the deepest faith and strongest convictions. In other words, it's the kind of struggle that many Europeans and Americans are ill-prepared for. While the mosques and Islamic schools have been delivering a purpose-driven message about Islam's manifest destiny, multiculturalist educators in the West have done everything they can to undermine their students' cultural foundations. According to multiculturalists, the worst crime is to deprive native peoples of their culture, yet all their efforts have been aimed at depriving Western students of their own multi-millennium cultural inheritance.

That's what seems to have happened to the Italian students. As *Katholisches.info* observed, "The theft of our own identity is proceeding on many levels…And now we are expected to tell our young people to take up weapons and defend themselves…In the name of what ideals and values are we to ask that of them? In the name of those ideas we never taught them, but denigrated in their eyes?"[57]

Those who are ashamed of their culture will not defend it—or, apparently, even themselves. If you believe in nothing important, then the prudent thing to do when faced with danger is to capitulate. As Alessandro Grotteri, the author of the *Katholisches.info* piece, puts it, "Decisive resistance comes from someone who is firmly founded in belief."

The end result of the dechristianization of Europe will very likely be the Islamization of Europe—unless, that is, Europeans are able to recover the faith that made Europe great in the first place. It was largely because of their Christian faith that Europeans of another era were able to resist Muslim forces at Tours, Lepanto, Malta, and Vienna, and to retake Spain from Muslim hands.

Absent that faith, there seems little hope for Europe. Without the cultural confidence that the Christian faith once provided, the various secular nostrums for combatting "violent extremism" while avoiding "Islamophobia" seem doomed to fail. Even the might of NATO will prove of little help because NATO is not equipped to fight a cultural or spiritual war. NATO can't readjust the birthrate imbalance (itself a result of dechristianization). It can't reverse the slow but steady Islamic takeover of schools, school boards, municipal councils, public streets, and squares. And NATO certainly can't provide Europeans with the transcendent beliefs that make "decisive resistance" possible.

But a number of recent surveys show that Christianity is also on the decline in America. Increasing numbers of Americans now identify as "no religion" or "agnostic" rather than as Christian. And the education system—our public schools, our universities—is hardly teaching the next generation that Western civilization is anything to be proud of, much less something worth dying for. American children are more likely to learn from their teachers that Western culture is racist, sexist, colonialist, imperialist—the root of so many evils that it ought to be a source of shame, not pride. Muslims believe strongly that Islam is the superior faith to which other faiths and cultures should submit. They believe, in short, that they have a right to rule. What do Americans believe?

People who lose their grip on transcendent realities soon lose their grip on earthly realities as well—or, to repeat the epigram attributed to Chesterton, "When men choose not to believe in God...they then become capable of believing in anything." It's a sign of how detached from reality we've become that European and American elites would much prefer that young people learn transgender values rather than transcendent ones. As the palpable reality of an Islamist takeover draws ever closer, the only value that they're willing to defend is the reality-denying proposition that boys can be girls and girls can be boys.

Actually, the attitude of the elites toward gender differences and their attitude toward Islam are connected. If you accept the proposition that your gender is whatever you wish it to be, then why not conclude that Islam is whatever you wish it to be? That is more or less what's happened. European and American elites have constructed a make-believe version of Islam in their own minds. For them "Islam" means "peace"; "jihad" is a "spiritual struggle"; and jihadist terror "has nothing to do with Islam."

That their fantasy Islam bears little relation to reality does not disturb them. For them, words and thoughts and desires are more interesting than reality. The people who open the doors of the women's bathroom to all and sundry without regard for the real differences between men and women are the same people who want to open wide the doors of Europe to all comers without regard to the stark differences that separate Islamic and Western cultures.

The caliphs of old who had their sights set on conquering the West could only have dreamed about facing such clueless and spineless opponents.

CHAPTER 7

Western Enablers of Jihad

From their skillful disinformation campaign to the hijra and the "baby jihad," the stealth jihadists have many weapons in their arsenal. But absent the weakness—in some cases amounting to active collusion—of so many of our own institutions, they would not be succeeding. How do you account for this willing submission? In a word, "sensitivity." Above all, Western man wants to be thought sensitive. He would not, for example, be caught dead using the word "man" as in the sentence above or the pronoun "he" in this sentence. Someone (that's better) might take offense.

The trouble is, the Islamic world, for the most part, is not impressed with this sensitivity. Muslims take it as confirmation of Western weakness and fecklessness.

What the West sees as tolerance and sensitivity is seen by Muslims as submission—a validation of their belief that theirs is indeed the superior culture. Western appeasement will not garner more respect from the Muslim world, but it will bolster the jihadi recruitment campaign.

Gestures of compliance do not convince Islamists that we are an admirable people. Such gestures only convince them that they have the winning

Did you know?

★ An Evangelical pastor in Northern Ireland was put on trial for a sermon critical of Islam

★ G. K. Chesterton predicted the Islamization of England in a futuristic novel written in 1914

★ Police in the UK are arresting an average of one jihadist a day

We're Not Looking like the Strong Horse

"I saw the weakness, cowardice, and fear of American soldiers myself.... American forces receive the best training and have the most advanced weapons in the world, but they did not have the power to confront the Guard due to weakness of faith and belief."

—an Iranian commander, after the U.S. Navy crew surrendered in the Persian Gulf [1]

hand. Unless Western leaders get a better grip on the realities of Islamic culture, they will continue to set up their own citizens for one humiliation after another.

You can call the current conflict between Islam and the West a "clash of civilizations," but that's rather like describing the encounter between a sadist and a masochist as a clash. As I wrote in *Christianity, Islam, and Atheism*: "It's difficult to conceive of a more disastrous combination of events than the simultaneous emergence on the world stage of a fiercely passionate ideology dedicated to conquering the West, and of another, dangerously naïve ideology, eager to dismantle it from within." [2]

It's All Relative

But what exactly is the dangerous ideology fueling the surrender of the West? It goes by many names. We've already met it under the title of "political correctness." Other names for it are "relativism" and "multiculturalism." By "relativism" I mean the notion that one cultural expression is as good as another—as in "who's to say that Beethoven is better than the beat of a bongo drum?" By "multiculturalism" I mean the process by which a culturally confused society surrenders itself to a more confident and aggressive culture.

There are many culturally confused societies, but let's take England as an example. Once the model of civilized manners and habits, England's green and pleasant land is now host to customs and traditions that seem better suited to the tenth century. Sharia courts? Fine. The burqa? Why not? Polygamy? That's their custom. Female genital mutilation? Well, okay, but do it in a clinic. Next thing you know, there will be beheadings in the streets. Er, sorry, that's already happened.

How did it come about—this relatively sudden intrusion of the past into the present? Ironically, the return of some of the worst features of the past has been made possible by so-called forward-looking people—the ones who think that every new idea is *ipso facto* a neat idea. These would include all those who think that relativism and multiculturalism (which is really just a variation of relativism) are advanced forms of thinking. But, in fact, these "latest" ways of viewing the world have opened the door to the return of the scary past. They guarantee the return of the primitive precisely because they disallow any distinction between the primitive and the civilized. If you take the multicultural premise to heart, then you can't really make any judgments about the rightness or wrongness of any behavior, provided it has cultural support. Child brides? Honor killing? They're just cultural variations. Besides, with our record of imperialism, slavery, and sexism, who are we to judge?

The French have a proverb: "To understand all is to forgive all." But in our attempts to understand and accept all points of view, we are in danger of forgetting all—all, that is, of the very good reasons for which our culture has rejected those variations. Not to put too fine a point on it, some traditions deserve to be relegated to the past.

The trouble with trying to understand other cultures is that we often try to understand them from a narrow modern perspective that arose in the sixties and seventies. This perspective is materialistic, ahistorical, and therapeutic in outlook. It prizes relativism, diversity, and tolerance, and, although it retains a certain vague spirituality, it is essentially secular. From this viewpoint, religions are quaint traditions clung to for sentimental reasons, not driving cultural forces that mold and shape history.

Islam is the moving force behind many of the unpleasant protrusions of the past into the present. Yet our *bien pensants* have largely failed to understand it. Because they live mentally in a provincial secular time warp (the sixties and seventies) they are ill-equipped to understand religion.

Thus, we don't take Islamists at their word when they talk about their desire to wage jihad for the sake of Allah. Nor do we take seriously their determination to conquer the world for Islam. Modern people don't talk like that or think like that. Consequently, we tend to interpret their dissatisfaction in terms that are familiar to us. Whether it's Boko Haram in Nigeria, al-Shabaab in Somalia, or the Taliban in Afghanistan, we assume that what really explains the jihad is poverty, oppression, or ignorance. Send them some foreign aid and some teachers, and all will be well.

When we do listen to representatives of Islam, we only pay attention to those who are willing to confirm our pre-existing impressions. Islamic apologists who maintain that Islam is a religion of peace and justice and that violence has nothing to do with Islam are the ones who get a hearing, because what they say fits so comfortably into our established narrative.

That narrative is largely determined by fashion, not facts. It's fashionable to think of the spirituality of Third World peoples as being somehow superior to Christianity and Judaism. It's not fashionable to talk about Islamic supremacism, jihad, or the return of the caliphate. But, as events are now showing, these fashionable ideas are already as out of date as bell bottoms and powder-blue tuxedos. It may have seemed funny a year or so ago to ridicule those who worried about sharia law or the reestablishment of the caliphate. It no longer seems quite so funny.

Unless we quickly update our thinking, the times will overtake us. Because we prefer to live mentally in the near past, the worst aspects of the far past have arrived on our doorstep. The list of Western institutions that are enabling jihad with their feckless appeasement of Islam is long. Let's look at some of them.

Western Governments: Enforcing Appeasement

In much of the Western world, Islam has acquired a most-favored status. In other words, Western authorities have bowed to the proposition that Islam must not be criticized. Consider two recent headlines:

- "Belfast pastor on trial for offending Islam"[3]
- "Quebec bill targets people who write against the religion of Islam"[4]

In August 2015, James McConnell, an Evangelical Christian pastor, was charged in a Belfast court with making "grossly offensive" remarks about Islam. Local Muslims had complained that on May 18, the Reverend McConnell had preached a sermon to his large congregation describing Islam as "heathen" and "satanic." McConnell, who rejected an "informed consent"

★ ★ ★

It Depends on Whose Ox Is Being Gored

Al-Wazzan seems to be endorsing genocide. Why isn't *he* on trial for hate speech? Writing in the *Belfast Telegraph*, Susan Breen, an atheist journalist, raised that very question: "The fact that Dr. Al-Wazzan will be in the witness box, and not in the dock himself, reinforces Christians' belief it is they alone who are being victimized and persecuted in our society."[5]

warning that would have allowed him to avoid prosecution, faced six months in prison.

In an interview with the *Belfast Telegraph*, McConnell denied that he hated Muslims: "My church funds medical care for 1,200 Muslim children in Kenya and Ethiopia. I've no hatred in my heart for Muslims, but I won't be stopped from preaching against Islam."[6] Ironically, Dr. Raied al-Wazzan, the director of the Belfast Islamic Center and the chief complainant against

McConnell, does seem to bear some animus against Christians. Speaking to the BBC in January 2015, he said, "Since the Islamic State took over, [Mosul] has become the most peaceful city in the world."[7] That, after the Islamic State had killed or expelled all of Mosul's Christian community of 60,000.

The Reverend McConnell, who thankfully was not convicted, is certainly better off living in Northern Ireland than in Mosul. But the UK seems increasingly inhospitable to Christians and their "inflammatory" opinions. And Pastor McConnell would probably not have fared much better in other parts of the Western world.

Take Canada. We've grown accustomed to thinking of our neighbor to the north as a more liberal place than the U.S. But these days it's difficult to distinguish a liberal from a fascist. Canadian Human Rights Commissions have already put two prominent Canadian citizens—Mark Steyn and Ezra Levant—on trial for criticizing Islam. Fortunately, Steyn and Levant prevailed and even managed to bring about a repeal of the Canadian law which gave Human Rights Commissions the authority to conduct Star Chamber–style inquiries.

But the appeasers are at it again. In the summer of 2015, a bill was introduced that would give new powers to the Quebec Human Rights Commission (QHRC) to combat hate speech and any speech that promotes "fear of the other." The Commission's president, Jacques Fremont, explained he would use the powers to sue "people who would write against...the Islamic religion...on a website or on a Facebook page."[8]

Pastor McConnell's remarks could be construed as promoting "fear of the other"—as can anything but the most innocuous remarks about Islam. And it's not just pastors in pulpits who need to worry. The "human rights" establishment in Canada wants the powers that be to prosecute any Canadian citizen who expresses an incorrect opinion on a website or Facebook page.

That sort of thing is already happening in Europe. Take the case of Geert Wilders, the Dutch MP who has been highly critical of Islam. He's been under police protection ever since 2004,[9] and he and his family are forced to move from safe house to safe house on a regular basis. But in addition to bodyguards, Wilders is also in need of lawyers. That's because he's been hauled before courts on a regular basis ever since 2008 on charges that he has defamed Islam with "hate speech." Wilders's real sin, of course, is to warn against the threat to the West from Islam. It's a threat that anyone with common sense can now see. Even his prosecutors recognize the danger. Because of the numerous threats to his life, his trial is being conducted in a bunker under Shiphol Airport.[10]

The upshot is that it's becoming increasingly difficult to discuss one of the most important issues of our time. The Islamist movement poses a major threat to our civilization. The danger is that, for fear of ending up in court, few will dare to openly acknowledge the threat.

You may counter that it's only the ultra-provocative who end up in court—that the Reverend McConnell, for instance, would never have faced prosecution if he had chosen his words more carefully—something a bit less provocative than "heathen" and "satanic."

But first, what business is it of the government what he says? Short of inciting a mob with pitchforks and torches to attack the local mosque or church, the representatives of one religion ought to be free to criticize another religion. Freedom of religion should include the right to say what you think is wrong with another religion. Or, as McConnell put it, "I would defend the right of any Muslim cleric to preach against me or Christianity."[11] Letting the state sit in judgment on sermons is tantamount to letting the state tell the church what it can and cannot believe.

Second, as we have seen, there is no end to the things that Muslim leaders find offensive. In Saudi Arabia, it's offensive for Christians to build a

A Book You're Not Supposed to Read

G. K. Chesterton had a knack for anticipating future trends, but when he anticipated the Islamization of England in his 1914 novel *The Flying Inn*, it seemed so far outside of the realm of possibility that it was difficult to take it as anything but a flight of fancy.

The book has a whimsical, Pickwickian quality. It follows the rambling adventures of two British stalwarts, Patrick Dalroy and Humphrey Pump, as they try to stay one step ahead of the law, dispensing free liquor as they go in an England where alcohol has been banned. The "Flying Inn" is their motorcar, which they have furnished with a large keg of rum, a cask of cheese, and a pub sign.

Chesterton was remarkably prescient not only in imagining that Islamization might happen, but also in envisioning how it would happen—through the instrumentality of a deracinated governing class. The reason that alcohol is banned in Chesterton's tale is that some upper class elites have become enamored of Islam and everything Islamic—including the prohibition of drink. Chief among these elites is Lord Ivywood, a Nietzschean diplomat who has enlisted the aid of a mysterious Turk, Misyra Ammon, to spread the new gospel among the jaded upper class, which finds exotic Islam to be more exciting than its own traditions and religion.

As Ammon patiently explains to his sophisticated audiences, England was originally an Islamic country. This is evident, he says, in the existence of numerous pubs with Islamic names—"The Saracen's Head," for example—as well as in the English fondness for the word "crescent"—as in "Grosvenor Crescent," "Regent's Park Crescent," and "Royal Crescent." Like today's multicultural elite, Chesterton's "smart set" are all too happy to hear that this exotic culture is superior to their own, and are quite willing to accept that virtually all scientific and technical discoveries were first made by Muslims. As one of the English characters puts it: "Of course, all our things came from the East.... Everything from the East is good, of course."

Much of what Chesterton foresaw has already come to pass. As in Chesterton's story, our multicultural elites are quite willing to believe that Muslims discovered or invented just about everything under the sun. Recently, Recep Tayyip Erdogan, the president of Turkey, claimed that Muslims were the first to discover America. This claim should resonate with Western educators. Multiculturalists would love to believe that America was discovered not by a light-skinned European Christian, but by a dark-skinned Muslim. It would fit in nicely with their decades-long campaign to undermine the Western tradition. Thanks to his teachers, the average Western student doesn't know much about history, but he does know that he was born into a rotten culture with an appalling history of racism, sexism, and imperialism.

In the England of Chesterton's imagining, polygamy is just a gleam in Lord Ivywood's eye. Nowadays, it is a well-established institution in the UK. Although polygamy is still against the law, it is, in fact, a growing practice among the Muslims of Great Britain. Instead of enforcing the law, culturally sensitive police and courts look the other way, and the welfare agencies do their best to provide material support. A Muslim man with four wives can expect a welfare check for each of them.

church. In some Muslim countries, it's offensive when Christians use the word "Allah," even though that is the word they have traditionally used for God.[12] When Pope Benedict quoted a medieval emperor's assessment of Muhammad, Muslims around the world rioted in protest. At this point, most pastors in Canada, Europe, and the UK will have figured out that anything other than greeting-card type platitudes about Islam is considered offensive. And so most will choose to remain completely silent on the issue.

Let's hope that Christian pastors will exercise prudence when speaking about Islam. But for them to remain silent about the threat from jihad will lead many Christians to conclude that there is no real danger to church or society. There's a fine old hymn called "Sleepers Awake," but in many parts of the Christian world, they seem to be humming Brahms's lullaby 24–7. Unless Christians wake up to the global Islamist agenda, they will soon have far more to fret about than facing a Belfast judge or a Canadian human rights commission.

The Police: Taking the Wrong Side in the Clash of Civilizations

The police in Europe and the UK can still be quite tough, but their toughness is in the cause of cultural soft-headedness.

In a sense, the rapes in Cologne and other European cities on New Year's Eve 2015 were the logical conclusion to Europe's inability to resist other Islamic advances. European leaders had opened their borders, their welfare coffers, and their public housing to well over a million Muslim immigrants (75 percent of whom were male) in less than a year. Coming from cultures where yielding is a proof of weakness, the Muslim invaders concluded that they could take what they wanted—both the welfare and the women.

More and more, it seems that Westerners will stand for just about any humiliation at the hands of Muslims. The one thing they won't allow is any resistance to the jihad. Apparently no Western value is worth defending—including the traditional notion that women should be protected from rampaging males. At one time in the chivalrous West, both men and women acknowledged that there are differences between the sexes, that one of those differences is physical strength, and that, as a consequence, there are circumstances in which men have a duty to protect women. But Europeans have now dispensed with those quaint notions. They now seem to believe that everyone—men and women, native Germans and Muslim migrants—will naturally behave in harmonious ways if only given the chance. When you put that assumption into practice, what you get, of course, is smaller, more multiculturally sensitive police forces.

According to one report, police in Cologne were unable to control events on the night of the sexual assaults because they were "overwhelmed."[13] In other words, they lacked the manpower to be of much help that winter's night. "Manpower." It's a curious word. Even today it would seem odd to say that a police force lacked "womanpower." Although men-only police forces are a thing of the past, it's still understood that "manpower" and "womanpower" are not quite the same thing.

In fact, the Cologne police lacked manpower in two senses of the word. They were lacking in numbers that particular night, but even when in full force they seemed to lack the instinctive masculine response that was once expected of civilized males. As I pointed out in *Christianity, Islam, and Atheism*, "the multiculturalist code is essentially an emasculating code. It has the effect of paralyzing the normal masculine response of coming to the protection of those in danger."[14] In the case of the Cologne police, this paralysis would include not having had the foresight to anticipate that German women would be at heightened risk once a million-man army newly arrived from misogynist cultures had made its appearance.

The problem is that the police were more committed to protecting multicultural pieties than to protecting ordinary citizens from Islamists gone wild. Thus, the initial police report of the evening's events read, "A mood of exuberance—largely peaceful celebrations." That's "largely peaceful" if you don't count the thousand marauding Muslims outside the train station and the cathedral.[15] Apparently the authorities' top priority was protecting the sensitivities of the newcomers from the outrage of "Islamophobia." As for the common folk, they are expected to do their best to understand the other culture and adjust to it. If they protest, the penalties can be severe.

★ ★ ★

Meet Your Cell Mates, Mate

The throw-anyone-who-protests-to-the-wolves tactic is not confined to Germany. When Tommy Robinson, a leader of the counter-jihad movement in England, was jailed—for the horrific crime of having exaggerated his income on a mortgage application—he was put into a cell containing several Muslims who beat him brutally, as the prison warders knew they would.[18]

No doubt there are some tough fellows in the Cologne police force, but their toughness has been enlisted in the service of political correctness. When, a week after the New Year's Eve assaults, the anti-immigration group PEGIDA rallied to protest the attacks, a massive force of Cologne police wearing riot gear broke up the demonstration using water cannons and pepper spray.[16] The people in PEGIDA have become used to that sort of treatment. They have been repeatedly attacked by German politicians and the German press as "extremists," "xenophobes," "racists," and "Nazis."[17] And German police have on several occasions left them to the mercy of the brutal and usually much larger leftist or "anti-fascist" gangs. These "antifa" groups use brownshirt tactics to suppress any protest against Islamization or the leftist policies—such as mass immigration—that promote Islamization. Numerous anti-Islamization rallies and marches in Europe have been broken up by much larger groups of young antifas throwing punches and sometimes bricks and bottles.[19]

The German police, however, have nothing on their UK counterparts. The British police force has become one of the most politically correct organizations on the planet. The London Metropolitan Police Authority recruitment target for 2009–10 required that 27 percent of all new recruits be black and minority ethnic, and 41 percent female. Forty-one percent female? In England, the police don't carry guns, so they have had to rely a lot on manpower in the physical strength sense of the word. Apparently that's not necessary anymore now that the bobbies and bobbettes have become ultra-sensitive. Well, not equally sensitive to all. If you say something critical about the religion of peace, you will quickly find yourself in front of a magistrate on charges of hate speech. When, for example, Parliamentary candidate Paul Weston stood in a public space and read aloud Winston Churchill's unflattering assessment of Islam from *The River War*, he was promptly arrested.

Even in America: Go to Jail, Go Directly to Jail

That's on the other side of the Atlantic. Surely the authorities in America would never abuse their power in this way? Tell that to Nakoula Basseley Nakoula. He was the obscure filmmaker whose fifteen-minute trailer for a film about the life of Muhammad supposedly sparked the Benghazi attack and rioting in the Arab world. Of course, you can't arrest a man for making a film, so the authorities dug up a minor violation of probation charge and sent half a dozen sheriff's deputies to arrest Mr. Nakoula in the middle of the night.[20]

According to then–Secretary of State Hillary Clinton, that was all you needed to know about the Benghazi affair: an American filmmaker caused it; culprit in jail; case closed. It was a convenient way of distracting attention from Clinton's own role in the Benghazi incident and her own curious enablement of Islamic policies. It's not well known, for instance, that the Clinton State Department worked closely with the Organization of Islamic Cooperation to help it (the OIC) achieve its objective of silencing speech critical of Islam.

In the Obama-Clinton era it was bad form to criticize Islam. In addition, it was bad manners to criticize its enablers. The press, for example, maintained a respectful silence about President Obama's overly accommodating attitude toward the Mulsim Brotherhood. Thus, it wasn't widely reported when former U.S. representative and retired lieutenant colonel Allen West claimed that Barack Obama "is an Islamist in his foreign policy perspectives and supports their cause." West wasn't saying that Obama was born in

Mombasa or that he wears a secret Muslim decoder ring, but that his policies suggest a deep sympathy with Islamist causes. West provided a list of particulars, including this eye-catching item: "The Obama administration has lifted longtime restrictions on Libyans attending flight schools in the United States and training here in nuclear science."[21] To which the obvious reply is, "What could possibly go wrong?"

Here are two other items on West's list (in his words):

- Returning sanction money, to the tune of billions of dollars, back to the theocratic regime led by Iran's ayatollahs and allowing them to march on towards nuclear capability
- Providing weapons of support to the Muslim Brotherhood-led Egyptian government—F-16s and M1A1 Abrams tanks—but not to the Egyptian government after the Islamist group has been removed[22]

If not many Americans have taken notice of the administration's Muslim Brotherhood bias, the Egyptian people have. When then–Secretary of State Hillary Clinton visited Alexandria in July of 2012, her motorcade was pelted by tomato-throwing protestors who charged that Washington had helped the Muslim Brotherhood come to power.[23] A year later, demonstrators at a huge rally against the Brotherhood government in Cairo roundly criticized Obama and Anne Patterson, the U.S. Ambassador to Egypt. A typical poster read, "Obama, stop supporting the Muslim Brotherhood fascist regime."[24] In December 2012, an Egyptian magazine, *Rose El-Youssef*, claimed that six American Islamic activists working within the Obama administration were Muslim Brotherhood operatives.[25] But while Egyptians were worried about Obama's pro-Muslim Brotherhood policies, Obama himself was worrying about the danger emanating from "those who slander the prophet of Islam."[26] And just to be sure there was no slandering on its watch, his administration ordered that FBI and Army training manuals be purged of all material offensive to Islam.[27]

Whether or not Obama is a secret Islamist (as another Egyptian newspaper claimed)[28] is almost beside the point. Judged by his policies, he might as well be. His administration has shown a distinct favoritism toward the Muslim Brotherhood and its offshoot organizations such as ISNA and CAIR.

A Book You're Not Supposed to Read

Londonistan by Melanie Phillips (New York: Encounter Books, 2007).

Attack of the Pod People

How do a nation's leaders become so detached from the best interests of the people they lead? *Londonistan* author Melanie Phillips describes the process. She argues that, in order to make room for other cultures, the elites have hollowed out their own culture so that "British society presented a moral and philosophical vacuum that was ripe for colonization by predatory Islamism."[29] She lays much of the blame on educators: "The British education system simply ceased transmitting either the values or the story of the nation to successive generations, delivering instead the message that truth was an illusion and that the nation and its values were whatever anyone wanted them to be."[30]

The end result? As UK prime minister David Cameron said in a speech launching a five-year plan to combat homegrown terrorism, "Many people born in Britain have little attachment to the country and that makes them vulnerable to radicalization."[31]

It's not as though Muslims who live in Britain don't eat fish and chips or root for their local football club. But, apparently, a not insignificant number can indulge in British pastimes and still feel unconnected to the country they live in. *Londonistan* describes how a separate and alien culture has developed in England as a result of Britain's experiment in multicultural-ism—an experiment that has been fostered by British elites in media, government, and even in churches.

Unfortunately, a similar process has been underway for a long time in the U.S. For many years, America has been deeply invested in the same multicultural experiment of elevating other cultures by denigrating its own. Our educational, media, and entertainment establishments have subjected young people to decades of anti-American, anti-Western, and anti-Christian conditioning. And as it turns out, the flip side of tolerance for "diversity" is intolerance for one's own culture and the things that make it distinctive.

The result? As Robert Spencer observes, "people who are ashamed of their own culture will not defend it."[32] Such people may even feel that attacks on our country are justified by our history of slavery, racism, colonialism, and imperialism. And the jihadists themselves will only be encouraged by the appeasement. Police in England are now monitoring 3,000 "Islamist fanatics"—with one arrest per day.[33]

The situation is not yet as desperate in America, but nevertheless we seem to be generating a steady supply of homegrown terrorists. On the surface, they blend in with the culture. Major Nidal Hasan was an Army psychiatrist, the Tsarnaev brothers in Boston were into sports and school, and Chattanooga shooter Muhammad Abdulazeez seemed in many respects to be the all-American boy. On the outside, they appeared to be ordinary Americans. On the inside they were more like the pod people in *Invasion of the Body Snatchers*—aliens with alien ambitions.

The worrisome thing is that our institutions of cultural formation seem to be on course to creating a whole nation of pod people—people with little attachment to their country or countrymen.

This detachment can take three forms. In some cases, individuals turn away from involvement in their culture to self-absorption. To assuage the loneliness of the unconnected self, they might turn to drugs or pornography or serial sex. They are unconscious of the larger world, except for the world of pop entertainment. Like the clueless young people interviewed on the Watters' World segment of the *O'Reilly Factor*, they may be unsure who the first president was, in which century the Civil War was fought, or who John Kerry is. None of that seems important to them. If a group of bearded men wearing long robes and speaking Arabic moved into the apartment above, they'd probably think, "that's cool" and light up another joint.

The second form that the detachment takes is a transfer of allegiance from one's own history and culture to a neo-Marxist perspective. A growing segment of our population has come to look upon its own culture as the root of all the world's evils. Unlike the self-absorbed detachers, they are politically engaged, but their political aims have to do with undermining traditional society and radically transforming it. The "Occupy Wall Street" movement is representative of this group.

The third group, the one that Prime Minister Cameron is primarily concerned about, is composed of those whose first loyalty is to the umma—the worldwide community of Muslim believers. They may live in the UK, France, or the U.S., but their allegiance lies elsewhere. They may have always felt this way, or they may have undergone a conversion. The majority even in this category pose no direct threat to the larger society; they simply prefer to lead their lives separate from it. But the separate communities they form do provide the soil in which the radicals take root. They are, to use another metaphor, the sea in which the jihadists swim. The radical Muslims themselves are in some ways similar to the anti-Western Westerners who repudiate the Western tradition. The radicals not only reject Western culture, they see it as evil and they want to bring it down.

Because they have the same goals—the destruction of Western and Christian civilization—the members of the second group often act as enablers of Muslim radicals. The leftist-Islamist alliance is a reality. The left side of the equation is made up of leftist professors who support the cause of Hamas, left-leaning foundations that finance the campaign against "Islamophobia" and left-leaning politicians who support the Muslim Brotherhood. And sometimes the alliance goes beyond moral and financial support and manifests itself in actual violence, as in the leftist "antifa" gangs that regularly attack anti-Islamization rallies.

As befits two movements with global ambitions, alliances between the jihad and the Left are cropping up all over the planet. When an organization called Reclaim Australia held a series of rallies to protest Islamization, they were met by violent "anti-racist" counter-demonstrators, some of them wearing face coverings. Here's an account of one such encounter in Melbourne: "I made my way onto Spring Street, where there was an even larger mob, maybe 500 or 600 people, some with megaphones...There were a few late comers or stragglers attempting to get through to the 'Reclaim Australia' section. It was futile. As soon as anyone in the mob identified a person as a Reclaimer, a large horde of 20 or 40 of the mob would rush to them, and in many incidents I witnessed, assault them, knock them to the ground, and kick them on the ground. It became a mob mentality. Anyone with an Australian flag had it stolen from them and was assaulted. Almost every assault I witnessed was by twenty or more on one."[34]

By comparison, the first group of detachers—those who are mainly into themselves—seems the least dangerous of the three. That's generally true. On the other hand, the self-absorbed sometimes become disenchanted with the pursuit of self and seek to find their identity in a larger cause. Sometimes they end up in church, sometimes in the radical Left,

★ ★ ★
Reinforcements from the Left

If you're worried about the advance of global jihad, it's not just the young Muslim browsing radical sites on the Internet that you need to worry about. You also have to worry about all those college grads who majored in Marxism and peace studies, and are dead set on ridding the world of "racists" and "fascists."

and sometimes in radical Islam. Judging by his blog posts, the Chattanooga jihadist, Muhammad Youssuf Abdulazeez, seems to have traveled this route. Having tried out drugs, drink, fast cars, and other vain pursuits, he finally found a purpose in jihad.[35]

But the main threat posed by those who seek constant diversion is that they are too distracted to notice the larger world and the dangers lurking in it. They are oblivious to anything outside their own pleasure zone. Thus, they can be of little help in resisting the twin threat posed by leftism and Islamism. The same can be said to a lesser degree of those we might call the semi-detached (or semi-attached, if you prefer). Such people don't reject Western and Christian values, but they are not actively engaged in promoting or defending them. They don't hate America, but they are too busy earning a living or raising a family to think much about existential threats to their society. Thanks to years of relentless indoctrination from the schools and the media, their links to core cultural principles are tenuous. The result is a certain passivity concerning events over which they supposedly have no control: "Ho-hum, I see there's been another jihad attack. I hope the authorities will do something about it."

An individual's will to resist tyranny depends to a large extent on the strength of his attachments—particularly attachments to family, church, and country. But the liberal state does everything it can to weaken those ties. And once the ties that bind are slackened sufficiently, it's difficult to care strongly about anything. If the current attacks on marriage, family, religion, and patriotism—up until recently the main glue of society—are as successful as social engineers hope, there will soon be nothing left worth fighting for.

Which raises a question: What happens when the leaders of a society are themselves detached from that society? What happens, for instance, when the leaders of the U.S. government begin to see themselves not as representatives of the American people but as members of a worldwide order of global elites—a sort of non-religious umma?

There was a brief controversy a while back when former New York mayor Rudy Giuliani raised this question by suggesting that President Obama did not love America. That line of inquiry didn't go very far because it was quickly put beyond the pale by those who control the levers of media. Yet there is very little evidence that Obama does love his country, and the same could be said for many others in government. Like the pod people, they know what they are supposed to say in order to assuage people's suspicions. But in pod-people fashion, they have been busy hollowing out the old culture and replacing it with alien institutions and strange new "traditions": gender-neutral schools, a transgendered military, a social justice warrior class, and a radical reconstruction of marriage. At the same time, the governing classes both in Europe and the U.S. have been introducing actual aliens (in the technical sense of the word) into their nations. In some countries, especially those that favor Muslim refugees and turn away Christians, this movement of peoples is beginning to look less like immigration and more like colonization. But, of course, colonization is what the pod people are all about.

If some of our leaders seem strangely detached from concerns over the safety, security, and integrity of our society, it may be a sign that the pod people are already in our midst.

CHAPTER 8

Information Wars

If there's one institution in America most responsible for the strange detachment with which Americans are meeting the existential threat of jihad, it's probably our system of education. From kindergarten to graduate programs, American schools are undermining students' attachment to their own culture and thus leaving them with little reason to resist the invasion of an alien one—and with little of the necessary will and character.

You've probably heard about the cancellation of a showing of the film *American Sniper* at the University of Michigan. The film was cancelled in response to a student petition protesting that the film was racist and anti-Muslim. The initiator of the petition told the *Detroit Free Press* that she felt "uncomfortable" watching it. The university responded by replacing *American Sniper* with *Paddington*—presumably on the premise that no one feels uncomfortable when watching a movie about a teddy bear. After the school's football coach, Jim Harbaugh, tweeted his support for *American Sniper*, the university relented and decided to show both films, although at different locations.[1]

Did you know?

★ The University of Michigan cancelled American Sniper out of respect for Muslim sensibilities—and showed a movie about a teddy bear instead

★ The Muslim terrorists in Tom Clancy's The Sum of All Fears were changed to white supremacists in the movie

★ The media suppressed facts that made it clear that the men who killed Drummer Lee Rigby were motivated by Islam

★ ★ ★

Peter Pan America

According to culture critic Roger Kimball, "If America's cultural revolution [of the 1960s] was anything, it was an attack on maturity: more, it was a glorification of youth, of immaturity." The result, wrote Kimball, was that the values and attitudes of the youth culture "were adopted by the culture at large."[2]

There are several morals to take away from the story. One is that football is still the most important institution on campus. Another moral—the one I would like to expound on—is that the infantilization of our society is complete. When a movie about a stuffed animal is considered age-appropriate for twenty-year-olds, it's a sign that our society is in trouble. When a movie about one aspect of the biggest story of our time is deemed a threat to the safe space of the same twenty-year-olds, it may be time for all of us to exchange our newspaper subscriptions for a lifetime subscription to Vermont Teddy Bear's annual editions of stuffed bears.

"Infantilization" may be a bit harsh. Let's just say, as sociologists have been saying for the last fifty years, that the preferred end-state of development for many Americans is adolescence. Although adolescents have many fine qualities, the mainstream culture tends to celebrate the more immature traits of the age group, such as self-absorption and a limited sense of personal responsibility. The results have been devastating. The widespread adoption of the youth culture zeitgeist led to, among other things, the divorce culture and the unwed mother culture, both of which led to more generations of mixed-up youth who chose, in their turn, to put growing up on permanent hold.

America has paid a steep price for its infatuation with youth culture, but it has somehow managed to avoid a final reckoning. Up until now, that is. While the counterculture in America and Europe was gradually becoming the established culture, another adolescent culture was beginning to assert itself in the Mid-East and Near-East. In many places, it was an adolescent culture in the literal sense of the word. For instance, the average age of a resident of the Gaza Strip is about eighteen.[3]

Although Islamic cultures are ancient, they nevertheless tend to exhibit some of the fantasy-based thinking of the adolescent. For example, a good many Muslim males, both young and old, are quite certain that seventy-two virgins have been reserved for them in paradise. And, like the adolescent mindset that ate the West, the Islamic mind tends toward excitability and even irrationality. Almost any perceived insult—an obscure video, a mild cartoon in a Danish newspaper—has the power to provoke paroxysms of anger. Much of the Muslim world also shares the view that Western imperialism, colonialism, and racism are at the root of the world's ills. In addition to endearing them to Western progressives, this simplistic explanation (largely borrowed from Western academics) has the advantage of relieving rioting Muslims of any sense of personal responsibility for their actions.

The re-emergence of Islam on the world stage is often attributed to three factors—rapid population growth, the success of the Iranian Revolution, and the Arab oil money that financed the spread of Islamic ideology to every corner of the world. But a fourth factor should be added—the concomitant spread of youth culture ideology in the Western world. Counterculture ideas helped to create the moral, spiritual, and population vacuum that Islam was quick to fill.

The biggest idea in the counterculture thought world is cultural relativism, a.k.a. multiculturalism—the notion that all cultures, religions, and customs are equally valid, so that other cultures and their cultural practices are beyond criticism.

But multiculturalism has another effect. It makes it difficult to see other cultures for what they are. One effect of adolescent self-centeredness is the belief that the "other," for all his otherness, is essentially made in one's own image and likeness. The youth culture (now middle-aged) looked out

★ ★ ★

A Different Kind of Youth Culture

Young people in the Muslim world may appreciate the rhythms of rock music, but they may also see little wrong with throwing rocks at adulterers.

and saw—or thought they saw—a global youth culture whose members were all equally dedicated to peace and love and the elimination of whatever divisions hindered the universal embrace.

But many of the world's youth are not like that. A young Muslim may be personally easygoing and inclined toward tolerance, but tolerance is not typically an important value in his culture, whereas honor—a concept that elicits laughs from sophisticated Western youth—is of ultimate importance. For males in the Muslim world, the concept of honor is bound up with control over women; for the sake of restoring family honor, a father may kill his daughter and a brother may maim his sister. Islam is an honor culture writ large. It differs from other honor cultures such as those found in tribal societies and street gangs by virtue of its universal claims. Islam elevates loyalty to the umma over other loyalties, but the same sensitivity to being disrespected is still there. Thus, the hair-trigger reaction to any insult against the religion or its prophet. Insofar as the Islamic mindset is an adolescent mindset, it is more like the mindset of an adolescent gang member than that of an adolescent flower child.

The honor-dominance dynamic which rules Islamic societies is in many respects the antithesis of counterculture values. Yet, without the triumph of the counterculture and its celebration of primitive values, it's unlikely that the Islamic revival would have been such a success. A society of grown-ups would have been able to see the Islamic resurgence for what it was and would have been able to resist it. But a nation in which the navel-gazers had somehow gravitated to the top was only able to view Islam through the prism of its own self-absorption.

The counterculturalists of the sixties and beyond were too busy actualizing themselves to have any but the vaguest ideas about history, philosophy, religion, or cultures. Thus they were suckers for simplistic ideas—the noble primitive, Marxism, the guilt of imperialists, and the justice of "liberationist" movements everywhere. We all know about the devastation to family life when the limited horizons of adolescence are carried over to adulthood, but how about the effect on political life? What happens when adults go into politics still clinging to an adolescent worldview? And what happens when the Western adolescent mindset meets the warrior adolescent mindset?

Much of the current deference to Islam and especially to its crazier manifestations can be explained by reference to this adolescent view of history and culture. In a piece for *National Review*, historian Victor Davis Hanson points out that our seemingly inchoate foreign policy only makes sense when you keep in mind that President Obama "has an adolescent, romantic view of professed revolutionary societies and anti-Western poseurs." Obama's "juvenile view" of the revolutionary non-West, says Hanson, explains why in any dispute he always comes down on the side of the more revolutionary party—Erdogan in Turkey, the Muslim Brotherhood in Egypt, al-Qaeda in Libya, the guardians of the Revolution in Iran, and the Castros in Cuba. Never mind that these revolutionary leaders are ruining their countries. Obama "has a starry-eyed crush on those who strike anti-Western poses" and who claim to speak for the people.[4]

Meanwhile, his equally starry-eyed secretary of state is betting the family farm on the trustworthiness of Iran's ideologically driven leaders. During the negotiations for the nuclear deal with Iran, it was rumored that, if all else failed, Kerry, a true son of the sixties, would employ the folk song and bear hug diplomacy that had worked so well to quell the fears of the French after the *Charlie Hebdo* massacre. Whether or not it will be a teddy bear hug accompanied by the presentation of a stuffed Paddington remains to be seen. It would be a mistake to assume that just because a man has reached septuage-narian status, his brain is no longer stuffed with adolescent pipedreams.

The skirmish between *Paddington* and *American Sniper* is part of a larger pattern. Last year, the University of Michigan at Dearborn cancelled the showing of *Honor Diaries*—a documentary about the violent treatment of women in Islam.[5] "Honor Diaries" seems like a strange title for a film describing female genital mutilation, forced marriage, and death at the hands of relatives. Until, that is, you remember that Islam is an honor culture where doing the honorable thing by a woman does not necessarily mean marrying her.

Unsurprisingly, the film was perceived as an attack on the honor of Islam, and the university administrators came under intense pressure from Muslim activist groups to cancel the "Islamophobic" production—and they dutifully did. On college campuses, protecting the honor of Islam often seems to be a higher priority than protecting the rights of women.

Respect for the culture of the "other" and respect for the rights of women are both part of the multicultural agenda subscribed to by academics. But what do you do when the two principles collide? The answer seems to be that you reserve your sensitivity for the group that is most likely to cause you bodily harm if you cross it. Perhaps the faculty and students at University of Michigan are dimly aware that in some crucial respects, the Islamic honor culture is not unlike the gang culture that rules parts of nearby Detroit. In short, it's best not to disrespect them.

There's a good deal of talk on university campuses of providing spaces where students can feel "safe" and "comfortable." This usually means allowing no space whatever for anything that might trigger the unsafe feeling. But it's highly unlikely that university officials are seriously worried that a Clint Eastwood film is going to catapult students into a state of shock. What they're really worried about is that Islamic brownshirts are going to create a genuinely unsafe environment.

At another Michigan campus—Eastern Michigan University—a showing of the Eastwood film was shut down after thirty-five protesters moved into the theater and marched onto the stage. Judging by the names of the protest leaders (Ahmed Abbas, and so forth), one surmises they were mostly Muslim students. In explaining the decision to cancel the second showing of the film, administrators said they "wanted to make sure whatever happens, students would be safe."[6] But safe from what? From a film that no one was compelling them to watch? Or from the sharp edge of a culture that seems increasingly intent on forcing others to abide by its rules?

★ ★ ★

Ladies and Gentlemen, Place Your Bets

Who seems most likely to prevail? Generations that have been indoctrinated in the belief that even the worst excesses of the multicultural "other" must be respected? Or generations that have been indoctrinated to believe that jihad for the sake of Allah is life's highest aspiration?

A society in which "safe spaces" are cancelling out free speech will not, in the long run, be able to provide either freedom or safety. For the time being, the perpetual adolescents in our society will still be able to rally for legalized pot, the right of gays to eat their cake and have it too, and other momentous causes of the day. But time may be running out for them.

The Paddington generation has been largely successful at winning battles in the domestic culture war. But that is because their opponents are constrained by the rules of civility and Christian forbearance. It's unlikely they'll fare as well in the looming intercultural war with Islam.

A word of caution: when your teddy bear arrives from the factory, be careful what you name it. Nine years ago, Gillian Gibbons, an English woman teaching six-year-olds in Sudan, allowed her students to name the class mascot—a teddy bear—"Muhammad." She was promptly arrested, found guilty of "insulting religion," and thrown in jail, while outside a crowd of 10,000 protestors demanded her execution. Luckily, the British government prevailed upon the Sudanese government to pardon her and release her back to England. It took only one multicultural misstep and suddenly Miss Gibbons found that all of Sudan was an unsafe space for her.[7] Note to the University of Michigan: is it really safe to show *Paddington*? It might remind Muslim students of an ugly Islamophobic incident that happened only nine years ago in Sudan. Seems rather insensitive.

Political Correctness in La La Land

The Sum of All Fears is a 2002 thriller based on the Tom Clancy novel of the same name. In the book, Islamic terrorists detonate a nuclear bomb in Denver at the Super Bowl. For the movie, the terrorists have been transformed into white supremacist neo-Nazis.

The Pilot's Wife is a made-for-TV film from the same year, about terrorists who blow up a trans-Atlantic airliner. Are the terrorists Muslims? Don't be silly. They are good Irish Republican Catholics. The pilot is a devout Catholic (well, maybe not all that devout, since he's also a bigamist) who gets mixed up with the IRA—apparently for religious reasons.

In one scene, the airline agent who is investigating the crash has a Eureka moment and says something to the effect of, "The Catholic thing, the Irish connection. I should have guessed." The filmmakers seem to take it for granted that blowing up planeloads of people is standard behavior for Irish Catholics who take their religion too seriously. To drive the point home, the next scene takes place in an Irish cathedral where a young Irish woman with a Celtic-style cross pendant gracing her neck confirms the investigator's suspicions about the Catholic-terrorist connection. To hear her talk, you'd think that fighting for the cause is a moral obligation for Catholics.

The 2014 film *Jack Ryan: Shadow Recruit* depicts a terrorist sleeper cell in Dearborn, Michigan, that aims to detonate a nuclear bomb under Wall Street. In the real world, Dearborn is home to the largest mosque in North America and has the highest concentration of Muslims per capita of any

U.S. city. It is jokingly referred to as "Dearbornistan." You would expect, therefore, that if there were a sleeper cell of terrorists in Dearborn, some of them might be Muslims. Uh-uh. In the film, the terrorists are Russian Orthodox Christians operating out of a Russian Orthodox Church. That may seem odd, but once you remember that Hollywood has the highest per capita concentration of politically correct panderers, it all makes sense.

Non-Stop, released the same year, is an action thriller about an unidentified terrorist on board a trans-Atlantic flight who begins to murder one passenger every twenty minutes. When the terrorist is finally identified and dispatched before he can blow up the plane, he turns out to be— are you ready?—an American combat veteran. Not only that, but an American vet who lost his father in the 9/11 attack on the World Trade Center, and therefore has an urgent need to wake Americans up to the lack of security at airports.

An interesting sidelight to the story is that one of the initial suspects is a Muslim doctor wearing Muslim garb and a full beard. As it turns out, he is one of the heroes. He tends to the dying and lends a hand to the air marshal protagonist (played by Liam Neeson). Why such an obvious red herring? Probably so the filmmakers can play "gotcha" with the rubes in the audience who are so unsophisticated as to think that a Muslim—let alone a Muslim doctor—could possibly be a terrorist.

Speaking of doctors, Bowen, the villain in *Non-Stop*, is badly in need of psychiatric help.

★ ★ ★
First, Do No Harm

In the real world, some of the planet's most notorious terrorists are Muslim doctors. Ayman al-Zawahiri, the head of al-Qaeda, is a doctor,[8] Major Nidal Hasan, the Fort Hood killer, is a doctor,[9] and so also is Bashar al-Assad, who studied ophthalmology before taking over the reins in Syria.[10] Bilal Abdullah, the ringleader of the 2007 terrorist attack at Glasgow International Airport, was a doctor,[11] as was his coconspirator Mohammad Asha.[12] These facts, of course, prove nothing as far as the majority of Muslim doctors are concerned. But neither does the presence of the noble Muslim doctor onboard the *Non-Stop* flight prove anything about which belief system tends to produce the most terrorists.

He suffers from a lethal case of "Islamophobia"—which, according to the experts, is an irrational fear of Islam, leading inevitably to discrimination and intolerance against Muslims. Bowen takes it even further than that. He is so fearful about the threat from Islam that he is willing to blow up a planeful of people, himself included, just to call attention to the threat. The film's producers seem to subscribe to the notion that "Islamophobia" is the chief threat to world security. Where could they have gotten that impression?

No doubt the producers of *Non-Stop* see themselves as providing a public service by pointing out the logical consequences of this irrational hatred. Moreover, they are doing their part in educating the public about the phobic nature of this malady by showing that there is no real basis for this fear: it's all in our heads. The good Muslim doctor on board proves that point, doesn't he?

It is fitting that the main action of *Non-Stop* takes place up in the air because the filmmakers seem to have lost all contact with earthly reality. Back on planet earth, the picture looks a little different.

In the world of liberal filmmakers (but I repeat myself) there is no danger from Islam or Islamists, only from people who mistakenly fear Islam. With apologies to Franklin Roosevelt, "The only thing we have to fear is fear of Islam." The Hollywood takeaway from all the real-life Islamist attacks on planes—the four 9/11 airliners, the Russian passenger jet downed over the Sinai, the failed attacks by the "shoe bomber" and the "underwear bomber"—is that we should keep an eye out for the

Islamophobes among us. Well-informed citizens might, understandably, come to a different conclusion.

The Media: Hiding the Real Threat

If, that is, citizens *were* well-informed about the profiles of actual terrorists. Unfortunately, our media is doing its best to cover up that information. According to Reporters Without Borders, the U.S. has dropped to forty-sixth place in press freedom. The lowered ranking is based on the conviction of the WikiLeaks informant, the effort to punish NSA leaker Edward Snowden, and the Justice Department's monitoring of reporters.[13]

Unmentioned by the report, though, is an equally serious cause for concern. Most press censorship in the U.S. is self-imposed. The masters of the media are quite willing to suppress certain news stories without any government encouragement. This can be accomplished in several ways: by not reporting a story, by providing only minimal coverage, or by shaping the story to fit a pre-existing narrative. There may be "eight million stories in the naked city," as the old television series informed us, but the news producers are the ones who decide which stories you will hear and what slant they will be given.

The media is by and large committed to the narrative that Islam is a religion of peace. Hence, they tend to underreport incidents of Islamic terrorism, or else they shape the story to fit the narrative that the violence has nothing to do with Islam. For example, did you know that the group of knife-wielding assailants who slashed to death thirty-one people and injured 141 at a crowded Chinese train station on March 1, 2014, were Muslim jihadists?[14] The fact that the killers were Muslims appears in some reports, usually at the end of the story, but the main impression given by most of the reporting is that the assailants were "separatists" making a political statement about the repression of ethnic minorities. The words "jihad" and "jihadists" are notable by their absence from most reports.

Did you know that Michael Adebolajo and Michael Adebowale, the murderers of British soldier Lee Rigby, have Muslim names? After their conversion to Islam they took the names Mujaahid Abu Hamza and Ismail bin Abdullah, respectively.[15] But in this case and others, the mainstream media refrained from using the jihadists' Muslim names. After the killing, Abu Hamza forced a passerby to video-record his message to the public. While several TV stations carried the message, most of them cut out the part where he referred to passages from the Koran as justification for his act. Also largely unreported was the fact that Abu Hamza handed a blood-stained note full of Koran quotations to a bystander. Almost all news reports, however, did manage to give a lot of space to Prime Minister David Cameron's assurance that the killing had nothing to do with Islam.[16]

Cameron said more or less the same thing in reaction to the terror attack at a Nairobi Mall that left over sixty dead: "They don't represent Islam or Muslims in Britain or anywhere else in the world." The media, however, couldn't very well pretend that there was no Islamic angle to the massacre, since the terrorist spared Muslims who were able to recite from the Koran.[17] Nevertheless, some details were not widely reported, including the fact that the terrorists themselves took time off for prayer in the midst of their deadly assault.[18]

The above are cases in which the media chose to slant the news by leaving out key details that might connect Islamic beliefs to terrorism. There are numerous other examples—the Fort Hood shooting, the Boston Marathon massacre, the Times Square bombing—in which the stories were tailored to fit the controlling narrative. Just as significant, though, are the stories that go unreported or underreported. It is not unfair to say that by giving the silent treatment to the vast majority of incidents, the mainstream media has managed to effectively cover up the sheer magnitude of Islamic violence worldwide. The streaming headlines at the bottom of your TV screen that detail the daily toll taken by jihadists represent only a fraction of the actual occurrences.

Did you know that on February 12, 2007, Sulejmen Talovic, a young Bosnian-Muslim man, opened fire on shoppers in the Trolley Square Mall in Salt Lake City, killing five and wounding four others before he was shot and killed by police? Talovic, who was named after the sixteenth-century Muslim jihadist-turned-sultan Suleiman the Magnificent, was a religious Muslim who attended mosque and had once boasted that his grandfather was "in the

jihad." The day before the attack he said that "tomorrow will be the happiest day of my life," and he wore a Koran necklace at the time of the shooting. Some witnesses at the scene heard him shouting "Allahu Akbar!" Nevertheless, according to Tim Fuhrman, the FBI special agent in charge of the case, "We were unable to pin down any particular motive."[19] If you remember the Trolley Square shooting at all, were you under the impression that the shooter was a Muslim who was clearly motivated by jihadist impulses?

Here are some more examples of stories that were underreported.

- The French interior minister announced in January of 2014 that 1,193 cars had been burned across France on New Year's Eve. Previous French governments had hushed up the numbers of car burnings—over 40,000 a year—by "youths" whose religion is carefully left out of news reports[20]
- The number of women who have been subjected to female genital mutilation in the UK is well over 100,000[21]
- In September of 2013, over 60,000 Christians were forced to flee their homes when Muslim terrorists took over sections of Zamboanga, one of the largest cities in the southern Philippines[22]

- Since March of 2013, at least 450,000 Christians in the Central African Republic have been forced to flee their homes following the Islamic takeover there[23]

In all likelihood, you have heard little or nothing about these stories. The mainstream media has a habit of burying them among other stories, or of passing over them briefly lest anyone begin to see a pattern. Yet they are fairly significant stories. Suppose the shoe were on the other foot and it was Christian youth who were burning 40,000 cars a year in France? Or if 60,000 Muslims were forced to flee a city that was under siege by Christian terrorists? What would happen? The answer, of course, is that such events would be the lead item on the news every night, followed by special one-hour, in-depth programs and accompanied by morning-to-night analysis by panels of experts.

Here are some closer-to-home stories you might have missed. All of the following stories were covered to some extent by the media, but not to the extent that they were likely to stick in the memory for long. It is very unlikely, for example, that you would recall the case of Nuradin Abdi, who in 2007 was sentenced to ten years in prison for a planned jihad attack against an Ohio shopping mall.[24] Nor is it likely that you would remember the case of Derrick Shareef, who was sentenced in 2008 to thirty-five years in prison for plotting to explode grenades at a Rockford, Illinois, mall. A convert to Islam, Shareef was recorded saying that he wanted to kill infidels.[25] How about Tarek Mehanna? In 2009, the twenty-seven-year-old Massachusetts man was charged with conspiring to attack shoppers in U.S. malls. According to the complaint, Mehanna and his co-conspirators often discussed their desire to participate in "violent jihad against American interests."[26]

While it's unlikely that you will have a good memory of these trials, it's very likely you remember the George Zimmerman–Trayvon Martin case.

That shooting might have remained a local news affair, but influential people both in and outside the media decided to turn it into a major national story. Am I suggesting a conscious and deliberate suppression of some stories and a conscious inflation of others? Yes and no. In some cases, yes, the bias is quite deliberate. But many cases of lopsided reporting can probably be attributed to an automatic response. Some events will seem more important to the news editors because they fit into a preconceived narrative, and other cases will receive less attention because they don't fit the narrative. Indeed, if some cases were to be explored in depth, they might challenge and even explode the narrative. Hence, there is much less incentive to dig into such stories. The trial of Major Nidal Hasan, the Fort Hood shooter, was at least as significant an event as the trial of George Zimmerman and it took place, moreover, in roughly the same time frame. Yet it received nowhere near the coverage. The media was quite happy to focus on the supposedly racist motivations of Zimmerman, but quite reluctant to look into the blatant jihadist motivations of Major Hasan.

More stories you may have missed:

- In January 2013, a jury convicted Mohamed Osman Mohamud of attempting to detonate a 1,800-pound bomb at a crowded annual Christmas tree lighting in Portland, Oregon, in 2010. Undercover FBI agents said Mohamud spoke of the need to eliminate unbelievers, and said that he didn't mind that children would die[27]
- In December 2013, Terry Lee Loewen, a convert to Islam and an avionics technician at Wichita's Mid-Continent Airport, was arrested for attempting to drive an explosive-laden van into the airport. Although Loewen had repeatedly written about his love for Allah and the Koranic justification for his planned jihad, the FBI special agent in charge of the case

The Politically Incorrect Guide to Jihad

assured Kansas citizens that Loewen's actions had nothing to do with Islam[28]

- On March 17, 2014, Nicholas Teausant, a convert to Islam, was arrested and charged with attempting to provide material support to al-Qaeda and plotting an attack on the Los Angeles subway system. Teausant's Muslim name is Ased Abdur-Raheem, but for some mysterious reason, the news reports refrain from using it[29]

- In April 2013, two Muslim men were arrested in Canada for plotting to blow up a passenger train from New York to Ontario as it crossed the trestle over the Niagara River Gorge. One of the defendants, Chiheb Esseghaier, insisted in court that he be judged only by the Koran instead of by Canadian laws[30]

Do you remember hearing these stories or reading about them? If so, did you receive a clear impression at the time that the accused were Muslims? That they were devout Muslims? That their actions were inspired by their Islamic faith? While the mainstream media can't very well ignore a plot to blow up a major U.S.-to-Canada train line, they can minimize the coverage, and they can and do downplay the Islamic connection.

The average Western citizen can be forgiven if he is not up to speed on the numerous successful and attempted jihad attacks in the U.S., Canada, and Europe. There is abundant evidence that the opinion-makers don't want us to think too much about the subject. When an attack occurs or when one is foiled, the media give it a perfunctory nod and then almost immediately lose interest in the story. Are they hoping that we will lose interest too?

As political scientist Samuel Huntington observed, we are in a civilizational struggle with Islam. One of the major fronts in that conflict is the information war, and thus far Islam seems to be winning it hands down. Why? Because the Western media has adopted as its own Islam's narrative about itself—that it is a religion of peace that has been hijacked by a handful of misunderstanders. The result is that what information we get about Islam is filtered through a rose-colored prism. Whether consciously or through force of habit, the mainstream media has effectively taken Islam's side in the information war. Thanks to the media's pandering, Western citizens are ill-informed about Islam, and as a result they are unprepared for the more aggressive forms of jihad to which the information jihad is merely a prelude.

CHAPTER 9

Christian Enablers of Jihad

In *The Flying Inn*, G. K. Chesterton's prescient 1914 novel about the Islamization of England, the great cathedrals propose to replace the cross with a cross-and-crescent emblem, and intellectuals believe that the time has come "for a full unity between Christianity and Islam."

"Something called Chrislam perhaps," observes a skeptical Irishman.[1]

Believe it or not, today there really is a religious movement called "Chrislam." It began in Nigeria in the 1980s as an attempt to foster peace between Muslims and Christians by blending elements of Islam and Christianity. Its followers stress the commonalities between the two faiths, and they recognize both the Koran and the Bible as holy texts.

Nigerian Chrislam appears to be a relatively small movement.[2] There is, however, a much larger worldwide movement that can, in a sense, be considered a form of Chrislam. Its adherents minimize the differences between Islam and Christianity. They describe themselves as "people of the book" and members of the "Abrahamic faith tradition." They are fond of saying that "we all worship the same God." The main religious ritual of these Chrislamites is dialogue—a ceremony that will serve, they hope, to build

Did you know?

★ A Lutheran bishop in Sweden has proposed removing Christian symbols from a church to make it more welcoming to those "from other religions"

★ Jesus appears in the Koran to explain that he is not really God

★ The U.S. bishops' main interfaith dialogue partner is a Muslim Brotherhood front group

bridges between the two faiths. People who are dubious about these bridge-building efforts are dismissed as "bigots" and "Islamophobes."

And this kind of Chrislam, unlike the Nigerian version, isn't an eccentric offshoot from mainstream Christianity. It is now the Christian churches' default attitude toward the religion of Muhammad. And it is appeasing and enabling jihad.

Preemptive Surrender

While cross-crescent emblems haven't yet appeared on cathedrals, the Right Reverend Eva Brunne, Lutheran Bishop of Stockholm, made headlines recently for her proposal to remove the Christian symbols of the Seamen's Church in Freeport, "to make it more inviting for visiting sailors from other religions." According to the story, "the bishop wants to temporarily make the Seamen's Church available to all, for example by marking the direction of Mecca and removing Christian symbols...."[3] Temporarily? What if some of the visiting sailors decide to put down roots in Freeport? What if the local imam proposes that the Seamen's Church be turned into a mosque?

Islam may be the fastest growing religion, but Chrislam appears to be the fastest growing fad among sophisticated Christians. In Washington, the National Cathedral has opened its doors for Friday Muslim prayers.[5] And over in the UK, a Church of England bishop has recommended that Prince Charles's coronation service should be opened with a reading from the Koran. The gesture, he said,

★ ★ ★
Tolerance Doesn't Run Both Ways

Bishop Brunne is of a welcoming disposition, but she doesn't seem to have thought out the consequences of her embrace of Muslim refugees. She is Sweden's first lesbian bishop, and the first to be in an official same-sex registered partnership (with another priestess).[4] Given both her sexual orientation and the rapid progress of stealth jihad in Sweden, one suspects that the time is approaching when Bishop Brunne herself may be the refugee.

would be "a creative act of accommodation" to make Muslims feel "warmly embraced."[6]

Remember Father Ronald Rolheiser, the proponent of "greater solidarity with Islam"? When jihadists massacred fourteen innocent people after an office Christmas party in California, Father Rolheiser judged it an appropriate occasion to point out that "Muslims more than ever need our understanding, sympathy, support, and fellowship in faith."[8]

It's the Catholics' Fault

"Florida bishop blames Orlando massacre on Catholic 'contempt' for homosexuality"

—Breitbart news headline[7]

Catholic schools are also into Chrislamism. While the rest of America is wondering where Islamic jihadists will strike next, at Georgetown University the biggest concern is not with Islamic terrorism but with "Islamophobia." A year ago, the Jesuit university sponsored a "Conversation on Islamophobia," featuring a lineup of Islamic apologists all testifying to the societal threat posed by anti-Muslim hysteria.[9] For two decades, the folks at Georgetown's Alwaleed bin Talal Center for Muslim-Christian Understanding have worked diligently to put a friendly face on Islam and to demonize its critics. Alwaleed bin Talal? He's just a friendly Arab prince who has donated over $20 million to the center.[10]

Meanwhile, while Georgetown is worrying about people who worry about Islam, over at John Carroll University in Ohio, retired archbishop Michael Fitzgerald is teaching students about the wonders of the Koran. He urges Catholics to look for commonalities with their own religion, and he suggests that, in its own way, the Koran is a sacrament—"a sign of the presence of God."[11]

In the "Chrislam" that is taking over our churches, the details of the merger between Christianity and Islam haven't as yet been worked out. But to a certain kind of Christian, the details are unimportant. It doesn't matter to him that his head is in the sand as long as his heart is in the right place.

The churches' lack of concern over the Islamic hijra currently underway in Europe is a perfect example of this head-in-the-sand-posture. Jihadists are murdering Christians in nearly every Muslim-controlled country on the face of the earth—from Nigeria, to Egypt, to Yemen, to the ISIS-controlled territories in Syria and Iraq, to Pakistan. And yet Christian pastors see the invasion of the West by millions of young men from the Muslim world primarily as an opportunity for Christians to show their generous hospitality to the other.

Cardinal Reinhard Marx, the president of the German bishops' conference, made a special trip to the Munich train station to offer a highly publicized welcome to asylum-seekers.[12] And Pope Francis chose to wash the feet of Muslims on Holy Thursday, in what we have seen may very well be read by the newcomers as a gesture of submission to Islam. He also decided to take Muslim refugees over Christian refugees when he was doing his own personal part in the welcoming of immigrants.[13] One wonders what it will take to remind the Catholic Church of its centuries-long struggle with Islam. The modern Church was quick to understand the totalitarian nature of communism. Catholic clergy, academics, and journalists were, on the whole, much more astute about the communist menace than their secular counterparts. Yet they have been painfully slow in awakening to the dangers inherent in Islam. Many of the bishops who convened for the Synod on the Family in Rome in 2014 and 2015 were the same bishops who have been encouraging the importation of a very unchristian family structure into Europe.[14] Shouldn't they take stock of what kind of culture is being imported by the migrants they are welcoming with open arms?

Their welcoming attitude didn't emerge just in response to the recent wave of migrants and refugees. It's been the Church's semi-official policy for decades. But over the decades the situation has changed. What was once a trickle of immigrants is now a flood. What hasn't changed, however, is the bishops' assessment of the situation. They are still relying on rationales for immigration that are long past their sell-by date: that young immigrants will solve Europe's labor shortage, replenish its welfare coffers, and enrich its culture with their talents. In short, the bishops have never admitted the possibility that mass immigration has a decided downside.

Of course, the pragmatic arguments for welcoming migrants and refugees pale beside the moral arguments—especially when they come from the pope himself. In his message for the World Day of Migrants and Refugees, Pope Francis said that in welcoming the stranger "we open our doors to God...in the face of others we see the face of Christ himself."[15]

But given the magnitude of Muslim immigration into Europe, a question arises: can European Christians see the face of Christ in their fellow native Europeans? It's true that the Church has a duty to remind Christians of their obligation to help the needy, but is there a Christian duty to collaborate in the destruction of Christianity?

The Nigerian experiment in "Chrislam" hasn't slowed the jihad in that country. In fact, since Chrislam was invented in the 1980s, violent jihad has only increased, with bloody massacres, church bombings, and kidnapped girls forced into sex slavery all now regular features of life in Nigeria.

Will the informal sort of Chrislam that holds sway in our churches defuse the stealth jihad that threatens Europe and America? Not likely. Christian appeasement will only enable those who intend to subjugate the West to Islam.

The Mosque of Jesus, Son of Mary

The Muslim takeover of Christian churches is more than metaphorical. Holy Trinity Catholic Church in Syracuse, New York, was sold in December 2013 to a Muslim group and turned into a mosque. The Muslim organization requested that six stone crosses be removed from the top of the century-old historic church, and the Syracuse Landmark Preservation Board signed off on the alteration. However, as Syracuse.com explained at the time, everything evens out because the mosque was to be named the Mosque of Jesus, Son of Mary, "to build a bridge between the old and the new."[16]

So that's all right then. Or is it? The news story was written to the theme that Islam and Catholicism share much in common—two sides of the same coin, so to speak. A diocesan spokeswoman is quoted as saying that "the building is once again being used to meet the needs of a growing population on the North Side, just as Holy Trinity did as it served the Catholic faithful." In this telling, immigrant Muslims are just like immigrant Catholics of a hundred years ago. And the faiths are not really that far apart. After all, both believe in Jesus, the son of Mary.

But if that's so, why did the crosses have to come down? The reason, as explained by one of the Muslim organizers, is that "crosses are not an appropriate representation of the religion of Islam."[17] Why is that? Because the Koran maintains that Jesus was never crucified and therefore never rose from the dead (4:157).

In short, there are reasons to wonder if the Jesus, son of Mary that Muslims revere is the same Jesus that Christians revere. For instance, the Syracuse.com story reported that some of the Holy Trinity parishioners were worried that the massive stained glass windows that depict scenes from the life of Christ might be removed next.[18] And well they might worry. Many of the scenes from the life of Christ do not pass the "appropriate representation of Islam" test. Naturally, the Crucifixion scene would have to go, along with any representations of Christ's Resurrection, but so also would any depiction of Christ's Baptism or the Transfiguration. Both of these events identify Jesus not just as the son of Mary, but as the Son of God, and from the Islamic point of view that is a blasphemous thought. On top of that, Islam prohibits the artistic representation of prophets. Have you ever seen a portrait of Muhammad? Probably not. And if you have any ideas about sketching one of your own, you'd be well-advised to keep it in your private collection. All things considered, the future of Holy Trinity's rose-colored windows does not look too rosy. Currently, they are covered with translucent curtains. In the future? Well, let's just say that preservation of the Christian heritage has never been a high priority in the Islamic tradition.

In other words, there are real differences between Islam and Christianity that necessitated changes to Holy Trinity church before it could become the Mosque of Jesus, Son of Mary. The Muslims who bought the building were clear that the crosses needed to come down and the windows needed to be covered. But many Christians seem less clear about the differences. They much prefer to emphasize common ground than to think about differences.

The search for commonalities with Islam is the order of the day among Christians. A professor I know at a Catholic seminary took note of some major differences between Islam and Catholicism in his course, only to have the course canceled because it contradicted another course that extolled the similarities. That sort of thing is not unusual. The Catholic education system seems devoted to the proposition that Islam is a close cousin of Christianity—an exotic cousin to be sure, but one who shares the same essential principles with the rest of the family. You can see why Catholics might think that. It's uncontestable that Islam does bear a superficial resemblance to Catholicism. Muslims pray daily, they emphasize modesty, their clerics wear long robes, they go on pilgrimage to shrines, and their mosques are often beautiful structures that convey an atmosphere of deep spirituality.

But that's no excuse for ignoring the major differences. Catholic students learn that Muslims revere Jesus and Mary, give alms, and go on pilgrimages. They're less likely to learn that the Jesus Muslims revere is not the Jesus of the gospels, that the alms are only meant for other Muslims, and that Christians are not allowed to enter Mecca, the main destination for Muslim pilgrims.

The same half-truth approach is used to teach about jihad. Catholic students are usually taught that jihad is an interior spiritual struggle. Although that definition resonates with Catholics, it's not the way that jihad is typically understood in the Muslim world. As we have seen, the primary meaning of jihad is holy war against non-Muslims.

One way to understand Islam today is to understand its history. But, even though Islam was one of the great imperial and slave-holding powers of all time, textbooks used in Catholic colleges tend to present a rose-colored picture of Islamic history. Thus, history texts present a romanticized view of Islam's "Golden Age," and Islam's brutal conquests are typically portrayed as little more than a peaceful "expansion" into surrounding territories. Without a knowledge of Islam's bloody past, students are easy prey to the notion that today's violent jihad "has nothing to do with Islam."

It's not that Catholic students aren't learning about Islam, it's that they're learning only a heavily edited, Disneyfied version of it. But why are Catholics—and Christians in general—so ready to overlook the differences between their own religion and the beliefs of Muslims?

Are Muslims the "Natural Allies" of Christians?

Many Christians, particularly those of the liberal variety, have simply embraced multiculturalism, despite the fact that it amounts to a species of moral relativism that is incompatible with Christian beliefs. And others, including some conservatives, have cottoned on to the notion that Christians and Muslims could be comrades in arms in the battle against aggressive secularism. We have already seen Princeton professor Robert George urging that Muslims are Christians' "natural allies" because of their belief in "modesty, chastity, and piety."

Many Christians have pegged secularism as public enemy number one—and with some justification. Based on all the wreckage it has left in its wake, a good case can be made that secularism is Christianity's chief rival.

But in the fight against enemy number one, some Christians have adopted the questionable tactic of aligning themselves with enemy number two—an enemy that is quite possibly a greater threat than the secular one.

Enemy number two is Islam. Of course, Christians who want to ally themselves with Islam in an ecumenical jihad against secularism don't see it as an enemy. They see it as a fellow religion and a close cousin of Christianity. They like to point out that Muslims worship one God, claim Abraham as an ancestor, and honor Jesus and Mary. As one Catholic priest reminded me, an entire chapter of the Koran is named after Mary. He apparently thought that was proof positive of Islam's affinity with the Christian faith.

Contemporary Christians have developed their own rules of political correctness, and one of those rules is that it's not brotherly to think of another religion as an enemy. Yet since its inception, Islam has been an enemy of Christianity. Why do we expect things will be different now? Especially when today's

★ ★ ★

From Prohibition to the Culture War

The idea that Muslims are "natural allies" in a moral crusade is Chesterton's *Flying Inn* all over again. In that Edwardian novel, progressives agitating for the prohibition of alcohol believe that Christians and Muslims can work together to "deliver the populace from the bondage of the all-destroying drug."[19] Today, conservatives believe that Christians and Muslims can work together to fight pornography and restore sexual morality. And today, just as in the novel, many believe that we have much to learn from Islam. As Lord Ivywood puts it in *The Flying Inn*, "Ours is an age when men come more and more to see that the creeds hold treasures for each other, that each religion has a secret for its neighbor…and church unto church showeth knowledge."[20] Or, as contemporary Catholic author Peter Kreeft claims, "Islam has great and deep resources of morality and sanctity that should inspire us and shame us and prod us to admiration and imitation."[21]

persecution of Christians is unfolding in accordance with a familiar historical pattern?

Christians' eagerness to respect and defend Islam—to portray it as a religion with a lot in common with Christianity, and downplay its association with violent jihad—hasn't stopped the Muslim persecution of Christians. In fact, the era of interfaith dialogue has seen Muslim violence against Christians increase by leaps and bounds, with the result that Christian populations in the Muslim world are shrinking rapidly and some will likely be completely eradicated.[22] Meanwhile, the rosy picture of Islam put out by the churches has succeeded in sowing considerable confusion among rank-and-file Christians, who don't know whether to believe the evidence of their eyes or to rely on the soothing reassurances of their leaders.

Muslims, however, seem far less confused. In places where religiously observant Muslims are in the majority and especially in places where they hold political power, there is much more emphasis on the differences between the two faiths than on the similarities. Christians are looked upon as inferiors, and they are well-advised to keep crosses, icons, and statues out of sight. When observant Muslims are in power, they seem less interested in building interfaith bridges than in denying permits to build churches—or, in the case of the more zealous practitioners of Islam, burning them to the ground.

In the West, it's a different story. When Muslims are first establishing themselves in a community, they tend to emphasize the commonalities between the two religions, and thus we get mosques named "Jesus, Son of Mary" and billboards that proclaim "Muslims Love Jesus Too." Indeed, the supposedly shared love for Jesus is a primary recruitment tool for bringing Christians to Islam. A few years ago, Ibrahim Hooper, a spokesman for the Council on American-Islamic Relations, wrote an essay titled, "Muslims and Christians: More in common than you think," which is reprinted in many publications around Christmastime. Hooper says, "It is well-known...that

Christians follow the teachings of Jesus. What is less well understood is that Muslims also love and revere Jesus as one of God's greatest messengers to mankind."[23]

Muslims love Jesus too? If so, why do Muslims (official disclaimer: not all of them, of course) display so much contempt for Christians when they gain power over them? Why are they so quick to charge Christians with blasphemy? To desecrate their churches and religious symbols?

Could it be that Islam has a lot less in common with Christianity than the proponents of the "natural allies" theory make out?

Not the Same Jesus

We have already seen how central elements of Christianity—the Crucifixion, the Resurrection, and other events in the life of Jesus that identify him as the Son of God—are incompatible with Islam. In fact, while the Koranic portrait of Jesus borrows some elements from Christianity—the Virgin Birth, a handful of miracles—the differences are more striking than the similarities. The Jesus of the Koran is not a Jew or a Christian, he is a Muslim. He is not the Son of God, and to say that he is is the greatest of all blasphemies. He was not crucified. He did not rise from the dead. He is not the savior of mankind. And, although Ibrahim Hooper says that Jesus is "one of God's greatest messengers," his message differs markedly from that brought by Jesus of Nazareth. Other than the message that people should obey God, there is not much in common. The Muslim Jesus announces that he is a prophet sent by God; that he is not God and never claimed to be; and that he brings "news of an apostle that will come after me whose name is Ahmed [Muhammad]" (61:6). So, on the one hand you have the message, "I am the way and the truth and the life," and on the other hand you have the message, "I am a messenger." That's no small difference.

Those who are looking for more from the Jesus of the Koran—more wisdom, more development of doctrine—will be disappointed. The Muslim Jesus has remarkably little to say about anything. There is nothing like the Sermon on the Mount in the Koran. In fact, that one sermon in the Bible far exceeds in length the sum total of everything said by the Jesus of the Koran.

He also has remarkably little to do. When Christians hear that Jesus is in the Koran, they tend to assume that the Koran must contain some account of his life. But other than a strange and truncated account of his birth, there is nothing in the Koran that could remotely be called a life of Jesus.

The Jesus of the Koran is nothing more than a disembodied voice. There is no information about where he lived or when he carried out his ministry or who his disciples were. In short, there is no attempt to portray him as recognizable human being. Judging by the cursory attention given to Jesus in the Koran, Muhammad seems to have had little interest in him as a person.

Nevertheless, Muhammad couldn't afford to leave Jesus out of the picture. Why? Because if Christ is who Christians say he is, then there is no need for another prophet and another revelation. In other words, the claims made by Jesus of Nazareth, if true, would have put a major crimp in Mohammad's prophetic career. Muhammad's solution to this problem was to include Jesus in the Koran and recast him as a messenger, rather than as the Messiah, the Son of God.

The reason Jesus is so frequently referred to as "son of Mary" in the Koran is to reinforce the point that he is not the Son of God. Likewise, whenever Jesus appears in the Koran or whenever he is mentioned by Allah, it is almost always for the purpose of denying his divinity. Take chapter five, verses 113 to 117, one of the few places in the Koran where the narrative about Jesus rises (well, almost) to the level of a scene: "'Jesus son of Mary,' said the disciples, 'Can your Lord send down to us from heaven a table spread with food?'...'Lord,' said Jesus son of Mary, 'send down to us from heaven a table spread with food....'" (5:113–14).

The interesting thing is what happens next. Allah agrees to send the table, but first he interrogates Jesus: "Jesus son of Mary, did you ever say to mankind: 'Worship me and my mother as gods besides God?'" Jesus, the faithful Muslim, replies, "I could never have claimed what I have no right to. If I had ever said so, You would have surely known it" (5:117).

So a demonstration of Jesus' power to produce a tableful of food is used as an occasion to reject the central tenet of Christianity. Notice that the phrase "Jesus son of Mary" is used three times in the table scene. Was this

★ ★ ★
Not Worthy to Untie the Strap of His Sandals

John the Baptist said of Jesus, "He must increase, but I must decrease" (John 3:30). Muhammad preferred it the other way around. For him to increase, it was necessary that Jesus decrease. Thus, what we find in the Koran is a greatly diminished portrait of Jesus.

because Muhammad had a deep Christian-like love of Jesus and his mother? Or was there another motive? Given that almost every page of the Koran contains reminders of Muhammad's prophetic role, it seems highly likely that the Jesus-son-of-Mary motif was simply a device for enhancing his own importance by reducing the status of Christ. Muhammad's purpose in introducing Jesus into the Koran was to discredit the Christian claim that he is divine in order to enhance Muhammad's claim to prophethood.

The irony is that this self-serving stratagem has become the main plank for keeping Muslim-Christian dialogue afloat. One would think that Christians would be sore about Muhammad's appropriation of Jesus and Mary for his own purposes—that is, to deny the Sonship of Jesus. Instead, Christians tend to respond to this hijacking of Jesus with gratitude—as though Islam had granted them a great favor by deigning to recognize their founder. For example, the Vatican II document *Nostra Aetate* says that "The Church regards with esteem also the Moslems," and two of the five reasons given for the esteem are that Muslims "revere" Jesus and "honor Mary."[24] But as

★ ★ ★ ★ ★ ★

Do Christians and Muslims Worship the Same God?

One of the most interesting commentaries on the same-God question was published in 1956 in, of all things, a children's book. C. S. Lewis addressed the possibility of finding common ground with Islam in *The Last Battle*, the final book in *The Chronicles of Narnia*. Lewis doesn't use the terms "Islam" and "Christianity" in his fictional account, but it's quite obvious that the Narnians are meant to represent Christians and that their enemies, the Calormenes, are meant to represent Muslims.

In the book, many of the Narnians are deceived into believing that their God, Aslan, and Tash, the demonic god of the Calormenes, are only two different names for the same god: "All that old idea of us being right and the Calormenes wrong is silly. We know better now. The Calormenes use different words but we all mean the same thing. Tash and Aslan are only two different names for you know Who. That's why there can never be any quarrel between them. Tash is Aslan: Aslan is Tash."[25]

After a while, the hybrid god is simply referred to as "Tashlan." As time passes, however, the worship of Tashlan becomes for all intents and purposes the worship of Tash, and the Narnians find themselves enslaved by the Calormenes. Lewis has no use for the Chrislam—or, as he puts it—the "Tashlan" solution. He sees no

we have seen, the Koran's inclusion of Jesus and Mary may stem from an ulterior motive.

When Christians look at Islam, what they are really faced with is not a brother religion, but an either-or choice. Either the New Testament account of Jesus is true or Muhammad's account is true. Since they contradict each other, they both can't be true.

In the gospel accounts, Jesus is rather insistent that he is the Son of God, and the Koran is rather insistent that he is not. Assuming that you know of

★ ★ ★ ★ ★ ★

possibility of a reconciliation between the two faiths because Tash and Aslan are of radically "different kinds." They are, in fact, "opposites."[26]

But that doesn't mean that Calormenes can't be sincere seekers of God. One character in the story that stands out is Emeth, a young Calormene officer who has sought to serve Tash all his days, and whose great desire is "to know more of him."[27] Emeth's nobility is so evident that one of the Narnians remarks that "he is worthy of a better God than Tash."[28]

When Emeth finally encounters the true God, Aslan, he is abashed at his former service to Tash: "But I said, Alas Lord, I am no son of thine but the servant of Tash. He answered, Child, all the service thou hast done to Tash, I account as service done to me...Not because he and I are one, but because we are opposites, I take to me the services which thou hast done to him. For I and he are of such different kinds that no service which is vile can be done to me, and none which is not vile can be done to him. Therefore if any man swear by Tash and keep his oath for the oath's sake, it is by me that he has truly sworn, though he know it not, and it is I who reward him. And if any man do a cruelty in my name, then, though he says the name Aslan, it is Tash whom he serves and by Tash his deed is accepted."[29]

the many instances in the gospels where Jesus asserts his divinity, here are some Koranic passages that say the opposite:

God is but one God. God forbid that he should have a son! (4:173, trans. Dawood).

The Messiah, the Son of Mary, was no more than an apostle (5:75, Dawood).

Christians call Christ the Son of Allah.... Allah's curse be on them: how they are deluded away from the truth! (9:30, trans. Yusuf Ali).

They do blaspheme who say: Allah is one of the three in a Trinity (5:73, Yusuf Ali).[30]

And if the Jesus of the Koran is not the Jesus Christians worship, is Allah really the same as the God of the Bible? Christian authorities are insistent that Muslims and Christians do worship the same God. To quote from *Nostra Aetate* again, Muslims not only "value the moral life" but even "adore the one God, living and subsisting in Himself; merciful and all-powerful, the Creator of heaven and earth."[31]

The quandary for Christians is that, although the Allah of Islam is different in major respects from the Christian concept of God, no one wants to deny Muslims a place among the family of believers. After all, as the Catechism of the Catholic Church says, Muslims "profess to hold the faith of Abraham,"[32] and many are undeniably sincere in their desire to serve God. Saying that they don't worship the one God sounds too much like saying that their prayers are wasted. Thus, a good many Christians resolve the quandary by ignoring the theological difficulties and focusing instead on the worthy acts of Muslims, such as fasting and almsgiving.

But in fact the God described in the Koran is different in important respects from the Christian God. The differences between Allah and God the Father, as revealed by Jesus, are so radical that it would be a mistake to call them the same God. Nonetheless, it is still possible to say that at least some Muslims do worship the one God—in so far as they "seek God with a sincere heart," and try "to do his will as they know it through the dictates of their conscience," to quote the words of the Catechism about non-Christian believers.[33]

In *Nostra Aetate*, the council fathers wisely confined their discussion of Christian-Muslim relations to Muslims. Although there is one reference to the "faith of Islam," no mention is made of Muhammad or the Koran. Rather, the Church's "esteem" is for the "Moslems" and it is Muslims who "value the moral life and worship God." There seems to have been a conscious effort to avoid endorsing Islam and its prophet. It is one thing to acknowl-edge that individual Muslims can lead moral lives and that they can have a close relationship with God. It's another thing to imply, through word or gesture, that Islam is a valid faith and the Koran a reliable guide to salvation.

Is There Such a Thing as a Bad Religion?

Besides a different God, Islam proposes a radically different moral code and a radically different view of the afterlife—in fact the two overlap. This is, after all, a religion that was founded by a sex-slave-owning warlord who envisioned heaven as a harem. According to Father Rolheiser, Christians and Muslims will "share the same heaven."[34] But the fact is, Muslims have a somewhat racier concept of paradise than do Christians, and do not wish to share it with infidels who say that Jesus is the Son of God (9:30). "Share the same heaven"? Does that mean that Muslims look forward to sharing in the life of the Trinity (a concept they vehemently reject)? Or does it mean that Christian men can look forward to the company of seventy-two virgins apiece? There are also serious problems with the Islamic moral code. It requires apostates to be killed and it allows non-Muslims to be raped in war zones (which some Muslim equate with the whole non-Muslim world.)

Which raises a question. Is there such a thing as bad religion? Or is reli-gion by its very nature a good thing? Throughout most of history, most people wouldn't have hesitated to label some religions as bad. The Romans condemned the child-sacrificing religion of the Carthaginians, Christians condemned the Aztec religion for its human sacrifice, and Catholics con-demned Arians and Albigensians as heretics.

The contemporary take on this question is altogether different. With the exception of some rabid atheists, most people—even those of no particular faith—have a positive view of religion. And Christians, especially, seem well-disposed to people of other faiths. Serious Christians are much more likely to be worried about the dangers inherent in secularism than the dangers posed by another religion. The current attitude seems to be that in the battle against secularism, people of faith—no matter what their faith—ought to stick together.

One might expect that the return of militant Islam to the world stage would put a damper on this benign view of religion, but that doesn't seem to be the case. Many Christians still take the attitude that if you're a religion, you're part of the family and we'll stick up for you. As an example, recent popes have been adamant in their opposition to secularism, but have been reluctant to criticize Islam. For them, the major conflict of our age is not between religion and religion, but between religion and unbelief. Of course, there is plenty of justification for that view. The struggle between atheism and belief that was the chief preoccupation of Pope St. John Paul II was indeed the defining struggle of the twentieth century. He may have been concerned about Islam, but there was little indication that he saw anything inherently wrong with it—as he did with Nazism and communism. He once kissed the Koran, but one cannot imagine that he would ever have done the same with *Mein Kampf* or the *Communist Manifesto.*

As is suggested by his Regensburg address, Pope Benedict XVI had a more critical view of Islam than his predecessor, but on the whole he seems to have adopted the position that believers are in one camp and secularists in another. When asked in a lengthy interview with journalist Peter Seewald if he was now following a different policy from earlier popes who "thought it their duty to save Europe from Islamization," Benedict replied, "Today we are living in a completely different world in which the battle lines are drawn differently. In this world, radical secularism stands on one side, and the question of God, in its various forms, stands on the other."[35]

But what if we see the old battle lines drawn up again? What if the apparent end of the war between Islam and Christianity was only a temporary truce? Not to put too fine a point on it, what if Osama bin Laden's interpretation of Islam is closer to the original than that of moderate Muslims? In his interview with Seewald, Pope Benedict refers on two occasions to the "tradition of tolerant and good coexistence between Islam and Christianity" that prevails in large parts of Sub-Saharan Africa. And he sees this as a hopeful sign that rapprochement is possible between the two faiths.[36] The thing is, the Islam practiced in that region tends to be of the folk religion type, and it typically incorporates elements of other faiths. In other words, it's a far cry from authentic, made-in-Mecca, by-the-book Islam. While folklore Islam may be more compatible with Christianity, it does not have as strong a claim as does the Islam of the Middle East to be following the authentic tradition of the prophet. Islam is very much a by-the-book religion, and all the books— the Koran, the hadith, the sira, and the sharia law manuals—provide more textual support to militant Muslims than to moderate ones. Moderate Islam is a cultural custom, radical Islam is the authentic item.

Some scholars assert that both interpretations—the more peaceful and the more militant—are equally valid. But unless you believe that Islam is like a Rorschach test that can be interpreted in an infinite number of ways, one side or the other has to have the better of the argument.

Was Muhammad a False Prophet?

In his second letter to the Corinthians, Paul warns against anyone who "comes and preaches another Jesus than the one we preached" (II Corinthians 11:4). Jesus himself delivered a similar warning: "Beware of false prophets who come to you in sheep's clothing but inwardly are ravenous wolves" (Matthew 7:15).

Of course, Jesus couldn't possibly have had someone like Muhammad in mind. Or could he? Unless Christian leaders are quite certain that the

"Prophet" is not included in the warning, they would do well to avoid statements that lend credibility to the Islamic faith.

Would "false prophets" include Muhammad? It's an impolitic question to ask in these politically correct times, but, thanks to political correctness, these are also highly dangerous times. Since a good deal of the danger emanates from the religion Muhammad founded, it seems reasonable to ask if he was a false prophet. And if he was, does that mean that Islam is a false religion? And if it is, why are Christian leaders so keen on declaring their solidarity with Islam?

Ralph Sidway, the author of a piece on the "same God" question, puts the either-or nature of the choice in perspective: "Christianity and Islam cannot both be from the same source, which is what the *Same God Question* ultimately boils down to. If we treat each truth claim with respect, that each faith springs from a self-revelation of God, then it is clear the Allah of Islam is directly, and in a specific, vigorous manner, opposed to the revelation from the Christian God. And Jesus' own emphatic testimony about himself excludes any alternate revelation concerning the nature of God."[37]

Considering that the Jesus of the gospels and the Jesus of the Koran are fundamentally irreconcilable, how can both revelations possibly be from the same God? If Christ is God, then the Koranic account is a false account and Muhammad was a false prophet.

That may seem a harsh way to put it. And if you go around saying such things, you likely won't be invited to your parish's next interfaith outreach program. But there it is. The only alternative is to say that Muhammad is a true prophet. Do you really want to go there?

Well, I suppose one could conjure up another alternative. One could say that Muhammad was a so-so prophet: he got some things right

A Book You're Not Supposed to Read

The Islamic Antichrist by Joel Richardson (Washington, DC: WND, 2015).

and some things wrong, and he was part of the Abrahamic faith tradition, and so on and so forth. It's true, of course, that Muhammad did get some things right. But on the point of Christ's divinity the New Testament doesn't seem to allow for any half-right, half-wrong compromise position.

Sidway reminds us of two passages from the First Letter of John:[38]

> Who is a liar but he who denies that Jesus is the Christ? He is antichrist who denies the Father and the Son. Whoever denies the Son does not have the Father either; he who acknowledges the Son has the Father also (I John 2:22–23).
>
> Beloved, do not believe every spirit, but test the spirits, whether they are of God; because many false prophets have gone out into the world. By this you know the Spirit of God: Every spirit that confesses that Jesus Christ has come in the flesh is of God, and every spirit that does not confess that Jesus Christ has come in the flesh is not of God. And this is the spirit of the Antichrist, which you have heard was coming, and is now already in the world (1 Jn 4:1–3).

According to John, the spirit of the Antichrist denies the Son. But Islam not only denies the Son, it brands belief in the Son as a sin. And not just any sin, but the worst of all possible sins in Islam—*shirk* (the sin of attributing partners to God). So the central belief of Christians is, from the Islamic point of view, the greatest sin conceivable.

It can be argued that other religions fail to acknowledge the Sonship of Christ, but there is a difference. For example, while Jews don't believe in the divinity of Christ, that, for obvious chronological reasons, is not part of the revelation to the Jews. On the other hand, the "revelation" to Muhammad came 600 years after the birth of Christ and one of its central messages is the denial of the Sonship of Jesus. As Christian author Joel Richardson

★ ★ ★

Ravenous

Jesus warned against false prophets who look like sheep but "inwardly are ravenous wolves." That certainly seems an apt description of Muhammad. While it's not known exactly how many people he killed in the course of spreading Islam, it is known that on one occasion he presided over the beheading of between six and nine hundred captured men.[40] "Ravenous" also seems to fit most of his successors. Islam's 1,400-year history is largely a record of conquest and subjugation. By one estimate, approximately 270 million people have been killed in the name of Allah, making Islam the greatest killing force in history by far.[41] Unfortunately, too many Christians and too many of their shepherds live in a bucolic dream world where thoughts of wolves and false prophets are never entertained.

puts it, "While many religions and systems of belief exist that do not agree with the doctrines of Christianity...only Islam fulfills the role of a religion that exists to deny core Christian beliefs."[39] The reality is that Islam is not only based on a false revelation, it's based on a false revelation that's fundamentally hostile to Christianity.

It's difficult to square the evidence with the currently fashionable notion that Christianity and Islam are close cousins. But is it really necessary to open old wounds? Isn't it better to emphasize the things that unite us rather than the things that divide us? In commenting on the Catholic Church's relationship with Muslims in *Nostra Aetate*, the Council fathers urged all to forget the "quarrels and hostilities" of the past.[42] Shouldn't we heed their advice?

But just how far in the past are the "quarrels and hostilities" mentioned in *Nostra Aetate*? They are still with us today. And what is the source of those hostilities, except that Christians refused and still refuse to accept the revelations given to Muhammad?

Anyone who keeps up with Raymond Ibrahim's reporting, including his monthly "Muslim persecution of Christians" series will realize that Islamic persecution of Christians is far more extensive than is generally reported. We hear about the more spectacular attacks—the suicide attack on All Saints Church in Peshawar, which left more than eighty dead;[43] the mall in Nairobi where Christians were separated out from Muslims, then tortured and killed;[44] the attack on Garissa University in Kenya that targeted Christian students and left 147 dead[45]—but, according to Ibrahim, "these attacks are but the tip of the iceberg of widespread hostility for and violence against non-Muslim 'infidels,' Christians chief among them."[46]

From the Islamic point of view, Christians who persist in unbelief in the prophet merit the severe punishment that follows. So there is good reason to beware of false prophets.

A Book You're Not Supposed to Read

Crucified Again: Exposing Islam's New War on Christians by Raymond Ibrahim (Washington, DC: Regnery, 2013).

Who You Gonna Believe, Me or Your Lying Eyes?

While there have certainly been places and times when Muslims and Christians have lived together in peace, the hope that a bridge can be built between the two religions is a bridge too far. There is good reason—in fact, there are many good reasons—for Christians to revisit the simplistic and dangerously misleading notion that Muslims and Christians share the same beliefs and values.

The first negative consequence of this stand-by-my-Islam approach on the part of Christian leaders is that it creates confusion for many in their flock. The average Christian who keeps abreast of the news and who is not committed to upholding any particular narrative about Islam will have noticed by now that there *is* something wrong with Islam. And as more is revealed about Islam and sharia law, it will become more and more difficult for that average Christian believer to give credence to the notion that all the many problems with Islam have nothing to do with the real Islam. Continued expressions of deep respect for Islam by church leaders won't do much to increase respect for Islam, but they might serve to lessen the respect that

Christians have for their own leaders. As the gap between what these leaders say and what the news reveals increases, their credibility will come into question.

Such an approach also tends to devalue the sacrifices of those Christians in Muslim lands who have had the courage to resist submission to Islam. It must be highly discouraging to be told that the religion in whose name your friends and relatives have been slaughtered is prized and esteemed by Christians who are living safely in Europe and America.

Moreover, this semi-official endorsement of Islam also does a disservice to the many Muslims who have their doubts about traditional Islam, and to the many Muslims who suffer under the weight of sharia law. When the faith traditions that Muslim parents hand down to their children involve genital mutilation, forced marriages, honor killings, and amputations, Christians should think twice about making statements or gestures that seem to validate that faith.

Another unintended consequence of the Christian tendency to put the best possible face on Islam is that it strengthens the atheist-secularist argument that all religions are cut from the same cloth. Christians are frequently accused by their foes of being intolerant "haters." If Christian leaders keep making excuses for a religion that actually *is* intolerant, those charges may begin to stick. The stock of atheists such as Richard Dawkins, Sam Harris, and Christopher Hitchens received a considerable boost in the wake of 9/11. That's because they were able to convince a lot of people that religion inevitably leads to violence. And their portrayal of Islam and Christianity as twin brothers—the one only slightly less violent and misogynist than the other—may well have contributed to the recent sharp decline in Christian numbers. Merely from a tactical standpoint, then, Christian leaders ought to be cautious about doing or saying things that reinforce this simplistic view of Christianity. If they want to avoid even more defections from the church, they need to think twice about emphasizing their common ground with Islam. At a time when even liberals are beginning to question Islam, it may be time for the church to consider the benefits of distancing itself from its "fellow" Abrahamic faith.

Finally, Christian appeasement and even positive encouragement of Islam are enabling jihad. It is leaving Christians in ignorance of and wholly unprepared for the kind of persecution being suffered by Christians in Iraq, Syria, Nigeria, Libya, and other parts of the Muslim world. Christians who think that Islam means "peace," that jihad is a spiritual struggle, and that Islamophobia is the greatest threat to national security are in for a rude surprise.

Christians have been lulled into complacency by the oft-repeated emphasis on the similarities between their faith and the faith of Muslims. This puts them at a disadvantage not only in regard to armed jihad, but also in regard to cultural jihad—the stealthy, steady incremental advance of Islamic law and culture. Once it has advanced sufficiently, Muslims will not be seeking fellowship with Christians. They will be seeking dominance over them.

This brings us back to what Stephen Coughlin has to say about interfaith dialogue in *Catastrophic Failure*. He contends that ISNA and other Muslim Brotherhood groups are simply using the bishops to further their agenda of bringing sharia law to America. From reading his account, one can't help but think that the bishops have been a tad naïve about their dialogue partners.[47]

Take this statement from the USCCB on "Dialogue with Muslims": "Perhaps most importantly, our work together has forged true bonds of friendship that are supported by mutual esteem and an ever-growing trust...Through dialogue we have been able to work through and overcome much of our mutual ignorance, habitual distrust and debilitating fear."[48]

But is it really wise for the bishops to put so much trust in their dialogue counterparts? "Habitual distrust" is the last thing the bishops need to worry about. They seem, rather, to suffer from a bad case of habitual trust. Keep in mind that many if not most of the dialogue partners for whom they feel an "ever growing trust" are members of groups that were designated as unindicted co-conspirators in a large-scale terrorist finding scheme. It's good that the bishops have managed to overcome "debilitating fear," but shouldn't they retain a little healthy fear about organizations with such a shady past?

Christ instructed his disciples to be "as wise as serpents and as innocent as doves." Church leaders seem to have mastered the "innocent as doves" part. What we need now is some assurance that they can also be "as wise as serpents."

The war against jihad is in part a spiritual struggle. The stealth jihadists understand that very well. They seek, in the words of Pakistani brigadier general Malik, to "dislocate" our faith.[49] But the people best equipped to fight such a battle—our spiritual leaders—scarcely understand that a war is on. Indeed, many of them are unwittingly supporting the cultural jihadists in their long march through the institutions. Unless that changes, the long march may soon become a full-on charge, followed by a rout.

PART III

Defeating
Jihad

CHAPTER 10

Strategies for Victory

How do we defeat jihad?

First we've got to get serious. We have to realize that we are in the midst of a worldwide struggle involving armed conflict in at least a dozen nations and stealth advances in dozens more. Analogies to World War II are in order. We don't face squadrons of fighter planes and bombers or fleets of battleships and aircraft carriers as we did then, but we face an equally determined enemy, driven by an equally fanatic ideology.

Moreover, this enemy has access to weapons the Germans and Japanese didn't possess—nuclear devices, biological weapons, and cyber warfare capacities, to name a few. Who needs a fleet of battleships when one EMP missile fired from one cargo ship in the Atlantic could knock out power— perhaps for years—along most of the East Coast of the United States? That would have the effect of sending us rather abruptly back to the middle of the nineteenth century. Except that we would lack the knowhow of getting along without electric lights, refrigerators, cellphones, and computers.

World War II was a two-front war, but the current war is being fought on many fronts—in Iraq, Syria, Afghanistan, Yemen, Libya, Nigeria,

Did you know?

★ "Moderate" Muslims aren't waiting to see which side in the war on terror is the most tolerant, they're waiting to see which side is winning

★ Two-thirds of Muslims in the UK would not report someone with terrorist ties to the police

★ The U.S. Navy already has fewer ships today than it had in 1917, and the Army is being reduced to pre–World War II size

Somalia, the Central African Republic, the Philippines, and elsewhere. That's not to mention the two-front combination of armed jihad and stealth jihad. The Nazis had the occasional well-placed spy or saboteur working to destroy democracies from within, but Islamists have been far more effective at tunneling behind the borders of their enemies. Indeed, they have set up shop within many of our key institutions.

What's more, this new enemy has a potential recruitment pool that is exponentially larger than that available to our World War II enemies. The population of Japan at the start of the Second World War was roughly 73 million; the population of Germany was about 70 million. By contrast, the global Muslim population is about 1.6 billion.

The "Vast Majority" Myth

But of course the vast majority of Muslims are peaceful and reject violence—at least that's what the authorities in Europe and America want us to believe. That proposition is worth examining because if it's not true there is cause to worry. Of course, you should be worried even if it is true. Even if only a small percentage of the world's 1.6 billion Muslims are prepared to use violence, that still works out to a large number. But if the vast-majority thesis doesn't hold up, you might want to order a Kevlar vest from Amazon, or, if you're the accommodating type, you could start practicing the *shahada*—the Islamic declaration of faith.

There is a good deal of polling data to suggest that the vast majority of Muslims are not just your standard-issue vast majority. For example, as we have seen, Pew polls of public opinion in Pakistan and Egypt show that the vast majority (about 80 percent) favor stoning for adultery, amputation for theft, and death for apostates. So even if a majority in these countries are not personally inclined to violence, they have no problem with the violent application of sharia law.

But rather than rely on polling data, let's look at some other ways of assessing the "vast majority" proposition. For some perspective, here are some other "vast majority" propositions:

Proposition 1. The vast majority of people are peaceful until they're not.

Proposition 2. The vast majority of people go with the flow.

The vast majority of people in any society are peaceful most of the time. But people who are peaceful today will not necessarily be peaceful tomorrow. It's probably safe to say that the vast majority of Hutus were behaving peacefully before the Rwanda genocide of 1994…and then they stopped behaving peacefully. Using clubs, machetes, and, occasionally, guns, the Hutu managed to kill about 800,000 Tutsis in the space of a hundred days. It's likely that the vast majority did not take part in the killings, but, by all accounts, a sizeable number did, and an even greater number were complicit. According to reports, most of the Tutsi victims who lived in rural villages were murdered by their neighbors.[2]

So, in line with Proposition 1, the majority of the Hutu were peaceful until they were not.

★ ★ ★
Until He Wasn't

A photo in the *Daily Mail* showed a smiling young man in Muslim garb holding a large sign that read "I am Muslim…do you trust me enough for a hug?" If that were the end of the story, we could all reassure ourselves that he had thoroughly grasped the cherished Western concept "arms are for hugging." But shortly afterward, Craig Wallace, a.k.a. Muhammad Mujahid Islam, sent an online death threat to a Tory MP who had voted to authorize military action in Syria.[3] Wallace was peaceful…until he wasn't.

★ ★ ★
The Guns of August

Before World War I, the vast majority of Europeans were behaving peacefully. Then came 1914, and the European nations went to war with each other. The majority, of course, remained at home and were never involved in battle, but it seems safe to say that most of them fully backed their own side in the conflict and welcomed news of enemy casualties. Given the right circumstances, the majority of almost any population will willingly put itself on a war footing and turn its homeland into a home front. The question is, is there something about Islamic cultures that make them even more susceptible to warlike attitudes more of the time?

And, in line with Proposition 2, the majority of the Hutu went with the flow—the flow, in this case, being in the direction of mayhem. It should be noted, however, that there were powerful incentives to go with the flow. Moderate Hutus who declined to join in the killing were often killed by their fellow Hutus.[4]

Although women took part in the slaughter, probably the majority of them did not. And if you combine the women with the children, the elderly, and the moderates, it is reasonable to assume that the majority of Hutus did not participate in the carnage. That is small comfort to the hundreds of thousands of dead Tutsis, though. The more you think about it, the less comforting it is to know that the vast majority of any population won't take up arms against you.

History is full of examples of peoples and nations who were peaceful and then were not. Let's briefly consider the ancient Spartans. Were the vast majority of Spartans peaceful? In the sense that the great majority, including women, children, and the elderly were not at war all the time, yes. Still, we would be mistaken to call them a peaceful people. Sparta had a warrior culture, and it cultivated a warrior mentality in its citizens.

The Spartans were a unique case, but in so far as Islam has a tendency, it tends in the direction of Sparta rather than, say, in the direction of Sweden—a land that was once host to a warrior culture of its own. But the Vikings are long gone, and their peaceful descendants look like they will be the first European nation to fall to Islam—a culture that has been more or less at war with the rest of the world since its inception.

Why is the sharia penalty for apostasy death? Because Islam understands itself to be an army. And the penalty for deserting an army in war-time is death. But for Islam, all times are war-times. The basic division in the Islamic faith is between the House of Islam and the House of War. The essential mission given to Muslims is to bring the House of War (all non-Islamic nations) under the control of the House of Islam. One of the chief appeals of ISIS and company is their promise to return Islam to those glorious days when Muslims spread the faith by force.

It may well be that a great many Muslims today just want to be left alone to go about their business. But one of the built-in features of Islam is that, if you're a Muslim, it won't leave you alone. It wants to force you to be good. The only way to know if you're good, though, is if you conform to sharia. Thus, where Islam is practiced in its purest form, the virtue police patrol the streets and everyone understands that if he converts to another religion, he can be executed for apostasy—that is to say, desertion.

This is where the second proposition comes in: the vast majority of people go with the flow. The flow of Islam today has returned to its historical channel. It flows in the direction of militancy. Many of the secular governments in the Muslim world have been overthrown, or are in danger of falling to militant theocrats. The caliphate has been re-established in the form of the Islamic State, and the combined might of Russia and the Western powers has been unable to defeat it. Moreover, the seeming impotence of the West

> ★ ★ ★
> ## Role Model for Jihadists
>
> Like the Spartans, the first Muslims were warriors. Their leader was both a prophet and a warlord. Since Muslims are still expected to model their behavior on Muhammad, it's not surprising that Muslim cultures will be more prone to violence than, say, cultures that take Jesus or Buddha as their inspiration. Our own culture is completely sold on the importance of having role models to emulate, but hasn't yet grasped the consequences that follow when 1.6 billion people take Muhammad as their primary role model.

★ ★ ★
A Not So Tiny Group of Extremists

Not long ago in Pakistan, 100,000 people attended the funeral of a man who had murdered an opponent of the blasphemy laws.[5] The murder victim was what we would call a moderate, but his murderer seems to have been far more honored by the Muslim population at large. About the same time, representatives of more than thirty-five religious parties and groups called for the revocation of a new Pakistani law protecting women from abuse.[6] Meanwhile, the Nigerian Senate rejected a gender equality bill because Muslim senators said it was un-Islamic.[7] If the "moderate" Muslims subscribe to more or less the same tenets as the violent Muslims, are they really all that moderate?

---

is matched by its decadence, and, according to your local imam, the two go together. The current parlous state of the West is just the sort of punishment that Allah visits on those who ignore his laws.

"Not Currently Killing Others" Is a Poor Gauge of Moderation

"Moderate" Muslims may not be willing to kill, but they may be willing to support those who do. After the bombings in Brussels, it was revealed that the terrorists enjoyed wide support in the Muslim district where they had hidden—according to a *New York Times* article, 90 percent of teens there considered the attackers to be "heroes."[8] On the other side of the Channel, a poll of UK Muslims revealed that two thirds of them would not report someone with terrorist ties to the police.[9]

Imagine that you're one of those moderately disposed Muslims who just wants to go about his own business. You look around and see that all the predictions of the more militant mullahs and imams are coming true. You want to be left alone, but you also want to be a good Muslim. And more and more it seems that being a good Muslim is what the militants say it is. After all, they can buttress their case with dozens of passages from Islamic scripture. And even if you're not inwardly persuaded, there are still those outside pressures to be considered. Just as the extremist Hutu killed off the moderate Hutu, extremist Muslims have a habit of murdering moderate Muslims who won't go along with the program. After a while, the radical position won't seem so radical. In fact, it will start to make sense

Now that the Islamic State has established a caliphate, all the arguments for the more militant form of Islam have been strengthened. Nothing succeeds like success, and the many successes of ISIS seem to prove that Allah's power is behind them. Father James Schall puts it this way: "Briefly, the assigned mission of Islam is to conquer the world for Allah. Submission to Allah is the highest human good. Any means to carry it out is good if it is successful. Carrying out this mission, in this view, is a Muslim's vocation. With the re-establishment of the caliphate, this mission can now recommence."[10]

★ ★ ★
Personalized Religion

Are there any Muslims who would qualify for the more rigorous definition of moderate? There are indeed. But they are nowhere near a majority, and their moderation often reflects a lack of commitment to mainstream Islamic beliefs. Moderate Muslims are like "cafeteria Catholics." They pick and choose those aspects of Islam that suit their inclinations and ignore the rest. For them, as for many a liberal Christian, religion is often a personal construct that bears little resemblance to the official version.

In short, the rebirth of the caliphate may be the signal that obedient and orthodox Muslims have been waiting for.

The vast majority of people go with the flow. Or, to change the metaphor, they wait to see which way the wind is blowing. In Islam, the wind is blowing once again in a radical direction. As we know from history, a relatively small number of radicals can pull the majority along with them. The problem is compounded in Islam because, judging by the numerous terrorist attacks in every part of the globe, we may no longer be facing a relatively small number of radicals. It is also likely that the violent radicals now have the sympathy of far more Muslims than we in the West will admit. Schall again: "Many Muslim countries are 'peaceful' only in the sense that their governments, usually

★ ★ ★

Debunking the Debunkers

A 2015 study by the New America Foundation claimed that right-wing extremism is to blame for more terrorism than Islam.[11] A blogger at "Loon Watch: The Mooslims! They're Heeere" had gone even further, creating a pie chart purporting to show that 94 percent of terror attacks are by non-Muslims.[12] How did they get those results? By ignoring facts inconvenient to their conclusions.[13] The Loon Watch debunker got debunked when a writer at the Religion of Peace blog pointed out that Muslims were responsible for the overwhelming majority of actual deaths from terror attacks in the U.S.—94 percent—between 1980 and 2005.[14] Plus, as Ian Tuttle points out in *National Review*, "to look at the West in isolation is misleading," considering that the nations with the most terror attacks are "70 percent majority Muslim countries."[15] Religion of Peace keeps a running total of Islam-inspired terror attacks worldwide since September 11; that total is now at 28,420.[16] As unwelcome as the truth may be to debunkers on the left, it's still the case that while not all Muslims are terrorists, nearly all terrorists are Muslims.

military dictatorships, keep down that radicalism that would overthrow them and is overthrowing them in many places. Muslim masses wait to see who is winning. They know even within Islam that they cannot afford to be on the losing side."[17]

It is often argued that if Western societies take a hard line toward Islamic aggression, both militarily and culturally, it will have the effect of driving the moderates into the radical camp. So we yield to demands for burqas in public, censor the "Islamophobes" in our midst, and avoid using "offensive" terms such as "radical Islam." But the majority of Muslims aren't waiting to see which side is the most tolerant or which side takes in the most refugees; they are waiting to see which side is winning. As long as the West continues on its current course of accommodation and appeasement, the moderates will continue by some strange alchemy to morph into radicals.

Want to Win the Propaganda War?
Win the Shooting War

I have suggested that one of the best ways to fight terrorism is by undermining the terrorist's ideology. For example, by undercutting the belief that seventy-two virgins await the young martyr in paradise, you undermine the jihadists' will to fight.

But the standard method of fighting terrorists—with guns—cannot be safely abandoned. The propaganda war works best when it is reinforced by the shooting war. The more convincingly force is applied on the battlefield, the more convincing will be the ideological arguments.

If, for example, you're an ISIS fighter and you see your buddies on the battlefield fall victim to an occasional bomb or bullet, that won't necessarily shake your faith in the brides-to-be. As long as the war is going well, and as long as there's a senior officer or two around to assure you that your fallen comrades are now enjoying their reward in paradise, your basic assumptions can remain intact. If, on the other hand, you look around and see nothing but death and destruction and no surviving officers to make sense of it all, you may begin to doubt the whole enterprise.

Most people, of whatever religion, like to think that God is on their side of the battle, but in Islam belief and battlefield success are more closely linked than in, say, Christianity. Indeed, the seemingly miraculous military successes of Muhammad and the caliphs who followed him were taken by Muslims to be a proof that Islam is the true religion. Conversely, the religion of Islam has never fared well when its imperialistic ambitions have been thwarted. After Napoleon's

★ ★ ★
Undermine Jihadist Recruiting

A devastating defeat for ISIS on the battlefield will have a salutary effect on people far away from the Middle East. The fellow in Brussels or Brisbane or Boston who's thinking of joining the jihad will now have second thoughts—not only about ISIS, but also about the ideology that fuels it. Even fanatics can become realists in the face of overwhelming facts. In short, doubts can be accelerated by defeats.

invasion and occupation of Egypt, and the subsequent European conquests and colonization of the Muslim world, Muslims began to seriously question the efficacy of Islam. As Raymond Ibrahim observes, "It was one thing to hold unhesitatingly to Islam and Sharia when Islam was conquering and subjugating non-Muslims, as it had done for well over a millennium. It was quite another thing for Muslims to remain confident in the Islamic way when the despised Christian infidels were conquering and subjugating the lands of Islam with great ease—displaying their superior weapons and technology, not to mention all the other perks of Western civilization."[18]

During the colonial and post-colonial era, Muslim nations looked increasingly to the West as a model of emulation, and increasingly away from Islam. Religious fanaticism declined, the jizya collection and the dhimmi laws were abolished, and, according to Ibrahim, "By the middle of the twentieth century, the Middle East's Christians were widely seen, particularly by the educated elites and those in power, as no different from their Muslim counterparts."[19]

The point is that this more moderate Islam of the not so distant past was made possible by Western military power and by the secular strongmen who succeeded the colonial rulers. Likewise, the recent renewed appeal of fundamentalist Islam has been made possible by shows of force by the other side: the overthrow of the Shah in Iran, the defeat of the Russians in Afghanistan, the bombing of the World Trade Center, (and numerous other successful terror attacks), the Arab Spring revolutions and, most recently, the march of ISIS across Syria and Iraq.

Such victories against technologically and numerically superior forces have created a psychological momentum that makes militant Islam all the more appealing to potential recruits. Psychological momentum, however, can be halted

★ ★ ★
When Islam Was Funny

Islam had been so thoroughly defanged by the mid–twentieth century that, if Americans thought about it at all, they thought of it in terms of comedy movies like *The Road to Morocco* or Broadway musicals like *Kismet*.

and reversed by decisive battlefield defeats. The idea that nothing is ever accomplished by war is not quite true—as evidenced by the current pacifist inclinations of our former enemies, Japan and Germany.

Crushing Their Dreams

In fighting ISIS, we are battling an armed force that has considerable symbolic significance for other Muslims. Because of the Islamic State's ability to inspire both lone-wolf and well-organized terror attacks around the world, it's crucial not only to degrade and contain ISIS, but to defeat it, and to defeat it definitively, so as to crush the dreams of would-be jihadists.

As military historian Victor Davis Hanson has observed, successful military leaders strive not only to defeat the enemy, but also to discredit his ideology.[21] This does not mean the killing of every last man on the enemy side, but it involves the killing of the enemy's dreams. After the defeat of Nazi Germany, Allied generals forced Nazi officials and thousands of nearby residents to take humiliating tours of the concentration camps and, in some cases, to bury the dead prisoners. The prosecution of Nazi officials at the Nuremberg trials also helped to ensure that the Nazi dream would never rise again. After definitive defeat and humiliation, Nazism was so thoroughly discredited as an ideology that, for decades after, no one—except for a few on the fringes—wanted to be associated with it in any way.

The Islamic State itself seems to fully understand the symbolic side of war. The crucifixions and ritual beheadings are not senseless acts, they are

A Watery Grave

"After the big battle at Omdurman near Khartoum...[General] Kitcher went to the tomb of the Mahdi—he had died before then—broke the tomb open, dragged the body out and he threw it into the Nile. See, he understood you humiliate and you damage their prestige and you say, if I may quote Bin Laden, 'We're the strong horse and you're the weak horse.'"

—Richard Miniter, author of *Losing bin Laden*[20]

acts calculated to send a message. On one occasion, after capturing 250 Syrian soldiers, the Islamic State militants forced the prisoners to strip to their underwear and then paraded them in front of cameras before marching them to the place of execution.[22] The message? Those who resist ISIS will suffer both defeat and dishonor; they fight for a worthless cause.

The ISIS campaign of psychological warfare, barbaric as it is, has had the intended effect. Rallies to support ISIS have popped up in numerous Western cities, other Muslim groups have pledged their solidarity, and more and more Muslims are flocking to join its army.

Perhaps we should take note. If and when we get around to defeating ISIS, let's hope we administer a psychologically definitive and humiliating defeat—one that shows up not only the impotence of their fighting force, but also the emptiness of their vision. Else ISIS will rise again in some other form under some other name.

Exactly how this would be done is difficult to say. We are not, hopefully, going to descend to the level of displaying severed heads. And parading troops in their underwear is inconsistent with our concept of human dignity. Indeed, the whole idea of imposing a humiliating defeat goes against the grain of our highly developed sensitivities. Nonetheless, it seems time to reconsider our politically correct policy on waging war with terrorists. Maybe we should think of a different message to send than that war is simply a misunderstanding, and that after we've defeated you quietly and without fanfare, we will give you a clean cell and a copy of the Koran untouched by infidel hands because, of course, your religion has nothing to do with your terrorist behavior.

If we wish to avoid endless wars with jihadists, we should conclude our war with the Islamic State in such a way that Muslims around the world will rethink the notions of Islamic jihad and Islamic martyrdom. It's not as improbable as it sounds. We have already seen that it wasn't so long ago, historically speaking, that Turks, Egyptians, and other Muslims who read the writing on the wall did rethink Islam. Faced with a West that was not only militarily powerful but also culturally confident, they opted for a more muted form of Islam. But is the West as militarily powerful as it once was?

Strategies to Defeat Jihad

I'm no military strategist, but there are some obvious steps that we ought to be taking if we want to defeat the jihadis:

• Build our military back up—or at least quit gutting it

In Chesterton's futuristic novel about the Islamization of England, reclusive Turkish warlord Oman Pasha has taken the estate next to Lord Ivywood's and, with Ivywood's assistance, is secretly building a Turkish army in England. And while Ivywood and Pasha have been quietly bringing in a Turkish army, "the British army is practically disbanded."[23]

Today it's not clear whether Turkey, which has the second-largest military in NATO (and the eighth-largest in the world), will come down on the side of the West or on the side of the Islamists. And meanwhile, the Western powers are gutting their militaries. The U.S. is drastically reducing the size and strength of our defense. We plan to shrink the Army to pre–World War II levels. The number of ships in the Navy is already lower than it was in 1917.[24] And, according to reports, the Obama administration has been quietly conducting a massive purge of top military officers.[25] Just at the point when the rest of the world is arming to the teeth, the American solons think it's safe to bid a farewell to arms. The armed forces of our allies are not what they used to be, either. They can be relied on to march in the local gay pride parade, or help out with Ebola patients, or even launch an occasional "overseas contingency operation," but major wars on multiple fronts are another matter. Just at the point when Islam is

Prescriptions From Dr. Gorka

- "The White House must scrap the arbitrary rules about what materials can and cannot be used to educate our warfighters, our analysts, and our FBI agents about the jihadist threat."

- "Resist the continuous lobbying and subversive tactics of groups such as the Council on American-Islamic Relations (CAIR) and the Muslim Public Affairs Council…"

—National security expert Dr. Sebastian Gorka in *Defeating Jihad: The Winnable War*[26]

advancing by stealth jihad and armed jihad all over the world, the West is letting down its guard, both literally and metaphorically.

• Ground our counterterrorism strategy in reality, not fantasy

The February 11, 2016, edition of *FrontPage Magazine* contains an insightful piece by Daniel Greenfield on our failed counterterrorism strategy. Our policy, he wrote, is based on an artificial distinction between "Good Islam" and "Bad Islam." Our aim, he continued, is to "convince Good Islam to have nothing to do with Bad Islam."

Ironically, as Greenfield observed, "our diplomats and politicians don't verbally acknowledge the existence of Bad Islam." Instead they claim that the "bad Muslims" (the terrorists) aren't really Muslims at all. To paraphrase various world leaders, the terrorists have "nothing to do with Islam," "speak for no religion," and have completely "perverted" the meaning of Islam. Technically, they're not bad Muslims, because they're no kind of Muslim. At least, that's what the theory says.[27]

In other words, our strategy is based on a circular argument: if you start with the premise that Islam is a peaceful religion, then those who break the peace cannot, by definition, be followers of Islam. They must be motivated by something else: grievances over Western imperialism, lust for power, or even some kind of psychological defect.

Our counterterrorism policy should be aimed not at helping good authentic Islam win out over bad terrorist Islam, but at weakening faith in Islam altogether. The truth is, as Greenfield puts it, "Good Islam and Bad Islam are two halves of the same coin...we're trying to convince Dr. Jekyll to help us fight Mr. Hyde. And Dr. Jekyll might even help us out, until he turns into Mr. Hyde."[28]

The proof of this thesis lies in our fear that the slightest criticism of Islam will force the moderates (good Muslims) to join the extremists (bad Muslims). But if Muslims can so readily convert from Jekyll to Hyde, can there have been much difference between the two in the first place? Nobody worries that an insult to Christianity or even to Jesus is going to suddenly turn moderate Christians into masked terrorists. The almost universal fear that moderate Muslims can be easily driven into the radical camp is an acknowledgement that the distance between the two is not that great.

In short, Good Islam and Bad Islam are not separated by a gulf; they are on a continuum. Many of the things that the "bad" Muslims do are done by our allies, the "good" Muslims. Thus, as Greenfield points out, "Our Good Islam allies in Pakistan fight Bad Islam's

Moderate Nazis?

"When it comes to Nazism, the world agreed that it is a supremacist ideology. Those who followed it to the core were 'bad guys'—such as Adolf Hitler. As for the 'good Nazis' [such as Oscar Schindler] who helped shelter persecuted Jews and performed other altruistic deeds, the world acknowledges that they were not following a 'moderate' form of Nazism, but that their commitment to Nazism was nonchalant at best.

"This is the correct paradigm to view Islam and Muslims with: Islam does contain violent and supremacist doctrines. This is a simple fact. Those who follow it to the core were and are 'bad guys'—for example, Osama bin Laden. Still, there are 'good Muslims.' Yet they are good not because they follow a good, or 'moderate,' Islam, but because they are not thoroughly committed to Islam in the first place."

—Raymond Ibrahim, author of *Crucified Again*[29]

More Is Not Better

"We can see consistently that more exposure to Islamic theology leads to more extremism."

—Moorthy S. Muthuswamy, author of *Defeating Political Islam*[31]

terror, when they aren't hiding Osama bin Laden. Bad Islam in the Islamic State beheads people and takes slaves and Good Islam in Saudi Arabia does too.... The moderate Iranian government signs a nuclear deal and then the extremist Iranian government calls for 'Death to America.'"[30]

We should stop projecting our own values and beliefs onto Islam. As Greenfield puts it, "moderate Islam isn't what most Muslims believe. It's what most liberals believe that Muslims believe." Moderate Islam or Good Islam is an invention—"an imaginary religion that they imagine Muslims must practice because the alternative is the end of everything that they believe in."[32]

Our counterterrorism policy must not be based on this pleasant fiction.

• Take the threat of nuclear jihad seriously

Pakistan has nuclear weapons, and Iran is acquiring them. What if, as seems increasingly likely, France and England concede more and more political power to Islamists? Both countries are nuclear powers with advanced delivery systems. Given the rapid rate at which the old order of things is being turned upside down, it is not inconceivable that these weapons could someday fall into the hands of Islamic radicals. We've seen that London has already elected its first Muslim mayor. How far away are the UK's first Muslim parliamentary majority and Muslim prime minister?

In the nearer term, it's likely that ISIS will be defeated in Iraq and Syria and that the Western world will breathe a collective sigh of relief. Many will assume that with the defeat of the supposedly un-Islamic Islamic State, things will return to normal—or, at least, to what passes for normal in the Middle East. As long as the beheadings, crucifixions, sex slavery, and destruction of churches come to a stop, Western citizens—many of them, at least—will be able to convince themselves that the danger is over.

We may soon see how the West will react to the rout of ISIS because the long-awaited boots-on-the-ground are now on the ground. Except that they're Iranian boots. Well, to be exact, Shi'ite militia and Iraqi troops led by Iranian Revolutionary Guard Commanders.[33]

A Book You're Not Supposed to Read

The Complete Infidel's Guide to Iran by Robert Spencer (Washington, DC: Regnery, 2016).

If the Iranian-led forces succeed in ridding Iraq and Syria of the Islamic State, what then? So much energy has been invested in the idea that ISIS is an evil aberration—a perversion of true Islam—that many will assume that moderate, mainstream Islam is back in the saddle. The fact that ISIS will have been defeated by other Muslims will reinforce the erroneous notion that most Muslims are just as opposed to jihad violence as its victims.

And while the defeat of ISIS by Shi'ite forces will almost certainly constitute a change for the better for the Christians in Iraq, from the perspective of global security the replacement of ISIS with Iran will likely turn out to be a frying-pan-into-the-fire type of scenario. An Iranian-led victory will greatly increase the strength and prestige of Iran in the Middle East and also on the world stage. Not that Iran is currently lacking in power and influence. ISIS may seem more frightening, but Iran is immeasurably more dangerous. Tehran is already in effective control of four major capitals in the Mid-East— Baghdad, Beirut, Damascus, and Sana'a.[34] In addition, Iran possesses medium- and long-range missiles and is on the verge of producing nuclear weapons.[35] The development of EMP weapons is also within its capabilities.

What's more, the Iranian government is just as firmly committed to jihad as the Islamic state. That the religion of Allah should be the religion of the whole world, by force if necessary, is an uncontroversial idea among Iran's mullahs, generals, and government officials. The only disagreements are over timing. After all, it was the Iranian Revolution of 1979 that re-introduced militant Islam to the world. And the Islamic Republic of Iran has done more to export terrorism than any other Muslim nation.[36]

The other feature Iran shares with ISIS is an apocalyptic mindset. This makes it doubly dangerous. More than any other Islamic state, Iran is governed by leaders who believe that the end times are imminent—leaders who seem anxious, moreover, to do what they can to shorten the wait. Like many Christians, Iranians believe in a Second Coming. Unlike most Christians, they believe it is just around the corner. Along with Christians, Shi'ite Muslims think that the end times will bring the return of Jesus to earth, although he won't be the Jesus that Christians expect. And the Muslim Jesus won't be the main attraction. That honor is reserved for the Mahdi—the Twelfth Imam who, according to Shia beliefs, has been in a state of "occultation" in the celestial cities of Hurqalya and Jabulsa since the ninth century. When he returns, the Mahdi will lead a revolution to establish Islamic rule and a reign of peace throughout the world. Then jihad can cease. The problem is, Iran's leaders believe the Mahdi can be woken from his trance state only by cataclysmic events.[38]

What sort of cataclysmic events? How about a nuclear attack on the Little Satan (Israel), followed by the detonation of an EMP device over the capital of the Big Satan (America)?

Sound crazy? To the Western ear, perhaps, but according to Denis MacEoin, a scholar who has contributed to the major encyclopedias on Islam and Iran, the yearning for the Mahdi's triumphant return "runs through the veins of all [Shia] believers."[39]

And even if no nation state ever launches a nuclear attack on us, we still have to worry about suitcase bombs. According to author Joe Cirincione, "Over the past five years the FBI, working in conjunction with local authorities in Moldova, have interrupted four attempts made by nuclear smugglers to sell radioactive materials to Middle Eastern extremists, including ISIS."[40]

• Bring down the price of oil with fracking and nuclear power

Iran, the Islamic State, and Saudi Arabia—the biggest exporter of full-strength Islam (and therefore jihad ideology) to the world[42]—all run on oil. To balance their budgets, most OPEC nations need the price of oil to be $85, and Iran needs it to be over $120.[43] If we are serious about stopping jihad, we should bankrupt the jihadists and their sponsors in the Middle East by developing the technology that would drive the price of oil to collapse.

• Use foreign aid as leverage

We've seen how President Obama was happy to send arms to the Muslim Brotherhood government of Egypt, but slow to arm the secular government that replaced it. And the nuclear deal with Iran has fecklessly released frozen

---

★ ★ ★

No Need to Worry, after All

Against MacEoin's informed analysis of the Iranians' apocalyptic bent, we have President Obama's assurance that according to their Supreme Leader, "it would be contrary to their faith to obtain a nuclear weapon."[41] Oh, well then, that's all right.

What Oil Money Buys

"It is no exaggeration to say that the resurgence of political Islam...has been mostly due to Saudi funding and proselytizing activities.... American scholar and terrorism analyst Alex Alexiev calls this 'the largest worldwide propaganda campaign ever mounted.'"

—**Moorthy S. Muthuswamy, author of *Defeating Political Islam*[44]**

Iranian assets and opened the floodgates to Western investment in Iran.[45] Our foreign aid budget is in need of a major overhaul in the direction of helping our friends rather than our enemies. In particular, we should provide support to the relatively moderate governments of Egypt, Jordan, and the UAE. This is not inconsistent with a policy of simultaneously criticizing Islamic ideology and theology. Several Muslim leaders seem to realize that Islam is a retrograde force. Egyptian president El-Sisi has been particularly outspoken in his criticism of traditional Islam.

• Wage cyberwar

Jihadists are more adept at cyberwar than most realize. As a recent headline puts it: "Jihad groups acquiring cyber capability to bring major cities to standstill."[46] We need to go on the cyber offensive. For example, we ought to be replicating our success with the Stuxnet virus, which did major damage to Iran's nuclear program.[47]

• Educate for victory

School textbooks and curricula need to be revamped to teach accurate views of Islamic history, not the romanticized PC version.

• Discredit political correctness

The PC mindset that has crippled our society's ability to defend itself has to be debunked, discredited, and ridiculed.

• Pull our heads out of the sand and prevent terror attacks on American soil

The U.S. Army is more than a match for any invading force of Middle Eastern jihadists. But military power can be offset by asymmetrical warfare—in other words, the type of warfare that terrorists favor. A small team of terrorists can incinerate the World Trade Center or paralyze Madrid or Mumbai, and there's not much that F-16s or nuclear submarines can do about it.

ISIS, Hezbollah, and Hamas have well-equipped fighting forces, and all are capable of carrying out terrorist operations far from their home bases. And ISIS, especially, is in the business of using social media to inspire "lone wolf" terrorists in the West to commit murder and other acts of war sabotage in the infidel countries where they live, including the United States.[48] Security agencies and social media companies should work together to limit the ability of jihadists to communicate their message and to communicate with one another. At the same time, these companies should stop censoring the valuable work of counterjihad organizations and individuals.[49]

If we don't want more Americans to be knifed, shot, or blown up by jihadists in our own country, we need to monitor social media more carefully, monitor mosques, infiltrate Islamist groups, and cultivate and reward informants within the Muslim community here. We also need to secure our borders, ports, and harbors, and consider a moratorium on Muslim immigration to the United States. Americans are ashamed that we turned Jews away from our shores in the Nazi era. This time around, we should willingly take in the people our enemies are persecuting—in other words, Christians and Yazidis from the Middle East.

A Book You're Not Supposed to Read

"Who's guarding the fort? National security takes back a seat to diversity in this dark comedy about political correctness run amok in the military. Gays, Muslims, and security threats are multiplying at Fort Camp, but no one seems to notice. When Captain Cassandra tries to sound the alarm about an imminent coup, he finds himself caught up in a multicultural maelstrom filled with an assortment of odd—and dangerous—characters: a handsome Muslim colonel who controls the chemical weapons depot, a president who prefers to set pink lines instead of red ones, a pretty anarchist for Islam, and a general who displays a 'Coexist' poster on his office wall. The stakes are high, but at Fort Camp and in Washington the nation's defenders are on low alert."

—killing PC with comedy, as demonstrated in my novel *Insecurity* (Franklin: Post Hill, 2014)

Visa Card Benefits

"At least 40 percent of illegal immigrants now in the United States may have come as legitimate visa holders and simply failed to leave."

—Van Hipp, author of *The New Terrorism*[51]

And we need to arm our armed forces. Fourteen died at Fort Hood partly because the only U.S. soldier on the spot with a lethal weapon in his hand was a soldier of Allah. Thanks to absurd regulations, the members of our military are generally prohibited from carrying weapons on U.S. Army bases.[50] That makes every soldier on base a sitting duck.

Jihad can be defeated. But not if we're not really trying.

A final point. The Good Islam–Bad Islam dichotomy is, as Greenfield observes, a main plank in most counterterrorism strategies. All we need to do, the experts say, is to get the good, moderate Muslims to reject the perverted form of Islam practiced by the jihadists. But that will not be easy. In fact, separating the Islam subscribed to by the terrorists from the Islam subscribed to by the majority of Muslims may be an impossible task.

As we saw in earlier chapters, it's the same Islam. In asking Muslims to reject the ideology of the jihadists, we are asking them to reject big chunks of their own faith. Muhammad did many of the things that today's jihadists do. Are Muslims supposed to give up their belief that Muhammad is the perfect model of behavior? Are they supposed to excise from the Koran all the injunctions to fight unbelievers? How about the *Life of Muhammad*? If you were to cut out all the parts about raids, battles, beheadings, and selling slaves from ibn Ishaq's authoritative biography of the prophet, you'd be left with a fairly slim volume. Are Muslims supposed to reject the notion of virgins in paradise as a fairy tale? Many mainstream Muslims hold to that belief just as firmly as do the mujahedeen. In short, how likely is it that Muslims will reform their faith into something resembling Unitarianism?

A better alternative to reforming Islam is to abandon it altogether—albeit gradually. That may sound reckless, but, in fact, that's what many Muslims were doing prior to the Islamist revival of the late twentieth century. During much of that century, Muslims, especially educated Muslims, took Islam much less seriously than they do now. Turkey had abolished the caliphate and become a secular, Westernized state, and most Mid-East and North African nations were trying to follow suit. Once, when speaking before a large assembly, President Nasser of Egypt related how when a Muslim Brotherhood leader had demanded that he enforce the wearing of the hijab. Nasser replied, "Sir…you cannot make one girl, your own [college-aged] daughter wear it, and yet you want me to go and make ten million women wear it?" His remarks brought a burst of applause and laughter from the audience.[53] Such things are no longer a laughing matter in the Muslim world, but the fact that they once were should tell us something.

As Raymond Ibrahim and Ali Allawi have pointed out, educated Muslims in that era were not in the process of reforming their faith, they were in the process of losing it.[54] Instead of asking Muslims to reject bits and pieces of their militant religion, perhaps we should be exploring ways to encourage them to leave it. But that's a topic for another chapter—the next one, in fact.

The Not So Gradual Approach

"Muslims, leave Islam, opt for freedom, turn your backs on the imams. Free yourself."

—Geert Wilders[52]

CHAPTER 11

Psychological, Spiritual, and Ideological Warfare

Military victory is a necessary condition for winning the war against the jihadists. Wins on the battlefield are crucial—especially when the enemy you're fighting equates might with right. But military victory by itself is not enough to win the war against jihad. A battlefield defeat of ISIS, for example, does not necessarily mean the end of ISIS. The Islamic State might reestablish itself in Jordan or the Sinai or in Libya. Or it could shift its focus to terrorist strikes in the Mid-East, Europe, and America. And even if ISIS were to disappear completely, the basic problem would remain. The main problem is not ISIS or Boko Haram or al-Qaeda, but the Islamic doctrine of warfare. ISIS may not be the most powerful military force around, but it embodies a powerful idea. Much of its attraction hinges on its claim to be faithful to the original doctrine of jihad. Until that idea ceases to attract support from Muslims worldwide, jihadist terror will always be with us.

So ideological warfare is also crucial. And it goes hand in hand with success on the battlefield. A good example of this principle comes from the Cold War era. In *The President, the Pope, and the Prime Minister*, John O'Sullivan points out that before President Ronald Reagan, Pope John Paul II, and Prime

Did you know?

★ Reagan, Thatcher, and John Paul II turned the tide against communism by discrediting it as an ideology

★ In the twentieth century, Islam recovered from a crisis of faith; we should be steering it into another one

★ Any criticism or ridicule of Muhammad is met with fury because Muslims intuitively understand that all of Islam depends on their prophet's credibility

True Believers

"The reality is that the Islamic State is Islamic. *Very* Islamic. Yes, it has attracted psychopaths and adventure seekers, drawn largely from the disaffected populations of the Middle East and Europe. But the religion preached by its most ardent followers derives from coherent and even learned interpretations of Islam."

—Graeme Wood[2]

Minister Margaret Thatcher arrived on the scene, communists were expanding their power all over the globe. The trio changed all that, and they did it in large part by undermining and discrediting communist ideology.[1]

Today, we find ourselves in a situation not unlike the late seventies. Islamists are on the march around the globe and our leaders have reverted to the Carter-era policy of dialogue and appeasement. Political leaders refuse to name the ideology we are fighting except in the most generic terms ("violent extremism"), and our leaders refuse to admit that we are engaged in a spiritual and ideological war similar to the one that John Paul II fought against communism.

Which is too bad. Because unless the belief system that motivates the terrorists is challenged and discredited, the attacks will continue. One of the great advantages that Islamists enjoy in their fight to impose Islam on the world is the conviction that God is on their side. We need to make them think twice about that.

In past ideological struggles, we sought ideological victory—the discrediting of the belief system that inspired our enemies. If we don't do something similar in our global civilizational struggle with Islam (or, if you prefer, "Islamism"), we need to face the very real possibility that we will lose the war—both militarily and culturally. As I said in *Christianity, Islam, and Atheism*, "Ordinarily one keeps one's reservations about another's religion to oneself. But if we are in a fight to the death with Islamic ideology/theology, why wouldn't we want to examine it more carefully? Why wouldn't we want to call into question the revelation on which it is all based? And,

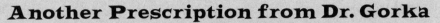

Another Prescription from Dr. Gorka

"Initiate a billion dollar covert psychological warfare campaign to support Muslim reformers across the Middle East, Asia, and North Africa...."

—Dr. Sebastian Gorka[3]

further why not seek ways to disillusion and demoralize the proponents of that ideology? In short, why shouldn't we want Islam to fail?"[4]

The other aim of ideological warfare is to convince your own side that it has something worth fighting for. That's difficult to do in a culture that keeps wanting to draw a moral equivalence between its own beliefs and those of every other culture. There is something very special about the Western Judeo-Christian heritage. Lately, we seem to have lost that sense. Now is the time to recover it.

The Information Wars

The war against militant Islam is, in part, a war of ideas, and it seems fair to say that we are losing badly on that front. That's odd when you think about it. After all, the Islamists are trying to promote oppressive seventh-century ideas and we, supposedly, are the champions of the most enlightened and up-to-date ideas. Unfortunately, one of those "up-to-date," enlightened ideas is that we have no right to judge other people's beliefs. So we don't call barbaric ideas barbaric. That would be unfair, uncivil, offensive, and insensitive.

Maybe so. But thirty years hence, how would you like to be the one to explain to your burqa-wearing granddaughter as she is married off to a man thrice her age that we lost the culture war against Islam because it would have been insensitive to fight back?

PC Policing

"Could the FBI's purge of training material relating to Islamic terrorism have led to the agency dropping the ball on Florida nightclub shooter Omar Mateen?"

—**Kerry Picket, The Daily Caller**[5]

The fear of being insensitive is a poor excuse for jeopardizing the future of your children and grandchildren. But sometimes you'll hear another, more practical argument against attacking the ideological and theological basis of Islam and thus undermining the faith of the jihadists—namely, that it won't work. Many take it for granted that a deeply held faith cannot be easily shaken by criticism, and Islamic beliefs seem as unshakable as they come.

Given that assumption, it would be a waste of time to try to sow the seeds of doubt in the minds of true believers. But deeply rooted beliefs are not always as deeply rooted as they appear. For instance, thirty-five years ago it seemed that the Catholic faith was deeply rooted in Ireland, but Ireland, like many other once solidly Catholic societies, has since experienced a significant decline in faith.

More to the point, Islam has also suffered a crisis of faith—and not that long ago. As we have already seen, the colonial era saw a drastic weakening of Muslims' enthusiasm for their religion. The zenith of Western power was the nadir of Islamic faith. By the early 1970s, Iranian and Egyptian women had abandoned their traditional garb for Western-style clothing, and Western entertainment was all the rage.[6] Muslims continued to observe their religion, but they did so in more or less the same fashion as a lukewarm Christian does—that is, more as a social obligation than a religious one. In the Muslim world, for most of the twentieth century, Islam could hardly be called a deeply rooted faith.

The radical Islamist movements of the twentieth century, such as the Muslim Brotherhood, were formed for the purpose of renewing the faith that was slipping away. And they were largely successful in doing so. The point to keep in mind, however, is that the "deeply rooted belief" we now see in the Muslim world is of fairly recent vintage.

Moreover, that deeply rooted belief rests on the very shaky foundation of the Koran. Jihadists do what they do because they believe that God commands them to do it. They also believe they will be richly rewarded for their endeavors in paradise. But what if the Koran was not written by God? What if it is a man-made fabrication—the invention of a self-serving schemer? Who wants to blow himself up in a suicide attack if the promised reward is nothing more than a clever recruitment tool made up for the purpose of replacing warriors lost in battle some 1,400 years ago?

My, How Times Have Changed!

"During the Colonial era and into the mid-twentieth century, all things distinctively Islamic—from Islam's clerics to the woman's 'hijab,' or headscarf—were increasingly seen by Muslims as relics of a backward age to be shunned. Most Muslims were Muslim in name only."

—**Raymond Ibrahim,** *Crucified Again*[7]

Did Muhammad actually receive a revelation? Was the Koran written by God? These seem like fairly central questions. And seeing that countless lives hang upon the answers, one would think that more people would be asking them. It's not as though these are strictly personal, private questions for the individual conscience to ponder. They are also, as with all publicly proclaimed religions, a matter for general discussion. Jihadists don't hide their lamp under a bushel. Muhammad-doubters, then, should not be reluctant to blow it out. One might even say that they have a public duty to try and extinguish it.

As long as Muslims believe that Muhammad received his marching orders from God, the Islamic jihad will continue. If we want to put a stop to the jihad, we need to put a dent in that belief. As we have seen time after time in history, even deeply rooted beliefs are susceptible to change. How many Nazis and subscribers to Japanese emperor worship have you met lately? If enough non-Muslims start asking certain questions and ask them insistently, there is a decent chance that Muslims can be returned to that state of doubt about Islam that prevailed in the Muslim world a mere sixty years ago.

By undercutting the jihadis' certitude, you also undermine their will to fight. Who wants to die for an illusion? Those of us who would prefer not to become a jihadist's ticket to paradise have a vested interest in sowing doubts in the minds of Muslim believers about the credibility of Muhammad, the authority of the Koran, and the reliability of the Islamic promises of paradise to those who die in the jihad. But how does one do that? Well, preferably from a safe distance. In war zones, leaflets could occasionally be dropped from planes instead of bombs. Elsewhere, the Internet and social media sites which have served so well to recruit jihadists could be used to win recruits for rationality.

Theologians, philosophers, and in fact public intellectuals of all kinds could also play a part in the debunking process. They could point out the contradiction inherent in trying to find a finite solution to an infinite yearning. Or they could simply refrain from rushing to the defense of Islam whenever serious questions are raised. In any event, we still seem to be a long way from addressing the contradictions in Islam. We have

★ ★ ★

Fool's Paradise: Dying for an Illusion

What should the content of the message for our leafleting and social media campaigns be? Nothing fancy. Just some simple questions to activate the grey cells. For example: "Won't you get tired of your seventy-two companions after the first few hundred years of eternity?" "Will Allah supply you with seventy-two more after that?" "Will all the women be equally attractive? If not, won't that cause problems?" "Will these companions be more like real women or more like beautiful robots?" "Do you want to spend eternity with robots?" "Isn't it likely that maidens in paradise is nothing more than a clever recruiting tool made up by Muhammad?" Or, to put it more bluntly, "How can you be such a sap?"

yet to go beyond the "no religion sanctions killing" and "we have deep respect for your beliefs" stage of confronting the realities of the Islamic faith.

Many security analysts say that we are in an ideological struggle with Islam—a propaganda war about which beliefs will ultimately prevail.[8] If so, we are going about it in an unusual way. In past ideological struggles, we sought ideological victory—that is, we sought to discredit the belief systems that inspired our enemies. We didn't accept their ideological premises, we challenged them.

★ ★ ★

Cold War Appeasement Redux

Back in the Cold War, some pacifists adopted the slogan "Better Red than dead." We don't have a similar slogan today, but if we did it might be something along the lines of "Better to appease than displease." It's not as catchy, but the sentiments are the same.

In the Cold War, for example, our aim was to shake faith in communism, not to validate and confirm it. We seem unwilling, however, to take a similar stance vis-à-vis the ideology of Islam. One obvious point of vulnerability is the Islamic idea of heaven as an adolescent boy's sex dreams come true. Although it would be greatly to our advantage to shake belief in the virgins-in-paradise deception (you do believe it's a deception, don't you?), we hesitate to go there. Perhaps we intuit that we can't shake the branch without shaking the whole tree. The heavenly garden of delights is a main theme of the Koran. To question it is to question the integrity of the Koran as a whole, and also to question the integrity of the man from whom the whole system flows. Politeness and multicultural pieties about respecting the other person's beliefs prevent us from wielding a potent ideological weapon.

For our own survival, we need to rethink the idea that the other person's deeply held beliefs can never be questioned. The Islamists' touching faith in the Stepford brides seems like a good place to start.

An Ideological House of Cards

It's estimated that some 270 million people have been killed in the name of Islam over the centuries—far more than the combined total of all those killed in the name of Nazism or communism.[9] It's not politically correct to compare Islam to totalitarian ideologies, but it's a fair comparison. Consider this entry from the 1910 edition of the Catholic Encyclopedia: "In matters political, Islam is a system of despotism at home and aggression abroad.... The rights of non-Moslem subjects are of the vaguest and most limited kind, and a religious war is a sacred duty whenever there is a chance of success against the 'Infidel.'"[10]

Our policy toward Islam should be based on the assumption that Islam is an ideological enemy like communism or Nazism. The idea is to wean people away from the ideology by undermining and discrediting it, and also by offering a better alternative. Because Islam has proven itself to be a totalitarian system, we should try to weaken it.

But it's difficult to give people second thoughts about their religion if you don't know the first thing about it yourself. All that is necessary to deconstruct and dismantle the political-religious ideology of Islam is readily available in the Islamic sources, but to be effective in the ideological war, we need to become acquainted with them, rather than relying on whatever Islamic apologists say about Islam.

Once you've studied up on Islam, the first thing you realize is that the key to sowing the seeds of disbelief is Muhammad himself—he who must not be maligned. The prophet is Islam's main prop. The whole religion rests on his veracity. If he is discredited, Islam is discredited. We often hear of the five pillars of Islam, but Muhammad is the essential pillar. And he is a surprisingly

★ ★ ★

Knowledge Gap

After the Orlando nightclub massacre, one longtime law enforcement officer admitted that "Never in all my years of training, and being involved in several investigative units, to include the FBI Task Force, would we have ever guessed a LGBT club be a target of an terrorist attack."[11]

fragile one. He is Islam's link to the Almighty, but also its weakest link.

Islamic leaders intuitively understand this. Which is why any cartoon or criticism of Muhammad is met with displays of rage and fury. An attack on Muhammad is an attack on the whole faith. Judging by news reports from the Muslim world, one is much more likely to be prosecuted for blasphemy against Muhammad than against Allah. To get an idea of Muhammad's centrality,

★ ★ ★
Yes, But

Imams and other Islamic leaders are willing to condemn terrorism, but can they be convinced to reject the explicit teachings of Muhammad (as found in the Koran and the hadith), which form the basis for jihad activity?

consider that there is no corresponding outcry among Muslims when Jesus is mocked or caricatured in a cartoon. Yet, according to Muslims, Jesus is also a great prophet and is, in fact, considered to be the greatest Muslim prophet after Muhammad. For strategic reasons, the Organization of the Islamic Cooperation's anti-blasphemy resolutions are formulated to protect all prophets from slander, but in practice the only prophet that matters is Muhammad.

Jesus has survived a good deal of mockery over the centuries. More to the point, he has survived the tests of critical and historical analysis that have been applied to Christian scripture. If anything, the examination has served to strengthen the case for the trustworthiness of the New Testament accounts. It's highly unlikely, however, that Muhammad could survive a similar examination. That is why, from a survivalist perspective, an examination is long overdue.

Did Muhammad even exist? Contrary to what is commonly supposed, the case for the historical Muhammad is not nearly as well-established as the case for people who lived long before him, such as Julius Caesar, Cicero, Alexander the Great, Aristotle, and Pericles. Some scholars have suggested that the stories about Muhammad are less fact than legend—very possibly invented by Arab conquerors who needed an historical and theological justification for their conquests. In any event, there is little historical or

Three Books You're Not Supposed to Read

Did Muhammad Exist? An Inquiry into Islam's Obscure Origins by Robert Spencer (Wilmington: ISI, 2014).

Mohammed and Charlemagne Revisited: The History of a Controversy by Emmet Scott (London: New English Review Press, 2012).

What the Modern Martyr Should Know: Seventy-Two Grapes and Not a Single Virgin: The New Picture of Islam by Norbert Pressburg (CreateSpace Independent Publishing Platform, 2012).

archaeological evidence to confirm the traditional story of Muhammad.[12] The question of his existence is an avenue of inquiry that merits further exploration. Yet, curiously, few seem willing to explore it. Was Muhammad more myth than man? If so, the next pertinent question is the one raised by Robert Spencer: "Are jihadists dying for a fiction?"

If Muhammad did exist as traditionally portrayed and if the canonical accounts of his life are accurate, then there are some questions about his character and credibility that need to be asked. Muhammad, as we have seen, is supposed to be the perfect man. So it comes as a shock to many Muslims when they discover that he was far from perfect. A youngster's first encounter with Muhammad is likely to come in the form of hagiographic stories that describe him as noble and saintly. It can be sobering to learn that Muhammad ordered mass executions of defenseless people, traded slaves, permitted rape, married a six-year-old, married his own daughter-in-law, and engaged in deceit and trickery. And that's only the short list.

Of course, when evaluating a prophet, the most important character trait to consider is honesty. Did Muhammad really receive a revelation from the angel Gabriel, or did he make the whole thing up? We have only his word for it. There is no other corroborating evidence. Here is where the historical-critical method comes in handy. Exhibit A is the Koran. It's supposed to be the eternal word of God. Muslims say that Muhammad couldn't possibly have invented it because he was (supposedly) illiterate. The proof that God wrote it, they say, lies in its inimitable style: who else but God could write so well? This is a little hard to swallow because, as we have seen, although there are beautiful passages in the Koran, much of it does look as though it was written by a semi-literate merchant. Well, that's a little harsh. It's more accurate to say that it seems to have been written by someone with a flair for poetic language, but with little sense of composition and with limited storytelling ability.

A Reformed Koran?

"The Koran cannot be reformed; or if it is reformed, it is no longer the Koran."

—Bill Warner, Director, Center for the Study of Political Islam[13]

If the tools of textual criticism were applied to the Koran, it would be difficult to avoid the conclusion that it is a fabrication—if not of Muhammad's making, then of someone else's. Whether out of fear or out of politeness, as we have seen, the Koran has not been subject to the searching examination that historians, archaeologists, linguists, and textual critics have applied to the Bible. To put it bluntly, it would never survive such an examination.

The Real Jesus

The same holds true of the Jesus of the Koran. He is not a believable character. In fact, he hardly rises to the level of a character. The portrait of him in the Koran is so one-dimensional that to call him a stick figure would not do justice to sticks.

Which brings us to the other Jesus—the real one. If Muhammad is the key to casting doubts about Islam, Jesus of Nazareth provides the path out of Islam. The penalty for converting away from Islam is death, so it takes a fairly compelling reason to convert—such as Jesus himself. According to various reports, a surprisingly high percentage of Muslim conversions to Christianity result from a dream or vision of Jesus—the Christian Jesus, that is.[14]

This suggests a promising avenue of approach for evangelists, apologists, and theologians. Instead of congratulating Muslims on revering the same Jesus we do, try to introduce them to the real story of the real Jesus. Most Muslims aren't familiar with the gospel story. Most have learned that the Bible should not be consulted because they are taught that Christians and Jews have thoroughly corrupted the text.[15] The true story, they believe, is the story of Jesus that's presented in the Koran. And since it's not a very interesting story, they can be forgiven if they think that Jesus is not a particularly compelling figure.

So one of the first orders of business is to convey the story of Jesus, whether through the gospels or in film or in simplified story versions. How exactly this message should be conveyed is a matter I will leave up to Christians who know more about media and communications than I do. But it is important to remember that Muslim countries have high rates of illiteracy. Audio and visual messages are more likely to have an effect than texts. One other thing to keep in mind is that Islam is a religion that emphasizes power. For that reason it seems important to underscore the power of Christ—the casting out of demons and moneychangers, the healing of the lame and blind, the raising of the dead, the fearlessness in the face of authorities, the final triumph over death itself. And, of course, Muslims need to be informed that at the Last Judgment, it is Jesus Christ, not Isa, who will do the judging.

A Muslim who becomes acquainted with both versions—the gospel account and the Koranic account—gets to see that Jesus of Nazareth is a far more compelling figure than the Isa of the Koran. What's more, he is a far more believable person than Isa.

The bottom line is that the case for Christianity is considerably stronger than the case for Islam. Theologically, Islam is a house of cards. It can't stand up to examination, which is why Islam's guardians go ballistic at the least hint of criticism. Nevertheless, we should start making the case while there is still time—before the questioning of Islam becomes a crime, or the Islamic world goes ballistic in the literal sense of the word.

Beating Them at Their Own Game

On October 20, 2014, a twenty-five-year-old convert to Islam named Martin Couture-Rouleau ran down two Canadian soldiers, killing one and injuring the other. In the police chase that followed, his car ran into a ditch and he was fatally shot by police as he came at them with a knife.

Rouleau's story is similar to that of other homegrown jihadists. He followed Islamic websites, he grew a beard, prayed constantly, and tried to convert his friends.

His Facebook page contains (mostly pictorial) arguments against atheism, Darwinism, capitalism, and corrupt Arab princes. The most revealing thing about it, however, is that it gives a glimpse into an ideological war against Christianity that most Christians are unaware of.[16] Christians may not know about it, but Muslim recruitment sites are full of slick anti-Christian apologetics.

For example, Rouleau's Facebook page contains an illustration of a seated Jesus extending his hand toward the viewer, with a multitude of followers pictured in the background. The text at the top of the picture reads, "It's like this: I created man and woman with original sin. Then I destroyed most of them for sinning. Then I impregnated a woman with myself as her child, so that I could be born. Later, I will kill myself as a sacrifice to myself to save all of you from the sin I gave you in the first place."

Without the text, it looks like a typical piece of devotional art. Jesus is smiling, and he appears to be kind, genuine, and welcoming. With the text, however, one notices a hint of the con man in his countenance. The smile could be the self-satisfied smile of the man who has just convinced you to sink all your money into his worthless Ponzi scheme.[17]

For those who are well-schooled in their faith, such aggressive apologetics do not constitute a stumbling block. But the great majority of Christians—particularly young Christians—are not well-catechized. With no solid grounding in the framework of their faith, they are easy prey to apologetics attacks of this kind.

The Jesus-as-pitchman ad is cleverly designed to play on doubts that people commonly have about Christianity. Who hasn't thought that this whole original sin business is grossly unfair? Why should I be punished for something I never did? If God knew what he was doing, why did he let things get so out of control? The implication of the "ad" is that one might consider opting for a more straightforward religion unencumbered by the doctrine of original sin—a religion such as Islam.

The "ad" is also pitched to play on youthful pride. "Don't be a dupe," it seems to say. "I will kill myself as a sacrifice to myself to save all of you from the sin I gave you in the first place"? The implicit message? "That's crazy talk, man! How can you fall for a line like that?"

The very different Islamic Jesus also shows up in Rouleau's Facebook page. In one picture he is prostrated in prayer with his forehead touching the ground in the manner of a good Muslim at prayer. The caption is from Matthew 26:59: "and he [Jesus] went a little further, and fell on his face, and prayed…" Below that in smaller letters are the words "Even Jesus (pbuh) bowing to the ground praying to his God." This is the true Jesus, the good Muslim prophet (peace be upon him) whose message, like Muhammad's, is to worship God alone.

So, for all those who might still have a sentimental attachment to Jesus, the message is that you can keep your Jesus—just make sure it's the real Jesus, not the false pretender created by power-hungry priests and popes.

This "real" Jesus shows up again in Rouleau's Facebook page juxtaposed with a black-robed priest. The Jesus figure delivers the uncorrupted message—"The Father is greater than I," "The Lord our God is one Lord"—while the priest delivers the falsified, contradictory message—"Jesus is equal to the Father," "God exists as three persons."

The final apologetics message comes in the form of two contrasting statements about God— one representing the Christian view, the other, the Muslim view. In the first frame, a standing, black-robed priest is reading from a book: "My god came from womb of a woman, he was breast-fed, had to defecate, played in the street with kids, and at the age of 33 he was beaten, spit upon, humiliated, mocked, stripped naked then hung on a cross, killed and then was buried."

> ★ ★ ★
> ## The Real Tough Guys
> One set of juxtaposed images on Rouleau's site even makes fun of wannabe gangsters with their wannabe honor cultures. The top photo shows a group of young black men, some with dreadlocks, some with hoods, some with a hint of beard, but all making gang-style hand signals. The bottom photo shows a group of more mature-looking, fully-bearded Muslim men seated on the bed of a large truck that is presumably taking them to the battlefront. They appear calm and confident, and they are carrying AK-47s. The message seems to be that the young blacks are merely "posers" by comparison. They deserve no respect because they are not real men—only boys who are playing at being men.[18]

In the next frame a devout Muslim kneeling in prayer says "My God is Allah, there is no other god beside Him, the King, the Holy, the One Free from all defects, the Giver of security, the Watcher over His creatures, the All-Mighty, the Compeller, the Supreme. Glory be to Allah. (High is He) above all that they associate as partners with Him."[19]

This exercise in persuasion is a direct appeal to a young man's sense of honor. For young men today, that does not mean throwing your coat over a

> ### ★ ★ ★
> ### An Act of Honor Wipes Away Shame
>
> It's been suggested that Omar Mateen, who murdered fifty at a gay club in Orlando, was himself a homosexual. If so, does that mean he was a bad Muslim? That his deeds were un-Islamic? Not really. In Islam, all of one's past sins can be wiped clean by an act of martyrdom. As Robert Spencer writes in regard to another young Muslim jihadist, Mohammod Abdulazeez (the Chattanooga killer), "If a jihadist knows he is about to wage a great jihad, he knows its value will outweigh anything evil he has done. He knows that he can assuage his guilty conscience over drinking and smoking marijuana and guarantee for himself a place in paradise."[20]

puddle so a young lady may walk safely across on it. It's more like the sense of honor found in gangs and tribal cultures. Honor means maintaining the good opinion of those whose opinion matters to you, and it's very much bound up with the concept of manhood. You maintain your honor by proving your manhood—by showing that you have power and control or, at least, by keeping up the appearance of power and control. Honor means demanding respect and avenging insults to one's sense of worth.

Islamic cultures are honor cultures, and the religion of Islam might justly be described as an honor religion. Allah is in charge and he exercises complete control. He is superior to any other conception of God.

What's the opposite of honor? Shame. In an honor culture, shame is the worst fate—worse than death. In honor societies, leaders or generals who have suffered a shameful defeat not uncommonly resort to suicide.

With all that in mind, consider the two contrasting statements about God on the Canadian terrorist's Facebook page. What's wrong with the Christian's God? He was shamed. He was beaten, mocked, and humiliated. Christians find comfort in God's humanity. He became one of us, shared in our weakness, sorrows, and sufferings. But that's not a selling point from the Islamic point of view. Someone who is mocked, spit upon, and crucified may be a god fit for a weak woman, but not for any self-respecting man. In contrast to the humiliated God-man of the Christians, Allah is "All-Mighty, the Compeller, the Supreme." Unlike the helpless victim in the Christian story, Allah is in complete control. Moreover, Allah does not let his prophets be shamed. According to the Koran (4:157) and other Islamic sources, the prophet Jesus did not suffer humiliation or crucifixion but was simply taken up to Heaven at the end of his mission.

So the overall appeal jihadists make to young men is, "Don't be a loser. Get on the winning side. Our cause is invincible because our God is invincible."

Who's the toughest gang on the planet? "We are," say the jihadis. This is the way dedicated and savvy Islamists are winning souls for Allah and the jihad.

But if we could turn the tables, making *Islam* something to be ashamed of, converts might start flowing in the other direction. Enter Father Zakaria Botros, an elderly Coptic priest whose Arabic-language TV show is broadcast from the U.S. to the Middle East. Father Botros says he wants to help reasonable Muslims who are searching for the truth to wake up to the truth about Islam. He does it by referring mainly to Islamic sources because, as he puts it, "Muslims have no greater enemy than their own scriptures...which constantly scandalize and embarrass Muslims."[21] Father Botros sometimes presents a catalogue of Muhammad's sexual habits and then asks his Muslim audience: "Is this the prophet I follow?"[22] It's a good question to put to the members of an honor culture, because if the leader you are following is a dishonorable man, then your own honor is at stake if you continue to follow him.

It helps that the Coptic priest is able to make his points in a very engaging manner. According to Muslim cleric Ahmed al-Qatani, 6 million Muslims convert to Christianity annually, many of them persuaded by Father Botros's public ministry.[23]

A hundred Fr. Botroses could do a lot to change Muslim minds without providing mobs an excuse to burn down the nearest church. A thousand would be even better. Not that every one of them needs to be an Arabic-speaking televangelist. David Wood is a Christian whose website, *Answering Muslims*, features short fireside chat–type videos aimed at English-speaking

Cold War strategists were not given to telling their Soviet counterparts, "We think the workers' paradise is a wonderful idea, but you really shouldn't put people in gulags. It's a betrayal of everything Marx stood for. Real communism doesn't sanction violence, you know." Instead, we opposed communism root and branch.

Muslims. Wood is thoroughly versed in Islamic theology, and he has a low-key "inquiring-minds-want-to-know" style that is hard to resist. His many informative and often entertaining videos are readily available on his site and on YouTube.[24]

What I am recommending is not an in-your-face *Charlie Hebdo* frontal assault on everything Muslims hold dear, but rather a slow process of desensitization by which Muslims get used to the idea of Islam being subject to criticism. Some of Father Botros's effectiveness lies in his ability to cite Islamic sources to which his Muslim audiences cannot very well object. But much of it resides in his ability to condition them to accept criticism of Muhammad. The first time a Muslim hears the flaws of Muhammad discussed, he might well be angry. But how about the third time? The twentieth time?

The sensitive approach has been a complete failure; maybe it's time for a little desensitization.

Of course there will be risks, but one of the advantages of a widely dispersed critique of Islam is that the risks are spread out. Moreover, theological and historical discussions, whether in print or on video, are not as eye-catching to Muslim mobs as intentionally offensive cartoons.

The case against Islam is, as Fr. Botros points out, embedded in mainstream Islamic sources. An article about the many wives (and concubines) of Muhammad might be offensive, but it would have the advantage of being factual. Or, for a somewhat less sensitive subject, how about a piece on the growing archaeological evidence that the story of Islam's "Golden Age" is considerably exaggerated?[25]

Fortunately, some in the mainstream media have begun to question the established narrative about Islam—Michael Coren of the Sun News TV network,[26] Bill O'Reilly,[27] Sean Hannity,[28] Megyn Kelly,[29] and Jeanine Pirro of Fox News.[30] They have begun to ask the essential questions: Are Muslim apologists telling the truth? Is Islam really a peaceful religion? Does the problem lie

> ★ ★ ★
> ## No Exit
> If Islam is to be reformed, one of the essential reforms would be to invalidate the apostasy laws which make it a capital crime to leave Islam.

only with a handful of radicals or is there something wrong with Islam itself? The drip-drip-drip effect of raising these questions night after night should not be underestimated. If enough people in the West were to engage in a low-confrontational ("I'm only raising the question") examination of Islamic tenets and do it often enough, the doubt level could be raised considerably.

And that is what we should aim at doing. The objective is not to make Muslims angry, but to make them uncomfortable with their faith. If enough questions are raised, some, at least, will begin to ask the same questions. To reiterate the main point, our aim should not be to separate Muslims from radical manifestations of their faith, but to separate them from their faith—albeit gradually.

Admittedly, sowing the seeds of doubt about Islam in the minds of Muslims is not a risk-free proposition. The policy calls for the dangerous work of discrediting Islam. It is, nevertheless, the safer alternative. A continuation of the current policy is likely to prove much more dangerous. And my proposal is based on the simple principle that honesty—even though it should be tempered with tactfulness—is still the best policy.

In other words, we need to find subtle ways of convincing Muslims of what Geert Wilders has put more bluntly. Just as we encouraged Eastern Europeans to free themselves from communism, we should be suggesting to Muslims in various ways to, as Wilders puts it, "Free yourselves and leave Islam!"[31]

The Nerve Centers of Radicalism

"This may be the most important long-term strategy in neutralizing political Islam—discrediting political Islamic theology and by extension the teachings of its clerics and its mosques which make up the nodes of the social network responsible for spawning jihad."

—Moorthy S. Muthuswamy, author of *Defeating Political Islam*[32]

The other side of the coin is to increase our faith in ourselves—that is, in our own cultural and religious heritage. As Mark Steyn observed, "There's no market for a faith that has no faith in itself."[33] Europe is fast losing ground to Islam because it lost faith in itself and in the religion that civilized it. It may be too late for Europe to reverse course, but it's not too late for Americans to learn the lessons.

As I noted earlier, one of the aims of ideological warfare is to convince your own side that it has something worth fighting for. But political correctness, which is itself a kind of religion, undermines that conviction. If the only thing you stand for is the bland belief that everything is equally okay, you really stand for nothing. When too many people think that way, their culture becomes easy prey for those with stronger beliefs.

To resist jihad, you need a reason to resist. That reason won't be found in modern multicultural pieties, but in the recovery of something older and deeper.

Acknowledgments

I would like to thank Harry Crocker for suggesting this book, and his team at Regnery for making it a reality. I am particularly grateful to my talented editor, Elizabeth Kantor, without whom this book would not have come to fruition. She deserves much of the credit for pulling it together into a coherent whole.

I am also indebted to Bob Shillman for his support of my endeavors. There are many others whose advice and encouragement contributed to this project, and they have my sincere thanks and appreciation.

Notes

Introduction: The Untold Story of Our Time

1. Soeren Kern, "Swedish Multiculturalism Goes Awry," Gatestone Institute, May 24, 2013, http://www.gatestoneinstitute.org/3729/sweden-multiculturalism; Ingrid Carlquist, "Sweden: Death by Immigration," Gatestone Institute, February 4, 2016, www.gatestoneinstitute.org/7363/sweden.death.by.immigration.

2. Douglas Murray, "'Religion of Peace' Is Not a Harmless Platitude, *Spectator,* January 17, 2015, http://www.spectator.co.uk/2015/01/religion-of-peace-is-not-a-harmless-platitude/.

3. Paul Sperry, "How US Covered Up Saudi Role in 9/11," *New York Post*, April 17, 2016, http://nypost.com/2016/04/17/how-us-covered-up-saudi-role-in-911/; and Clare M. Lopez, "History of the Muslim Brotherhood Penetration of the U.S. Government," Gatestone Institute, April 15, 2013, http://www.gatestoneinstitute.org/3672/muslim-brotherhood-us-government.

4. "Text of George Bush's Speech," The *Guardian*, September 21, 2001, http://www.theguardian.com/world/2001/sep/21/september11.usa13.

5. Lopez, "History of the Muslim Brotherhood Penetration"; Denis MacEoin, "Keith Ellison's Stealth Jihad. *Middle East Quarterly* 17:3 (Summer 2010): 31–40, http://www.meforum.org/2756/keith-ellison-stealth-jihad; Paul Bremmer, "Beware 'Stealth Jihad' in America," WND, October 27, 2015, http://www.wnd.com/2015/10/beware-stealth-jihad-in-america/;

Marilyn Stern, "ISNA'S Interfaith Overreach," *FrontPage Magazine*, September 28, 2015, http://www.frontpagemag.com/fpm/260271/isnas-interfaith-overreach-marilyn-stern.

6. See, for example, Foday Justice Darboe, "Terrorism Is un-Islamic," The Peace Worker, November 21, 2015, http://peaceworker.org/2015/11/terrorism-is-un-islamic/.

7. N. J. Dawood, trans., *The Koran* (London: Penguin Books), 2000. Unless otherwise noted, quotations from the Koran throughout the book are from this translation.

8. Andrew C. McCarthy, "Huma Abedin's Muslim Brotherhood Ties", *National Review*, July 25, 2012, http://www.nationalreview.com/article/312211/huma-abedins-muslim-brotherhood-ties-andrew-c-mccarthy.

9. Claudia Rosett, "Questions for the Pentagon: Who is Hesham Islam?" Foundation for Defense of Democracies, May 30, 2016. http://www.defenddemocracy.org/media-hit/questions-for-the-pentag.

10. Stephen Coughlin, *Catastrophic Failure: Blindfolding America in the Face of Jihad* (Washington, DC: Center for Security Policy Press), 2015, 19, 337, 376–78.

11. See, for example, Jessica Desvarieux, "Twelve Years Post 9/11, Islamophobia Still Runs High," Truth Out, September 11, 2013, http://www.truth-out.org/video/item/18759-twelve-years-post-9-11-islamophobia-still-runs-high%5d.

12. Robert Spencer, "Egypt's Mufti: Jihad Terrorists Are Misunderstanders of Islam and Qur'an," Jihad Watch, April 10, 2015, https://www.jihadwatch.org/2015/04/egypts-mufti-jihad-terrorists-are-misunderstanders-of-islam-and-quran.

13. Robert Steinback, "The Anti-Muslim Inner Circle," Southern Poverty Law Center, June 17, 2011, https://www.splcenter.org/fighting-hate/intelligence-report/2011/anti-muslim-inner-circle; "Hatewatch," Southern Poverty Law Center, https://www.splcenter.org/hatewatch.

14. Mark Steyn, "Last Laughs in Europe," Steyn Online, September 28, 2015, http://www.steynonline.com/7200/last-laughs-in-europe.

15. Dale Hurd, "ISIS's First Step: Conquer Rome, Defeat Christianity," CBN News, December 30, 2015, http://www1.cbn.com/cbnnews/world/2015/October/ISISs-First-Step-Conquering-Rome-Defeat-Christianity.

16.   William Kilpatrick, "Will a Future Pope Be Forced to Flee Rome?" Catholic World Report, January 21, 2015, http://www.catholicworldreport.com/Item/3645/will_a_future_pope_be_forced_to_flee_rome.aspx.

17.   Hannah Roberts, "ISIS Threatens to Send 500,000 Migrants to Europe as a 'Psychological Weapon' in Chilling Echo of Gaddafi's Prophecy that the Mediterranean 'Will Become a Sea of Chaos,'" *Daily Mail*, February 18, 2015, http://www.dailymail.co.uk/news/article-2958517/The-Mediterranean-sea-chaos-Gaddafi-s-chilling-prophecy-interview-ISIS-threatens-send-500-000-migrants-Europe-psychological-weapon-bombed.html.

18.   Conrad Hackett, "5 Facts about the Muslim Population in Europe," Pew Research Center, November 17, 2015, http://www.pewresearch.org/fact-tank/2015/11/17/5-facts-about-the-muslim-population-in-europe/.

19.   Ross Clark, "Muhammad Really Is the Single Most Popular Boys' Name in England and Wales, *Spectator*, http://blogs.spectator.co.uk/2015/08/mohammed-really-is-the-single-most-popular-boys-name-in-england-and-wales/.

20.   Mark Howarth, "The Changing Face of Britain: A Child in Birmingham Is Now More Likely to Be a Muslim Than Christian," *Daily Mail*, September 14, 2014, http://www.dailymail.co.uk/news/article-2755654/The-changing-face-Britain-A-child-Birmingham-likely-Muslim-Christian.html; Soeren Kern, " Austria: Muslims Outnumber Catholics in Vienna Schools," Gatestone Institute, March 26, 2014, website: http://www.gatestoneinstitute.org/4229/austria-muslims-vienna-schools.

21.   Ernest Hemingway, *The Sun Also Rises* (New York: Scribner, 2016), 109.

Chapter 1: The Resurgence of Jihad in the Twenty-First Century

1.   Cheryl K. Chumley, "Egyptian cleric on Islamic law: If you beat your wife, just don't touch her face," *Washington Times*, July 31, 2013, http://www.washingtontimes.com/news/2013/jul/31/egyptian-cleric-islamic-law-if-you-beat-your-wife-/.

2.   Imran Ali Teepu, "Islamic law and suspicion fuel polio resurgence," *USA Today*, November 30, 2013, http://www.usatoday.com/story/news/world/2013/11/30/pakistan-polio-resurgence/3591683/.

3.   Gerry Braiden, "Flu vaccine scheme halted over fears of Muslim parents," *Herald Scotland*, October 3, 2013, http://www.heraldscotland.com/news/13125738.Flu_vaccine_scheme_halted_over_fears_of_Muslim_parents/.

4. Alfredo Burlando, Anca Cristea, and Logan M. Lee, "The Trade Consequences of Maritime Insecurity: Evidence from Somali Piracy," *Review of International Economics*, 23(3).

5. Owen Gibson, "Migrant workers suffer 'appalling treatment' in Qatar World Cup stadiums, says Amnesty," *Guardian*, March 30, 2016, http://www.theguardian.com/global-development/2016/mar/31/migrant-workers-suffer-appalling-treatment-in-qatar-world-cup-stadiums-says-amnesty.

6. Daniel Greenfield, "Islamic State Has 3,500 Sex Slaves," *Frontpage Magazine*, January 19, 2016, http://www.frontpagemag.com/point/261527/islamic-state-has-3500-sex-slaves-daniel-greenfield.

7. Soeren Kern, "UK: Child Sex Slavery, Multiculturalism and Islam," Gatestone Institute, March 24, 2014, http://www.gatestoneinstitute.org/4226/uk-child-sex-slavery#print.

8. Sam Greenhill, Jill Reilly, and Kieran Corcoran, "ISIS Butchers leave 'roads lined with decapitated police and soldiers,'" *Daily Mail*, June 12, 2014. http://www.dailymail.co.uk/news/article-2655977/ISIS-militants-march-Baghdad-trademark-bullet-head-gets-way-control-north.html.

9. Katie Hunt, "4 found guilty of railway station knife attack in China," CNN, September 12, 2014, http://www.cnn.com/2014/09/12/world/asia/china-kunming-attack-trial/.

10. Associated Press, "Islamic group claims Volgograd attacks and threatens Sochi visitors," The *Guardian*, January 19, 2014, http://www.theguardian.com/world/2014/jan/20/islamic-group-claims-volgograd-threatens-sochi.

11. Nikolaus von Twickel, "Twin Moscow Metro Bombings Kill 39," *Moscow Times*, March 30 2010, http://www.themoscowtimes.com/news/article/twin-moscow-metro-bombings-kill-39/402801.html.

12. "Mumbai death toll tops 200," The *Guardian*, July 12, 2006, http://www.theguardian.com/world/2006/jul/12/india; Reuters, "Mumbai train bombings: Indian court sentences five to death for 2006 attacks," *Guardian*, September 30, 2015, http://www.theguardian.com/world/2015/sep/30/mumbai-train-bombings-indian-court-sentences-five-to-death-for-2006-attacks.

13. "July 7 2005 London Bombings Fast Facts," CNN, July 13, 2015, http://www.cnn.com/2013/11/06/world/europe/july-7-2005-london-bombings-fast-facts/.

14. Paul Hamilos, "The worst Islamist attack in European history," The *Guardian*, October 31, 2007, http://www.theguardian.com/world/2007/oct/31/spain.

15. "September 11th Fast Facts," CNN, September 7, 2015, http://www.cnn.com/2013/07/27/us/september-11-anniversary-fast-facts/.

16. Greenhill, Reilly, and Corcoran, "ISIS butchers leave 'roads lined with decapitated police and soldiers.'"

17. Matthew Bunn et al., *Steps to Prevent Nuclear Terrorism: Recommendations Based on the U.S.-Russia Joint Threat Assessment*, Belfer Center, September 2013; Zafar Nawaz Jaspal, "Nuclear/Radiological Terrorism: Myth or Reality?" Journal of Political Studies, 19(1): 91–111; Martin E. Hellman, "Risk Analysis of Nuclear Deterrence," *The Bent* of Tau Beta Pi, (Spring 2008): 14–22.

18. In the jihadist lexicon, "Rome" sometimes refers to the city, and sometimes to Christian Europe, as in "Holy Roman Empire." Islamists have long memories.

19. Andrew C. McCarthy, *Spring Fever: The Illusion of Islamic Democracy* (New York: Encounter Books, 2013), 72, 123–26.

20. Mark Steyn, *America Alone: The End of the World As We Know It* (Washington, D.C.: Regnery, 2008), xxix.

21. Roger Scruton, "Why Did British Police Ignore Pakistani Gangs Abusing 1,400 Rotherham Children? Political Correctness," *Forbes*, August 30, 2014, http://www.forbes.com/sites/rogerscruton/2014/08/30/why-did-british-police-ignore-pakistani-gangs-raping-rotherham-children-political-correctness/#3c10fcf75a7c.

22. Ingrid Carlqvist and Lars Hedegaard, "Sweden: Rape Capital of the West," Gatestone Institute, February 14, 2015, http://www.gatestoneinstitute.org/5195/sweden-rape.

23. Soeren Kern, "European 'No-Go' Zones: Fact or Fiction? Part 1: France," Gatestone Institute, January 20, 2015, http://www.gatestoneinstitute.org/5128/france-no-go-zones.

24. Leo Cendrowicz, "Paris attacks: Visiting Molenbeek, the police no-go zone that was home to two of the gunmen," *The Independent*, November 15, 2015, http://www.independent.co.uk/news/world/europe/paris-terror-attacks-visiting-molenbeek-the-police-no-go-zone-that-was-home-to-two-of-the-gunmen-a6735551.html.

25. Phillip Puella, "Italy's Muslims divided over Gaza prayer protests at cathedrals," Reuters, January 13, 2009, http://blogs.reuters.com/faithworld/2009/01/13/italys-muslims-divided-over-gaza-prayer-protests-at-cathedrals/.

26. Oriana Fallaci, *The Force of Reason* (New York: Rizzoli, 2006), 34–35.

27. Christopher Orlet, "Oriana in Exile," *The American Spectator*, July 18, 2005, http://spectator.org/48304_oriana-exile/.

28. Dale Hurd, "ISIS's First Step: Conquer Rome, Defeat Christianity," CBN News, December 30, 2015, http://www1.cbn.com/cbnnews/world/2015/October/ISISs-First-Step-Conquering-Rome-Defeat-Christianity.

29. Dennis Prager, "1,400 English Girls Raped by Multiculturalism," *National Review*, September 9, 2014, http://www.nationalreview.com/article/387428/1400-english-girls-raped-multiculturalism-dennis-prager.

30. Alexis Jay, *Independent Inquiry into Child Sexual Exploitation in Rotherham (1997–2013)*, Rotherham Metropolitan Borough Council, August 21, 2014, http://www.rotherham.gov.uk/downloads/file/1407/independent_inquiry_cse_in_rotherham.

31. Peter Williams et al., "Gunman Omar Mateen Described as Belligerent, Racist, and 'Toxic,'" NBC, June 15, 2016, http://www.nbcnews.com/storyline/orlando-nightclub-massacre/how-nra-has-responded-mass-shootings-over-years-n592551; Christian Datoc, "FBI Called Off Investigation of Orlando Shooter Because They Thought His Coworkers Were Racist," Daily Caller, June 13, 2016, http://dailycaller.com/2016/06/13/fbi-called-off-investigation-of-orlando-shooter-because-they-thought-his-coworkers-were-racist/.

32. John R. Schindler, "The Road to Orlando," *New York Observer*, June 13, 2016, http://observer.com/2016/06/the-road-to-orlando/.

33. Robert Spencer, "Who is responsible for Muslim rape gang scandal? Nick Lowles, Fiyaz Mughal & co." Jihad Watch, August 31, 2014, https://www.jihadwatch.org/2014/08/who-is-response-for-muslim-rape-gang-scandal-nick-lowles-fiyaz-mughal-co.

34. Tom Brooks-Pollock, "Rotherham researcher 'sent on diversity course' after raising alarm," *Telegraph*, September 2, 2014, http://www.telegraph.co.uk/news/uknews/crime/11069178/Rotherham-researcher-sent-on-diversity-course-after-raising-alarm.html.

35. James Simpson, "Southern Poverty Law Center – Manufacturing Hate for Fun and Profit," Breitbart, February 16, 2016, http://www.breitbart.com/big-government/2016/02/16/southern-poverty-law-center-manufacturing-hate-for-fun-and-profit/.

36. "Hatewatch," Southern Poverty Law Center, https://www.splcenter.org/hatewatch; Wajahat Ali et al, *Fear, Inc. The Roots of the Islamophobia Network in America, Center for American Progress*, August 26, 2011, https://www.americanprogress.org/issues/religion/report/2011/08/26/10165/fear-inc/.

37. Kenneth Timmerman, "Obama administration pulls references to Islam from terror training materials, official says," Daily Caller, October 21, 2011, http://dailycaller.com/2011/10/21/obama-administration-pulls-references-to-islam-from-terror-training-materials-official-says/?print=1.

38. David Badash, "McCain Slams Bachman, Others, over Claim Clinton Aide Part of Muslim Brotherhood," The New Civil Rights Movement, July 18, 2012, http://www.thenewcivilrightsmovement.com/mccain-slams-bachmann-over-claim-clinton-aide-part-of-muslim-brotherhood/politics/2012/07/18/43965; Edward Rollins, "Bachman's Former Campaign Chief—Shame on You, Michele," Fox News, July 18, 2012, http://www.foxnews.com/opinion/2012/07/18/bachmann-former-campaign-chief-shame-on-michele.html.

39. "NYPD Blind," *Wall Street Journal*, April 17, 2014, http://www.wsj.com/articles/SB10001424052702304311204579507393976730268.

40. Robert Spencer, *Arab Winter Comes to America: The Truth About the War We're In* (Washington, D.C.: Regnery, 2014), 12–13.

41. Robert Spencer, "Latest death threat to Robert Spencer: 'hahaha this bastard needs to get killed,'" Jihad Watch, July 24, 2012, https://www.jihadwatch.org/2012/07/latest-death-threat-to-robert-spencer-hahha-this-bastard-needs-to-get-killed.

42. Pamela Geller, "Pamela Geller 'WORTH RAPING AND CHOPPING': Mark Zuckerberg ALLOWS SAVAGE DEATH THREATS by Muslims but CENSORS Posts Critical OF Muslim Migrants," *Pamela Geller*, March 6, 2016, http://pamelageller.com/2016/03/pamela-geller-death-threats.html/.

43. Spencer, *Arab Winter Comes to America*, 12–13.

44. Timmerman, "Obama administration pulls references to Islam from terror training materials, official says."

45. Clare M. Lopez, Roland Peer, and Christine Brim, "New Study on Hate Crimes Debunks the Myth of a Growing Trend in Muslim Victimization," Center for Security Policy, March 29, 2011, http://www.centerforsecuritypolicy.org/2011/03/29/new-study-on-hate-crimes-debunks-the-myth-of-a-growing-trend-in-muslim-victimization-8/.

46. Ronald Rolheiser, "Our Muslim brothers and sisters," *Angelus,* December 3, 2015, http://www.angelusnews.com/voices/fr-rolheiser/our-muslim-brothers-and-sisters-9579/#.VzEJKvkgvNg.

47. "2015 Paris Terror Attacks Fast Facts," CNN, April 13, 2016, http://www.cnn.com/2015/12/08/europe/2015-paris-terror-attacks-fast-facts/.

48. Gordon Rayner, Henry Samuel, and Martin Evans, "Charlie Hebdo attack: France's worst terrorist attack in a generation leaves 12 dead," *The Telegraph,* January 7, 2015, http://www.telegraph.co.uk/news/worldnews/europe/france/11331902/Charlie-Hebdo-attack-Frances-worst-terrorist-attack-in-a-generation-leaves-12-dead.html.

49. Kim Hjelmgaard, Mary Vidon, and Katharine Lackey, "Gunman killed, 4 others dead at Paris market," *USA Today,* January 9, 2015, http://www.usatoday.com/story/news/world/2015/01/09/paris-hostage-supermarket/21489449/.

50. Paul Hamilos, "The worst Islamist attack in European history," *The Guardian*, October 31, 2007, http://www.theguardian.com/world/2007/oct/31/spain.

51. CNN, "July 7 2005 London Bombings Fast Facts."

52. Diantha Parker And Jess Bidgood, "Boston Marathon Bombing: What We Know," *New York Times*, January 1, 2015, http://www.nytimes.com/2015/01/02/us/boston-marathon-bombings-trial-what-you-need-to-know.html.

53. Cheryl K. Chumley, "Nidal Hasan, self-described 'Soldier of Allah,' touts jihad in letter to pope," *The Washington Times*, October 10, 2014, http://www.washingtontimes.com/news/2014/oct/10/nidal-hasan-self-described-solder-of-allah-touts-j/.

54. CNN, "September 11th Fast Facts."

55. "Cologne sex attacks: Women describe 'terrible' assaults," BBC, January 7, 2016, http://www.bbc.com/news/world-europe-35250903.

56. Prager, "1,400 English Girls Raped by Multiculturalism."

57. Ludovica Iaccino, "Top 5 Countries with the highest rates of rape," *IB Times*, January 29, 2014, http://ibtimes.co.uk/top-5-countries-highest-rates-rape-1434355.

58. Rolheiser, "Our Muslim brothers and sisters."

Chapter 2: Are ISIS and Boko Haram Un-Islamic?

1. "Tony Blair's speech on the Middle East: Full Text," *New Statesman*, April 23, 2014, http://www.newstatesman.com/politics/2014/04/tony-blairs-speech-middle-east-full-text.

2. William Kilpatrick, *Christianity, Islam, and Atheism: The Struggle for the Soul of the West* (San Francisco: Ignatius Press, 2012), 42–43.

3. "Transcript of President Bush's address," CNN, September 21, 2001, http://edition.cnn.com/2001/US/09/20/gen.bush.transcript/; AM, "Discover Which World Leaders Believes [sic] That Islam Is a Religion of Peace," Conservative Post, http://conservativepost.com/discover-which-world-leaders-believes-that-islam-is-a-religion-of-peace/.

4. Robert Spencer, "UK Home Sec'y Reid: Islam Means Peace," Jihad Watch, August 16, 2006, https://www.jihadwatch.org/2006/08/uk-home-secy-reid-islam-means-peace.

5. Robert Spencer, "'Palestinian' Muslim Texted Parents before Murdering Israeli Policewoman: 'My religion called upon me,'" Jihad Watch, February 14, 2016, https://www.jihadwatch.org/2016/02/palestinian-muslim-texted-parents-before-murdering-israeli-policewoman-my-religion-called-upon-me.

6. Associated Press, "Pope Francis Says Fundamentalist Terrorism Result of 'Deviant Forms of Religion,'" Fox News, January 12, 2015, http://www.foxnews.com/world/2015/01/12/pope-francis-says-fundamentalist-terrorism-result-deviant-forms-religion.html.

7. Jane Onyanga-Omara and John Bacon, "Aunt: San Bernardino Suspect 'Became More Devout,'" *USA Today*, December 6, 2015, http://www.usatoday.com/story/news/nation/2015/12/06/san-bernardino-shooting/76879058/.

8. "Older Bombing Suspect Became More Devout in Recent Years," NPR, April 22, 2013, http://www.npr.org/2013/04/22/178462390/older-bombing-suspect-became-more-devout-in-recent-years.

9. Howard Schneider, "Fort Hood Suspect Became More Devout after Mother's Death, Cousin Says," *Washington Post*, November 7, 2009,

http://www.washingtonpost.com/wp-dyn/content/article/2009/11/07/AR2009110701688.html.

10. Spencer, *Arab Winter Comes to America*, 16.

11. "Full text: bin Laden's 'letter to America,'" *Guardian*, November 24, 2002, http://www.theguardian.com/world/2002/nov/24/theobserver.

12. Ibid.

13. Justin Kaliebe, who attempted to join an al-Qaeda affiliate, in Spencer, *Arab Winter Comes to America*, 43.

14. Serdar Tatar, one of the Fort Dix mass murder plotters, "(USA) Fort Dix Mass Murder Plotter: 'I'm Doing It in the Name of Allah...,'" LiveLeak, September 28, 2008, http://www.liveleak.com/view?i=eaa_1222621709.

15. Major Nidal Hasan, on the date he killed fourteen people at Fort Hood, in Spencer, *Arab Winter Comes to America*, 4.

16. Robert Spencer, *The Complete Infidel's Guide to ISIS* (Washington, D.C.: Regnery, 2015), 178–179, 184.

17. Robert Spencer, "Nigeria: Muslim hacks daughter to death with machete for converting to Christianity," Jihad Watch, March 8, 2014, https://www.jihadwatch.org/2014/03/nigeria-muslim-hacks-daughter-to-death-with-machete-for-converting-to-christianity.

18. Joe Mozingo and Sarah Parvini, "A Christmas party with a trivia game—and then the shooting started," *Los Angeles Times,* December 5, 2015, http://www.latimes.com/local/california/la-me-1205-christmas-party-20151205-story.html.

19. Rocco Parascandola, Heidi Evans, and Bill Hutchinson, "Boston Marathon Bomb Devices Were Pressure Cookers Filled with Nails, Ball Bearings: Report," *New York Daily News*, April 17, 2013, http://www.nydailynews.com/news/national/boston-marathon-bomb-devices-made-pressure-cookers-filled-nails-ball-bearings-report-article-1.1318278.

20. Nigel Morris, "Murder of Soldier in Woolwich Was 'Betrayal of Islam' Says Cameron As He Insists Britain Will Stand Resolute against Terror," *Independent*, May 23, 2013, http://www.independent.co.uk/news/uk/politics/murder-of-soldier-in-woolwich-was-a-betrayal-of-islam-says-cameron-as-he-insists-britain-will-stand-8629067.html.

21. Andrew Griffin, "Isis Should Be Called The 'Un-Islamic State': British Muslims Call on David Cameron to Stop Spread of Extremist Propaganda," *Independent,* September 14, 2014, http://www.independent.co.uk/news/uk/home-news/isis-call-it-the-un-islamic-state-say-muslim-groups-as-another-hostage-is-murdered-9731823.html.

22. Daniel Halper, "Obama: 99.9% of Muslims Reject Radical Islam," *Weekly Standard*, February 2, 2015, http://www.weeklystandard.com/obama-99.9-of-muslims-reject-radical-islam/article/836303.

23. William Saletan, "The Pope's Catholic Problem," Slate, February 11, 2014, http://www.slate.com/blogs/saletan/2014/02/11/catholic_poll_on_abortion_gay_marriage_and_birth_control_europe_and_the.html.

24. Nuh Ha Mim Keller, ed. *Reliance of the Traveller: A Classic Manual of Islamic Sacred Law* (Beltsville: Amana Publishing, 1997).

25. "Poll of U.S. Muslims Reveals Ominous Levels Of Support For Islamic Supremacists' Doctrine of Shariah, Jihad," Center for Security Policy, June 23, 2015, http://www.centerforsecuritypolicy.org/2015/06/23/nationwide-poll-of-us-muslims-shows-thousands-support-shariah-jihad/.

26. Jordan Schachtel, "King of Jordan at UN: Struggle against 'Outlaws of Islam' Is a 'Third World War,'" Breitbart, September 28, 2015, http://www.breitbart.com/national-security/2015/09/28/king-jordan-un-struggle-outlaws-islam-third-world-war/.

27. "Pakistan: Growing Concerns about Extremism, Continuing Discontent with US," August 13, 2009, http://www.pewglobal.org/. See also "Muslim Publics Divided on Hamas and Hezbollah,"; and Pew Research Center, *Global Attitudes and Trends*, December 2, 2010, http://www.pewglobal.org/2010/12/02/muslims-around-the-world-divided-on-hamas-and-hezbollah/.

28. Dana Ford, Salma Abdelaziz, and Ian Lee, "Egypt's President Calls for a 'Religious Revolution,'" CNN, January 6, 2015, http://www.cnn.com/2015/01/06/africa/egypt-president-speech/.

Chapter 3: The Roots of Jihad

1. CNN, "Transcript of President Bush's Address."

2. Robert Spencer, *The Truth about Muhammad* (Washington, D.C.: Regnery, 2006), 184–85.

3. The Translation of the Meanings of Sahih Al-Buhkari: English and Arabic Edition, trans. Muhammad M. Khan (Riyadh: Darus-Salam Publications, 1997).

4. Ibn Ishaq, The Life of Muhammad, trans. A Guillaume (Oxford: Oxford University Press, 1967).

5. Sahih Muslim, trans. Nasiruddin Al-Khattab (Riyadh: Dar-us-Publications, 2007).

6. Ishaq, The Life of Muhammad; The Translations of the Meanings of Sahih Al-Buhkari, trans. Khan.

7. Aymenn Jawad Al-Tamimi, "Islamic State Justification for Burning Alive the Jordanian Pilot: Translation and Analysis," Aymenn Jawad Al-Tamimi's Blog, February 4, 2015, http://www.aymennjawad. org/2015/02/islamic-state-justification-for-burning-alive.

8. Robert Reilly, The Closing of the Muslim Mind (Wilmington: ISI Books, 2010), 74.

9. Daniel Greenfield, "Beheading Is Against Islam, That's Why Mohammed Owned A Sword Named 'Cleaver Of Vertebrae,'" FrontPage Magazine, September 30, 2014, http://www.frontpagemag.com/ point/242060/beheading-against-islam-thats-why-mohammed-owned-daniel-greenfield.

10. Keller, Reliance of the Traveller, 1.1–1.3.

11. Ibid., 2.1.

12. Eliot C. McLaughlin, "Local Man Planned Suicide Attack at Wichita, Kansas, Airport, Feds Say," CNN, December 13, 2013, http://www.cnn. com/2013/12/13/justice/wichita-terrorism-arrest/.

13. Bill Warner, A Self-Study Course on Political Islam: Level 1 (CSPI Publishing, 2011), 19.

14. "Pakistan Taleban Vow More Violence," BBC, January 29, 2007, http:// news.bbc.co.uk/2/hi/south_asia/6292061.stm.

15. Keller, Reliance of the Traveller.

16. Stephen M. Kirby, Letting Islam Be Islam: Separating Truth from Myth (CreateSpace, 2012), 294–299.

17. Qasim Rashid, "10 Fabrications Muslim Leaders Need to Stop Making About Ahmadi Muslims," Huffington Post, November 24, 2014, http:// www.huffingtonpost.com/qasim-rashid/10-fabrications-muslim-leaders-need-to-stop-making-about-ahmadi-muslims_b_5854492.html.

18. Ibn Ishaq, The Life of Muhammad, trans. A. Guillaume (Oxford: Oxford University Press, 1967), 219–690.

19. "The Perfection of the Koran," Miracles of the Qur'an, http://www. miraclesofthequran.com/perfection_01.html. See also, Keller, Reliance of the Traveller, 245.

20. Hamza Tzortzis, *The Inimitable Qur'an: Introduction to the Literary and Linguistic Excellence of the Qur'an*, SlideShare, http://www.slideshare.net/abdullahbinahmadmuslim/introducing-the-literary-and-linguistic-excellence-of-the-quran.

21. Kilpatrick, *Christianity, Islam, and Atheism: The Struggle for the Soul of the West*, 119.

22. Dawood, *The Koran*, x.

23. Ibn Warraq, *Why I Am Not a Muslim*, (Amherst: Prometheus Books, 2003), 24.

24. Thomas Jefferson, *Notes on the State of Virginia* (New York: Penguin Classics, 1998).

25. Keller, *Reliance of the Traveller*, 9.1.

26. Andrew G. Bostom, *The Legacy of Jihad: Islamic Holy War and the Fate of Non-Muslims* (Amherst: Prometheus Books, 2005).

27. David Frum and Richard Perle, *An End to Evil: How to Win the War on Terror* (New York: Random House, 2003), 107.

28. See, for example, Keller, *Reliance of the Traveller*, 9.0.

29. BBC interview with Anjem Choudary, YouTube, posted by "umer123khan," November 24, 2006, https://www.youtube.com/watch?v=maHSOB2RFm4.

30. Aaron Y. Zelin, "Al-Qaeda Disaffiliates with the Islamic State of Iraq and al-Sham," Washington Institute, February 4, 2014, http://www.washingtoninstitute.org/policy-analysis/view/al-qaeda-disaffiliates-with-the-islamic-state-of-iraq-and-al-sham.

31. Jeffrey Haynes, ed. *Routledge Handbook of Religion and Politics*, 2nd ed. (New York: Routledge, 2016).

32. Omar Sacirbey, "The Muslim Brotherhood's 'Intellectual Godfather,'" *Washington Post*, February 12, 2011, http://www.washingtonpost.com/wp-dyn/content/article/2011/02/11/AR2011021106019.html.

33. Haynes, ed. *Routledge Handbook of Religion and Politics*, 2nd ed.

Chapter 4: What's in a Name? What Jihad Really Means

1. Stepanksy et al., "Boston Bombing Suspects Tamerlan, Dzhokhar Tsarnaev Appeared to Lead Normal Lives," *New York Daily News*, April 20, 2013, http://www.nydailynews.com/news/national/boston-marathon-suspects-tamerlan-dzhokhar-tsarnaev-appeared-lead-normal-lives-article-1.1321715.

2. "MyJihad Chicago Buses Live Shots," MyJihad, http://myjihad. org/2012/12/chicago-buses-live-shots/.

3. Nonie Darwish, *Now They Call Me Infidel: Why I Rejected the Jihad for America, Israel, and the War on Terror* (New York: Sentinel Publishing, 2007), 201.

4. Keller, *Reliance of the Traveller*, o. 9.0.

5. "Palestinians celebrating the fall of the twin towers on 911," YouTube, posted by "Yank507," July 25, 2006, https://www.youtube.com/ watch?v=KrM0dAFsZ8k.

6. Ari Lieberman, "Palestinians Cheer While America Mourns," *FrontPage Magazine*, April 17, 2013, http://www.frontpagemag.com/ fpm/186152/palestinians-cheer-while-america-mourns-ari-lieberman.

7. Robert Spencer, "Pakistan: 100,000 Attend Funeral of Killer of Blasphemy Laws Foe," Jihad Watch, March 1, 2016, https://www. jihadwatch.org/2016/03/pakistan-100000-attend-funeral-of-killer-of- blasphemy-laws-foe.

8. Paul Joseph Watson, "Teacher Gets Police Visit After Tweeting about Muslim Children Celebrating Brussels Attack: Yogo Instructor Shocked at Support for Terror Bombings," Infowars, March 23, 2016, http://www. infowars.com/teacher-gets-police-visit-after-tweeting-about-muslim- children-celebrating-brussels-attack/.

9. "At UN, Cardinal Condemns Terrorism's Use of Religion," Catholic News Agency, September 26, 2014. http://www.catholicnewsagency. com/news/at-un-cardinal-condemns-terrorisms-use-of-religion-89405/.

10. Pamela Geller, "New Study: Wealthy, Better Educated Muslims More Likely to Wage Jihad," March 23, 2014, http://pamelageller. com/2014/03/new-study-wealthy-better-educated-muslims-likely-wage- jihad.html/.

11. Ibid.; and Corinne Lestch, "Tech-Savvy Terrorist from Boston Believed to Be Running ISIS' Social Media Arm," *New York Daily News*, September 4, 2014,http://www.nydailynews.com/news/world/tech- savvy-terrorist-boston-believed-running-isis-social-media-arm- article-1.1928004.

12. David R. Francis, "Poverty and Low Education Don't Cause Terrorism," National Bureau of Economic Research, http://www.nber.org/digest/ sep02/w9074.html.

13. "Risk Factors for Violent Radicalization: Youth, Wealth And Education," Medical News Today, March 21, 2014, http://www. medicalnewstoday.com/releases/274292.php.

14. National Commission on Terrorist Attacks, *The 9/11 Commission Report: Final Report of the National Commission on Terrorist Attacks Upon the United States Including the Executive Summary* (Baton Rouge: Claitor's Law Books and Publishing, 2004); William Kilpatrick, "Fool's Paradise: The Appeal of Jihad," *Crisis*, October 3, 2014, http://www. crisismagazine.com/2014/fools-paradise.

15. Stephen M. Kirby, *Letting Islam Be Islam* (CreateSpace Independent Publishing Platform, 2012), 285–288.

16. Louis René Beres, "The Jihadists' Promise: Power over Death," Gatestone Institute, September 23, 2014, http://www.gatestoneinstitute. org/4718/jihadists-power-death.

17. Kilpatrick, *Christianity, Islam and Atheism: The Struggle for The Soul of The West*, 148.

18. James V. Schall, "Taking the Islamic State Seriously," St. Augustine's Press, September 29, 2014, http://www.staugustine.net/blogs/rectify-names-a-blog-on-publishing/taking-the-islamic-state-seriously-september-29-2014/.

19. "Airline Denied Atta Paradise Wedding Suit," WND, September 11, 2002, http://www.wnd.com/2002/09/15172/.

20. "Islamic State Jihadis Justify Child Marriage by Invoking Muhammad's Example," Jihad Watch, September 23, 2014, https://www.jihadwatch. org/2014/09/islamic-state-jihadis-justify-child-marriage-by-invoking-muhammads-example.

21. Robert Spencer, "Video: Geller vs. Camerota: Free Speech Warrior Bests Advocate of Sharia Submission," Jihad Watch, May 4, 2015,https:// www.jihadwatch.org/2015/05video-geller-vs-camerota-free-speech-warrior-bests-advocate-of-sharia-submission.

22. Jeffrey Lord, "Garland, Texas: There's Some History Here," *American Spectator*, May 4, 2015, http://spectator.org/62599_garland-texas-theres-some-history-here/.

23. "Gunmen Open Fire on Guard at Controversial Muhammad Exhibit; Vatican Newspaper Weighs In," Catholic Culture, May 5, 2015, http:// www.catholicculture.org/news/headlines/index.cfm?storyid=24818.

24. Declan Walsh, "Pakistan minister Shahbaz Bhatti Shot Dead in Islamabad," The *Guardian*, March 2, 2011, http://www.theguardian.com/world/2011/mar/02/pakistan-minister-shot-dead-islamabad.

25. "Alexandria Church Bomb: Egypt Police on High Alert," BBC, January 3, 2011, http://www.bbc.com/news/world-middle-east-12107084.

26. "US bloggers banned from entering UK," BBC, June 26, 2013, http://www.bbc.com/news/uk-23064355.

27. "Robert Spencer," Southern Poverty Law Center, https://www.splcenter.org/fighting-hate/extremist-files/individual/robert-spencer.

28. National Review Editors, "What the Wilders Trial Means," *National Review*, October 18, 2010, http://www.nationalreview.com/article/250038/what-wilders-trial-means-editors.

29. See, for example, "Dutch far-right leader Geert Wilders goes on trial for inciting hatred," *The Guardian*, March 18, 2016, http://www.theguardian.com/world/2016/mar/18/dutch-far-right-leader-geert-wilders-goeson-trial-for-inciting-hatred.

30. Eugene Volokh, "Congressmen Keith Ellison and André Carson call for denial of visa to Dutch legislator Geert Wilders," *Washington Post*, April 29, 2015, https://www.washingtonpost.com/news/volokhconspiracy/wp/2015/04/29/congressmen-keith-ellison-and-andre-carson-call-for-denial-of-visa-to-dutch-legislator-geert-wilders/.

31. Steve Almasy, "After four years, American Cartoonist Molly Norris Still in Hiding after Drawing Prophet Mohammed," CNN, January 14, 2015, http://www.cnn.com/2015/01/13/us/cartoonist-still-in-hiding/.

32. Lindsay Wise and Jonathan S. Landay, "After Texas shooting: If free speech is provocative, should there be limits?" McClatchy DC, May 4, 2015, http://www.mcclatchydc.com/news/crime/article24784057.html.

33. Abdullah Yusuf Ali, trans., *The Holy Qur'an*, 5th ed. (Ware: Wordsworth Editions Ltd., 2011).

34. Raymond Ibrahim, "Western Ignorance of the 'Conditions of Omar,'" March 24, 2014, http://www.raymondibrahim.com/2014/03/24/western-ignorance-of-the-conditions-of-omar/.

35. Mark Steyn, "The Humiliation," Steyn Online, January 14, 2016, http://www.steynonline.com/7420/the-humiliation.

36. Baron Bodissey, "Groped and Molested in the Hauptbahnhof," Gates of Vienna, January 4, 2016, http://gatesofvienna.net/2016/01/groped-and-molested-in-the-hauptbahnhof/#more-38340.

37. Denis MacEoin, "The Spreading Scent of Cologne," Gatestone Institute, January 26, 2016, http://www.gatestoneinstitute.org/7285/scent-of-cologne.

38. Robert Spencer, "UK Waterpark Bans Bikinis, Orders Visitors to Wear 'Islamically Appropriate' Clothes," Jihad Watch, June 14, 2015, https://www.jihadwatch.org/2015/06/uk-waterpark-bans-bikinis-orders-visitors-to-wear-islamically-appropriate-clothes.

39. "Turn empty Catholic churches into mosques, French Muslim leader says," *RT*, June 15, 2015. https://www.rt.com/news/267358-churches-france-turn-mosques/.

40. Spencer, "UK waterpark Bans Bikinis."

41. RT, "Turn empty Catholic churches into mosques."

42. "Rising anti-Semitism forces Jews out of Paris suburbs," *The Local France,* May 31, 2016, http://www.thelocal.fr/20160531/french-jews-flee-paris-suburbs-over-rising-anti-semitism.

43. Giulio Meotti, "Europe: Allah Takes Over Churches, Synagogues," Gatestone Institute, May 22, 2016, http://www.gatestoneinstitute.org/8005/europe-mosques-churches-synagogues.

44. Soeren Kern, "The Islamization of France in 2015," Gatestone Institute, January 19, 2016, http://www.gatestoneinstitute.org/7256/france-islamization.

45. Peter Kreeft, *Ecumenical Jihad: Ecumenism and the Culture War*, new enlarged ed. (South Bend: St. Augustine's Press, 2016).

46. Dinesh D'Souza, *The Enemy at Home: The Cultural Left and Its Responsibility for 9/11* (New York: Broadway, 2007).

47. E. Michael Jones, *Culture Jihad in Tehran* (South Bend: Fidelity Press, 2013), https://www.amazon.com/Culture-Jihad-Tehran-Michael-Jones-ebook/dp/B00BUV1Q88/ref=sr_1_37?s=books&ie=UTF8&qid=146471514 6&sr=1-37&keywords=E.+Michael+Jones.

48. "Cardinal Timothy Dolan Tells Muslims 'We Love God and He Is the Same God,'" *The Christian Post*, June 19, 2013, http://www.christianpost.com/news/cardinal-timothy-dolan-tells-muslims-we-love-god-and-he-is-the-same-god-98359/.

49. Robert P. George, "Muslims, Our Natural Allies," *First Things*, February 2, 2014, http://www.firstthings.com/blogs/firstthoughts/2014/02/muslims-our-natural-allies.

50. Nonie Darwish, *Cruel and Usual Punishment* (Nashville: Thomas Nelson Publishing, 2008).

51. George, "Muslims, Our Natural Allies."

52. Jane Kramer, "Taking the Veil," *The New Yorker*, November 22, 2004, http://www.newyorker.com/magazine/2004/11/22/taking-the-veil.

53. Serge Trifkovic, *Defeating Jihad: How the War on Terror May Yet Be Won, in Spite of Ourselves* (Salisbury: Regina Orthodox Press, 2006), 69.

54. Olivier Guitta, "Why France is right about the burqa," Reuters, March 2, 2010, http://blogs.reuters.com/faithworld/2010/03/02/opinion-why-france-is-right-about-the-burqa/.

55. George, "Muslims, Our Natural Allies."

56. Darwish, *Now They Call Me Infidel*, 80.

57. Wafa Sultan, *A God Who Hates: The Courageous Woman Who Inflamed the Muslim World Speaks Out Against the Evils of Islam* (New York: St. Martin's Griffin Press, 2011), 13.

58. Keller, *Reliance of the Traveller*.

59. George, "Muslims, Our Natural Allies."

60. Jack Moore, "U.N. Condemns Iran For Increase in Child Brides as Young as 10," *Newsweek*, February 5, 2016, http://www.newsweek.com/un-condemns-iran-increase-child-brides-young-10-423435.

61. "Iran lawmakers pass bill allowing men to marry adopted daughters," The *Guardian*, September 26, 2013. http://www.theguardian.com/world/2013/sep/26/iran-lawmakers-men-wed-adopted-daughters.

62. George, "Muslims, Our Natural Allies."

63. "American Muslims Overwhelmingly Backed Obama," *Newsweek*, November 6, 2008, http://www.newsweek.com/american-muslims-overwhelmingly-backed-obama-85173.

64. Bob Unruh, "Guess who U.S. Muslims are Voting for," WND, October 30, 2012, http://www.wnd.com/2012/10/guess-who-u-s-muslims-are-voting-for/.

65. Art Moore, "Did CAIR founder Say Islam to Rule America?," WND, December 11, 2006, http://www.wnd.com/2006/12/39229/.

Chapter 5: The Quiet Kind of Jihad

1. Matthew Holehouse, "Trojan Horse Plot Driven by Same 'Warped' Islamic Extremism as Boko Haram, Says Tony Blair," *The Daily Telegraph*, June 15, 2014, http://www.telegraph.co.uk/education/education-news/10900955/Trojan-Horse-plot-driven-by-same-warped-Islamic-extremism-as-Boko-Harams-says-Tony-Blair.html.

2. Katie Strick, and Ben Wilkinson, "Oxford University Press Bans Sausages and Pigs from Children's Books in Effort 'to Avoid Offence': Bizarre Clampdown Branded 'Nonsensical Political Correctness,'" *Daily Mail*, January 13, 2015, http://www.dailymail.co.uk/news/article-2908910/Oxford-University-Press-bans-sausages-pigs-children-s-books-avoid-offending-Jews-Muslims.html#ixzz47n7mLAMz.

3. Jane Harley, "No, we haven't banned books on pigs—but sensitivity is key in global publishing," *The Guardian*, January 15, 2015,http://www.theguardian.com/commentisfree/2015/jan/15/books-pigs-global-publishing-oxford-university-press-children.

4. Max Kutner, "Meet Farid Benyettou, The Man Who Trained Paris Attack Suspect Cherif Kouachi," *Newsweek*, January 8, 2015, http://www.newsweek.com/meet-farid-benyettou-man-who-trained-paris-attack-suspect-cherif-kouachi-298028.

5. John Leicester, "Inside the Grande Borne: A Lawless, Concrete Labyrinth where Paris Terrorist Amedy Coulibaly Grew Up," *National Post*, January 19, 2015, http://news.nationalpost.com/news/inside-the-grande-borne-a-lawless-concrete-labyrinth-where-paris-terrorist-amedy-coulibaly-grew-up.

6. Alissa J. Rubin, "The Arrest of Salah Abdeslam, a Paris Suspect, Ends Manhunt, Not Questions," *New York Times*, March 21, 2016, http://www.nytimes.com/2016/03/22/world/europe/arrest-salah-abdeslam-paris-suspect.html?_r=0.

7. "DOJ: CAIR's Unindicted Co-Conspirator Status Legit," IPT News, March 12, 2010, http://www.investigativeproject.org/1854/doj-cairs-unindicted-co-conspirator-status-legit.

8. Mauro, "UAE Doubles Down on Designation of CAIR as Terrorists."

9. Stephen Coughlin, *Catastrophic Failure: Blindfolding America in the Face of Jihad* (Washington, D.C.: Center for Security Policy Press, 2015), 164–68.

10. Patrick Poole, "A Detailed Look at the 'Purge' of U.S. Counter-Terrorism Training by the Obama administration," *The Blaze TV*, March 26, 2014, http://www.theblaze.com/blog/2014/03/26/a-detailed-look-at-the-purge-of-u-s-counter-terrorism-training-by-the-obama-administration/. See also Nick Short, "Muslim Brotherhood Controls Our National Security from the Inside," Western Journalism, September 21, 2015. http://www.westernjournalism.com/muslim-brotherhood-controls-our-national-security-from-the-inside/.

11. Robert Spencer, "Vermont: Restaurant Ad for Bacon Removed After Muslim Claimed It Offended Her," Jihad Watch, August 23, 2014, https://www.jihadwatch.org/2014/08/vermont-restaurant-ad-for-bacon-removed-after-muslim-claimed-it-offended-her.

12. "Recep Tayyip Erdogan: Turkey's ruthless president," BBC, May 5, 2016, http://www.bbc.com/news/world-europe-13746679.

13. President Obama, Twitter post, September 16, 2015, 9:58 a.m., https://twitter.com/potus/status/644193755814342656?lang=en.

14. Robert Spencer, "Cambridge Public Library Hosts 'Stand with Ahmed and Build Your Own Clock Day,'" Jihad Watch, October 19, 2015, https://www.jihadwatch.org/2015/10/cambridge-public-library-hosts-stand-with-ahmed-and-build-your-own-clock-day.

15. Anthony, "Reverse Engineering Ahmed Mohamed's Clock. . .and Ourselves," Art Voice, September 17, 2015, http://blogs.artvoice.com/techvoice/2015/09/17/reverse-engineering-ahmed-mohameds-clock-and-ourselves/.

16. Ben Shapiro, "The Real Story of #IStandwithAhmed," Breitbart, September 18, 2015, http://www.breitbart.com/big-government/2015/09/18/real-story-istandwithahmed/.

17. John Lott, "On Ahmed's Clock, President Obama Once Again Spoke Too Soon," Daily Caller, September 28, 2015, http://dailycaller.com/2015/09/28/on-ahmeds-clock-president-obama-once-again-spoke-too-soon/.

18. Pamela Geller, "Clockmeister Ahmed Mohamed's Sister Was Once Suspended from School for Threatening to Blow It Up," Family Security Matters, September 24, 2015, http://www.familysecuritymatters.org/publications/detail/clockmeister-ahmed-mohameds-sister-was-once-suspended-from-school-for-threatening-to-blow-it-up?f=must_reads.

19. Mark Steyn, "Get Lost, You Palace Guard Creeps," Steyn Online, September 19, 2015, http://www.steynonline.com/7188/get-lost-you-palace-guard-creep.

20. Shapiro, "The Real Story."

21. F. Peter Brown, "'Clock Boy' Ahmed's Father Just Got Caught Making a Stunning Claim about His Son's Clock Incident," Western Journalism, October 16, 2015, http://www.westernjournalism.com/clock-boy-ahmeds-father-just-got-caught-making-a-stunning-claim-about-his-sons-clock-incident/.

22. Kim Bellware, "Here's What Ahmed Mohamed Has Been Up to since His Clock Arrest," Huffington Post, October 18, 2015, http://www.huffingtonpost.com/entry/ahmed-mohamed-white-house_us_56239e6ae4b0bce34701009e.

23. Christopher Brennan and Ashley Collman, "'Clock Kid' Ahmed Mohamed Announces He Is Accepting Scholarship to Attend School in Qatar after Meeting Obama at White House," Daily Mail, October 20, 2015, http://www.dailymail.co.uk/news/article-3281836/Clock-Kid-Ahmed-Mohamed-announces-accepting-scholarship-attend-school-Qatar-meeting-Obama-White-House.html.

24. M. Zuhdi Jasser, "Exposing the 'Flying Imams,'" Middle East Quarterly 15:1 (Winter 2008): 3–11, http://www.meforum.org/1809/exposing-the-flying-imams.

25. Neil Munro, "Obama's 'Cool Clock' Muslim Boy Gets Award from Jihad-Tied CAIR," Breitbart, October 19, 2015, http://www.breitbart.com/big-government/2015/10/19/obamas-cool-clock-muslim-boy-gets-award-jihad-tied-cair/.

26. Jasser, "Exposing the 'Flying Imams.'"

27. Mark Steyn, "The Clock Ticks On," Steyn Online, October 20,2015, http://www.steynonline.com/7244/the-clock-ticks-on.

28. Robert Spencer, "The Implications of the Dismissal of Stephen Coughlin, Joint Staff, Pentagon," Jihad Watch, January 12, 2008, https://www.jihadwatch.org/2008/01/the-implications-of-the-dismissal-of-stephen-coughlin-joint-staff-pentagon.

29. Diana West, American Betrayal: The Secret Assault on Our Nation's Character (New York: St. Martin's, 2013), 10.

30. "Gen. Petraeus Dressed in Tribal Robes"—Yahoo Image Search Results, https://images.search.yahoo.com/search/images;_ylt=AwrBT9XqnFBXc WcAKrpXNyoA;_ylu=X3oDMTEyaHZjYzhtBGNvbG8DYmYxBHBvcwM xBHZ0aWQDQjE4NzlfMQRzZWMDc2M-?p=Gen.+Petraeous+Dressed+I n+Tribal+Robes&fr=mcafee.

31. "New Army Manual Orders Soldiers Not to Criticize Taliban," Judicial Watch, December 11, 2012, http://www.judicialwatch.org/blog/2012/12/ new-army-manual-orders-soldiers-not-to-criticize-taliban/.

32. Spencer, "The Implications of the Dismissal of Stephen Coughlin."

33. Catherine Herridge and Pamela Browne, "FBI tracked radical American cleric to Defense Dept. lunch, documents show," Fox News, September 12, 2013, http://www.foxnews.com/politics/2013/09/12/fbi-tracked-radical-american-cleric-to-defense-dept-lunch-documents-show.html.

34. Spencer, *Arab Winter Comes to America*, 9.

35. Ibid., 9–11.

36. "Ft Hood Report: FBI missed 'ticking time bomb,'" CBS News, February 3, 2011, http://www.cbsnews.com/news/ft-hood-report-fbi-missed-ticking-time-bomb/.

37. Spencer, *Arab Winter Comes to America*, 27–28.

38. Beenish Ahmed, "Why Converts To Islam Are So Susceptible To Becoming Terrorists," Think Progress, FEB 3, 2016, http:// thinkprogress.org/world/2016/02/03/3743136/muslim-converts/.

39. Greg Miller, "At CIA, A Convert to Islam Leads the Terrorism Hunt," *Washington Post,* March 24, 2012, https://www.washingtonpost.com/ world/national-security/at-cia-a-convert-to-islam-leads-the-terrorism-hunt/2012/03/23/gIQA2mSqYS_story.html.

40. Andrew C. McCarthy, "Competing Visions In "Palestine," *National Review*, January 5, 2011, http://www.nationalreview.com/ corner/256392/competing-visions-palestine-andrew-c-mccarthy.

41. Colin Moynihan, "A New York City Settlement on Surveillance of Muslims," *The New Yorker*, January 7, 2016, http://www.newyorker.com/ news/news-desk/a-new-york-city-settlement-on-surveillance-of-muslims.

42. Nancy Cordes, "Michele Bachman Refuses to Back Down on Claims about Huma Abedin," CBS News, July 19, 2012, http://www.cbsnews.com/news/ michele-bachmann-refuses-to-back-down-on-claims-about-huma-abedin/.

43. Kellan Howell, "'I'll see you guys in New York,' ISIS terror leader told U.S. troops in 2009," *Washington Times*, June 14, 2014, http://www. washingtontimes.com/news/2014/jun/14/ill-see-you-guys-new-york-abu-bakr-al-baghdadis-pa/.

44. Paul McLeary, "U.S. Resuming F-16, Tank Shipments to Egypt," Foreign Policy, March 31, 2015, http://foreignpolicy.com/2015/03/31/us-f-16-arms-abrams-shipments-egypt/.

45. Remarks by the president to the UN General Assembly, September 25, 2012, https://www.whitehouse.gov/the-press-office/2012/09/25/remarks-president-un-general-assembly.

46. Eric Trager, "Obama Wrecked U.S.-Egypt Ties," National Interest, April 8, 2015, http://nationalinterest.org/feature/obama-wrecked-us-egypt-ties-12573.

47. Ryan J. Reilly, "DOJ Official: Holder 'Firmly Committed' To Eliminating Anti-Muslim Training," Talking Points Memo, October 19, 2011, http://talkingpointsmemo.com/muckraker/doj-official-holder-firmly-committed-to-eliminating-anti-muslim-training.

48. Coughlin, Catastrophic Failure.

49. Ibid., 66.

50. Ibid., 164–69.

51. Ibid., 17, 402–5.

52. Ibid., 12–13, 465–72. Coughlin himself was removed from his Pentagon post when his research findings conflicted with the views of Muslim "experts."

53. Ibid., 17, 21, 337.

54. Ibid., 21. See also "Letter to DHS John Brennan on FBI's Use of Biased Experts and Training Materials," Muslim Advocates, October 19, 2011, https://www.muslimadvocates.org/letter-to-dhs-john-brennan-on-fbis-use-of-biased-experts-and-training-materials/.

55. Timmerman, "Obama Administration Pulls References to Islam From Terror Training Materials, Official Say."

56. Coughlin, 21.

57. Ibid., 408–16, 497.

58. Tim Kane, "Why Our Best Officers Are Leaving," The Atlantic, January/February 2011, http://www.theatlantic.com/magazine/archive/2011/01/why-our-best-officers-are-leaving/308346/.

59. General S. K. Malik quoted in Coughlin, 135.

60. Coughlin, Ibid., 135.

61. Ibid.

62. Ibid., 522.

63. Muhammad Shafiq and Mohammed Abu-Nimer, Interfaith Dialogue: A Guide for Muslims, quoted in Coughlin, 521, 532.

64. Coughlin, Ibid., 521, 543.

Chapter 6: Immigration and the "Baby Jihad"

1.   Sam Solomon and Elias Al-Maqdisi, *Modern Day Trojan Horse: Al-Hijra, the Islamic Doctrine of Immigration, Accepting Freedom or Imposing Islam?* (Afton: Advancing Native Missions, 2009).

2.   Mark Steyn, "No Man's Land," *Free Republic*, June 18, 2007, http://www.freerepublic.com/focus/f-news/1855177/posts.

3.   Soeren Kern, "Muslim Voters Change Europe," Gatestone Institute, May 17, 2012, http://www.gatestoneinstitute.org/3064/muslim-voters-europe.

4.   Robert Spencer, "Robert Spencer in FrontPage: Muslim Elected Mayor of London," Jihad Watch, May 9, 2016, https://www.jihadwatch.org/2016/05/robert-spencer-in-frontpage-muslim-elected-mayor-of-london.

5.   Geert Wilders, *Marked for Death: Islam's War Against the West and Me* (Washington, D.C.: Regnery, 2012), 162.

6.   Adrian Michaels, "Muslim Europe: the Demographic Time Bomb Transforming Our Continent," *Daily Telegraph*, last modified August 8, 2009, http://www.telegraph.co.uk/news/worldnews/europe/5994047/Muslim-Europe-the-demographic-time-bomb-transforming-our-continent.html.

7.   "Violent Muslim Protest Outside the Danish Embassy in London," YouTube video, posted by "makesyoumadd" on March 11, 2008, https://www.youtube.com/watch?v=qoMeUcC_M20.

8.   Peter Hitchens, "We Won't Save Refugees by Destroying Our Own Country," *The Daily Mail*, September 5, 2015, http://www.dailymail.co.uk/debate/article-3223828/PETER-HITCHENS-won-t-save-refugees-destroying-country.html.

9.   Robert Spencer, "Netherlands: Muslims Assault Elderly Jews, Authorities Searching for Motive," Jihad Watch, last modified September 6, 2015, https://www.jihadwatch.org/2015/09/netherlands-muslims-assault-elderly-jews-authorities-searching-for-motive.

10.   Soerne Kern, "Germany: Migrants' Rape Epidemic," Gatestone Institute, last modified September 18, 2015, http://www.gatestoneinstitute.org/6527/migrants-rape-germany.

11.   Elise Harris, "Strong Words From the Vatican as Migrant Crisis Spikes Worldwide," Catholic News Agency, last modified September 3, 2015, http://www.catholicnewsagency.com/news/strong-words-from-the-vatican-as-migrant-crisis-spikes-worldwide-65943/.

12. Soeren Kern, "European Concerns over Muslim Immigration go Mainstream," Gatestone Institute, August 15, 2011, http://www.gatestoneinstitute.org/2349/european-concerns-muslim-immigration; Kern, "Turks in Germany: The Guests Take over the House," Gatestone Institute, November 7, 2011, http://www.gatestoneinstitute.org/2566/turks-germany-guests-take-over-house.

13. "Child Sex abuse gangs could have assaulted one million youngsters in the UK," *Mirror*, February 5, 2015, http://www.mirror.co.uk/news/uk-news/child-sex-abuse-gangs-could-5114029.

14. Brendan James, "European Refugee Crisis 2015: 50% Of Asylum-Seekers Landing In Europe Are Syrian, UN Report Finds", *International Business Times*, September 6, 2015, http://www.ibtimes.com/european-refugee-crisis-2015-50-asylum-seekers-landing-europe-are-syrian-un-report-2084862; "Here's the One Fact that Dismantles the 'Syrian refugee myth,'" *The Political Insider,* September 8, 2015, http://www.thepoliticalinsider.com/heres-one-fact-dismantles-syrian-refugee-myth/.

15. Pat Condell, "The Invasion of Europe," last modified September 28, 2015, http://www.patcondell.net/the-invasion-of-europe/.

16. Adam Withnall, "Saudi Arabia Offers Germany 200 Mosques—One for Every 100 refugees Who Arrived Last Weekend," *The Independent*, September 10, 2015, http://www.independent.co.uk/news/world/europe/saudi-arabia-offers-germany-200-mosques-one-for-every-100-refugees-who-arrived-last-weekend-10495082.html.

17. Chase Winter, "Arab Monarchies Turn Down Syrian Refugees Over Security Threat," *Deutsche Welle*, January 25, 2016, http://www.dw.com/en/arab-monarchies-turn-down-syrian-refugees-over-security-threat/a-19002873.

18. "The Future of the Global Muslim Population: Region: Europe," Pew Research Center, January 27, 2011, http://www.pewforum.org/2011/01/27/future-of-the-global-muslim-population-regional-europe/.

19. Nick Gutteridge, "True Toll of Merkel's Open Door Migration Revealed: Germany Received TWO MILLION Migrants," *Daily Express*, last modified March 21, 2016, http://www.express.co.uk/news/world/654402/Another-blow-for-Merkel-Germany-sees-highest-levels-of-immigration-since-Second-World-War.

20. Daniel Greenfield, "Muslim in UK Threatens to Stab Son, Tells Court He Didn't Know It was Illegal," *FrontPage Magazine*, last modified September 15, 2015, http://www.frontpagemag.com/point/260109/muslim-uk-threatens-stab-son-tells-court-he-didnt-daniel-greenfield.

21. Jack Sommers, "Steve Emerson, Fox News 'Muslim Only Birmingham' Commentator, Defends His Record," Huffington Post, December 1, 2015, http://www.huffingtonpost.co.uk/2015/01/12/fox-news-steve-emerson_n_6457444.html.

22. Erik Wemple, "Fox News Corrects, Apologizes for 'No-Go Zone' Remarks," *Washington Post*, January 18, 2015, https://www.washingtonpost.com/blogs/erik-wemple/wp/2015/01/18/fox-news-corrects-apologizes-for-no-go-zone-remarks/.

23. Robert Spencer, "Paris Mayor Says She Will Sue Fox News Over No-Go Zones Coverage," Jihad Watch, January 20, 2015, https://www.jihadwatch.org/2015/01/paris-mayor-says-she-will-sue-fox-news-over-no-go-zones-coverage.

24. Soeren Kern, "European 'No-Go' Zones: Fact or Fiction? Part 2: Britain," Gatestone Institute, February 3, 2015, http://www.gatestoneinstitute.org/5177/no-go-zones-britain.

25. "Système d'information géographique de la politique de la ville," http://sig.ville.gouv.fr/Atlas/ZUS/.

26. Kern, "European 'No-Go' Zones."

27. Kern, "The Islamization of France in 2015," Gatestone Institute, January 19, 2016, http://www.gatestoneinstitute.org/7256/france-islamization; Oren Liebermann, "Au revoir and shalom: Jews leave France in record numbers," CNN, January 25, 2016, http://www.cnn.com/2016/01/22/middleeast/france-israel-jews-immigration/.

28. Kern, "European 'No-Go' Zones."

29. Mark Howarth, "The changing face of Britain: A child in Birmingham is now more likely to be a Muslim than Christian," *Daily Mail*, September 14, 2014, http://www.dailymail.co.uk/news/article-2755654/The-changing-face-Britain-A-child-Birmingham-likely-Muslim-Christian.html.

30. Ibid.

31. Jemma Buckley, "Birmingham Faces Changes with More Muslim Children than Christian," *Birmingham Post*, September 21, 2014, http://www.birminghampost.co.uk/news/local-news/birmingham-faces-changes-more-muslim-7800883.

32. Hitchens, "We won't save refugees by destroying our own country."

33. Robert Spencer, "Hungarian PM: 'Europe is not free. Because freedom begins with speaking the truth,'" Jihad Watch, March 19, 2016, https://www.jihadwatch.org/2016/03/hungarian-pm-europe-is-not-free-because-freedom-begins-with-speaking-the-truth.

34. Danusha V. Goska, "Western Europeans vs. Eastern European Responses to Mass, Unvetted, Muslim Immigration," *FrontPage Magazine*, last modified September 15, 2015, http://www.frontpagemag.com/fpm/260120/western-european-vs-eastern-european-responses-danusha-v-goska.

35. Barry Shaw, "Solving the European Migrant Problem," Gatestone Institute, September 13, 2015, http://www.gatestoneinstitute.org/6491/european-migrant-problem.

36. "Qaradawi Says Hitler Was Divine Punishment For Jews," The Global Muslim Brotherhood Daily Watch, last modified February 3, 2009, http://www.globalmbwatch.com/2009/02/03/qaradawi-says-hitler-was-divine-punishment-for-jews/.

37. ADL Global 100 Map, http://global100.adl.org/.

38. Vijeta Uniyal, "Germany's Appeasement of Radical Islam,"Gatestone Institute, September 10, 2015, http://www.gatestoneinstitute.org/6466/germany-radical-islam.

39. Soeren Kern, "Germany: Muslims Exempt from School Trips to Holocaust Sites?" Gatestone Institute, June 10, 2015, http://www.gatestoneinstitute.org/5929/germany-muslims-holocaust-education.

40. Jonathan Schanzer, "Hitler's 'Grossmufti von Jerusalem,'" *The Jerusalem Post*, September 4, 2008, http://www.jpost.com/Arts-and-Culture/Books/Hitlers-Grossmufti-von-Jerusalem.

41. Wilders, *Marked for Death*, 162.

42. Raymond Ibrahim, "Islam's 'Baby Jihad,'" *FrontPage Magazine*, June 11, 2015, http://www.frontpagemag.com/fpm/258300/islams-baby-jihad-raymond-ibrahim.

43. William Kilpatrick, *Christianity, Islam and Atheism: The Struggle for The Soul of The West*, 6.

44. "Latest survey finds 25% of French Teenagers are Muslim," The Briefing Room, March 14, 2016, http://www.gopbriefingroom.com/index.php?topic=198694.0; "French City with 40% Muslim population is the most dangerous city in Europe," *FrontPage Magazine*, January 4,

2014, http://www.frontpagemag.com/point/214086/french-city-40-muslim-population-most-dangerous-daniel-greenfield; "Antwerp: 40% of elementary school students are Muslim," Islam in Europe, October 14, 2009, http://islamineurope.blogspot.com/2009/10/antwerp-40-of-elementary-school.html; Vincent Cooper, "The Islamic future of Britain," *The Commentator*, June 13, 2013, http://www.thecommentator.com/article/3770/the_islamic_future_of_britain.

45. Mark Steyn, "It's Still the Demography, Stupid," Steyn Online, January 19, 2016, http://www.steynonline.com/7428/it-still-the-demography-stupid.

46. Anthony Watts, "Tipping Points and Beliefs—the 10% Solution," WUWT, July 27, 2011, https://wattsupwiththat.com/2011/07/27/tipping-points-and-beliefs/.

47. Ibrahim, "Islam's 'Baby Jihad.'"

48. Mark Steyn, "Belated Alarums," Steyn Online, October 2, 2014, http://www.steynonline.com/6583/belated-alarums.

49. Daniel Greenfield, "Muslim Convert Beheads 82-Year-Old Woman W/ Machete In London," *FrontPage Magazine*, September 4, 2014, http://www.frontpagemag.com/point/240295/muslim-convert-beheads-82-year-old-woman-wmachete-daniel-greenfield.

50. Victoria Ward, "Jihadi John's Victims: Who Were They?" *Telegraph*, November 13, 2015, http://www.telegraph.co.uk/news/worldnews/islamic-state/11992798/Jihadi-Johns-victims-who-were-they.html.

51. Sophia Rosenbaum, "Terrorists Foiled in Plot to Kill Queen Elizabeth," *New York Post*, November 7, 2014, http://nypost.com/2014/11/07/plot-to-assassinate-queen-elizabeth-thwarted-by-bobbies/.

52. Darwish, *Now They Call Me Infidel,* 91.

53. Ibid., 74; and Darwish, *Cruel and Usual Punishment*, 79.

54. Cheryl K. Chumley, "Afghan Parliament Upholds Right to Marry Children," *Washington Times*, June 10, 2013, http://www.washingtontimes.com/news/2013/jun/10/afghan-parliament-upholds-right-marry-children/.

55. Steven Erlanger, "Blaming Policy, Not Islam, for Belgium's Radicalized Youth," *New York Times*, April 7, 2016, http://mobile.nytimes.com/2016/04/08/world/europe/belgium-brussels-islam-radicalization.html?mabReward=CTM&_r=3&referer=http://www.breitbart.com/london/2016/04/11/majority-of-muslim-students-think-brussels-terrorists-are-heroes-say-teachers/.

56. Baron Bodissey, "Faced With ISIS, These Italian Students Would Convert to Islam," Gates of Vienna, April 1, 2016, http://gatesofvienna.net/2016/04/faced-with-isis-these-italian-students-would-convert-to-islam/.

57. Ibid.

Chapter 7: Western Enablers of Jihad

1. Adam Kredo, "Iran: 'American Sailors Started Crying After Arrest,'" *Washington Free Beacon,* January 16, 2016, http://freebeacon.com/national-security/iran-american-sailors-started-crying-after-arrest/.

2. Kilpatrick, *Christianity, Islam and Atheism: The Struggle for The Soul of The West*, 81.

3. Soeren Kern, "Belfast Pastor on Trial for Offending Islam," Gatestone Institute, August 18, 2015, http://www.gatestoneinstitute.org/6356/pastor-james-mcconnell-islam.

4. Robert Spencer, "Quebec N=Bill Targets 'People Who Write Against the Islamic Religion,'" Jihad Watch, August 15, 2015, https://www.jihadwatch.org/2015/08/quebec-bill-targets-people-who-write-against-the-islamic-religion.

5. Suzanne Breen, "It's Not Only Pastor McConnell in The Dock, Freedom of Speech Is There As Well," *Belfast Telegraph*, June 8, 2015, http://www.belfasttelegraph.co.uk/opinion/news-analysis/its-not-only-pastor-mcconnell-in-the-dock-freedom-of-speech-is-there-as-well-31430397.html.

6. Kern, "Belfast Pastor on Trial."

7. "Mosul Most Peaceful City in World, Claims Belfast Muslim," BBC, January 10, 2015, http://www.bbc.com/news/uk-northern-ireland-30753698.

8. Kyle Shideler, "Quebec's Proposed Imposition of Blasphemy Laws Will Affect Us All," *Townhall*, Aug 28, 2015, http://townhall.com/columnists/kyleshideler/2015/08/28/quebecs-proposed-imposition-of-blasphemy-laws-will-affect-us-all-n2045062.

9. Dale Hurd, "Marked for Death: One Man's 10-Year War with Islam," CBN News, October 29, 2014, http://www1.cbn.com/cbnnews/world/2014/October/Marked-for-Death-One-Mans-10-Yr-War-with-Islam.

10. Baron Bodissey, "Geert Wilders in the Dock: 'Freedom of Speech is the Only Freedom I Still Have,'" Gates of Vienna, March 19, 2016, http://gatesofvienna.net/2016/03/geert-wilders-in-the-dock-freedom-of-speech-is-the-only-freedom-i-still-have/.

11. Kern, "Belfast Pastor on Trial for Offending Islam."

12. Christopher Howse, "The Christians who call God 'Allah,'" *Daily Telegraph*, January 30, 2010, http://www.telegraph.co.uk/comment/columnists/christopherhowse/7110855/The-Christians-who-call-God-Allah.html.

13. Mark Steyn, "Checkpoint Charlie Hebdo," Steyn Online, January 8, 2016, http://www.steynonline.com/7407/checkpoint-charlie-hebdo.

14. Kilpatrick, *Christianity, Islam, and Atheism*, 176.

15. Steyn, "Checkpoint Charlie Hebdo."

16. "German Police Fire Water Cannons at PEGIDA Protesters In Cologne," RT, January 9, 2016, https://www.rt.com/news/328379-police-pegida-cologne-rally/.

17. Robert Spencer, "Germany: 17,500 march against Islamization, sing Christmas carols; lawmakers and media smear them as 'pinstripe Nazis,'" Jihad Watch, December 24, 2014, https://www.jihadwatch.org/2014/12/germany-17500-march-against-islamization-sing-christmas-carols-lawmakers-and-media-smear-them-as-pinstripe-nazis.

18. Bodissey, "Totalitarian Britain and Political Dissident Tommy Robinson," Gates of Vienna, January 15, 2016, http://gatesofvienna.net/2016/01/totalitarian-britain-and-political-dissident-tommy-robinson/#more-38465.

19. Baron Bodissey, "A brief history of the transatlantic counterjihad, Part VI," Gates of Vienna, November 30, 2011, http://gatesofvienna.net/2011/11/a-brief-history-of-the-transatlantic-counterjihad-part-vi/; Bodissey, "The German Awakening," Gates of Vienna, December 22, 2014, http://gatesofvienna.net/2014/12/the-german-awakening/.

20. Shaun Waterman, "Benghazi Scapegoat Remains in Prison for Film," *Washington Times*, May 13, 2013, http://www.washingtontimes.com/news/2013/may/13/benghazi-scapegoat-filmmaker-remains-prison/.

21. Allen West, "Six (Only Six?) Examples Obama Is Purposely Enabling the Islamist Cause," Allen B. West: Steadfast and Loyal, August 13, 2014, " http://www.allenbwest.com/allen/six-six-examples-obama-purposefully-enabling-islamist-cause.

22. Ibid.

23. Suzi Parker, "Hillary: It'll Take More Than Tomatoes to Rattle Her," *Washington* Post, July 16, 2012, https://www.washingtonpost.com/blogs/she-the-people/post/hillary-clinton-in-egypt-pelted-with-tomatoes-and-taunts-of-monica/2012/07/16/gJQA8E7HpW_blog.html.

24. Emet m'Tsiyon. "Egyptians Charge Obama with Supporting Terrorists—They're Right," Zion Truth, July 31, 2013, http://ziontruth. blogspot.com/2013/07/not-everybody-would-like-to-agree-that.html.

25. John Rossomando, "Egyptian Magazine: Muslim Brotherhood Infiltrates Obama Administration," Investigative Project on Terrorism, January 3, 2013, http://www.investigativeproject.org/3869/egyptian-magazine-muslim-brotherhood-infiltrates#.

26. White House Office of the Press Secretary, "Remarks by the President to the UN General Assembly," The White House, September 25, 2012, https://www.whitehouse.gov/the-press-office/2012/09/25/remarks-president-un-general-assembly.

27. Patrick Poole, "A Detailed Look at 'the Purge' of U.S. Counterterror Training by the Obama Administration," The Blaze, March 26, 2014, http://www.theblaze.com/blog/2014/03/26/a-detailed-look-at-the-purge-of-u-s-counter-terrorism-training-by-the-obama-administration/; Essam Abdallah (with an introductory note by Steven Emmerson), "Islamist Lobbies' Washington War on Arab and Muslim Liberals," The Investigative Project on Terrorism, February 16, 2012, http://www. investigativeproject.org/3453/islamist-lobbies-washington-war-on-arab#.

28. Sharona Schwartz, "Egyptian Newspaper's Explosive Allegation: President Obama Is a Secret Muslim Brotherhood Member," The Blaze, September 3, 2013, http://www.theblaze.com/stories/2013/09/03/egyptian-newspapers-explosive-allegation-president-obama-is-a-secret-muslim-brotherhood-member/.

29. Melanie Phillips, *Londonistan*, revised ed. (New York: Encounter Books, 2007), xviii.

30. Ibid, 62–63.

31. Associated Press, "British PM launches 5-year anti-extremism plan," CBS News, July 19, 2015, http://www.cbsnews.com/news/british-pm-launches-5-year-anti-extremism-plan/.

32. Robert Spencer, *Religion of Peace?: Why Christianity Is and Islam Isn't* (Washington, D.C.: Regnery Publishing, 2007), 3.

33. James Slack, Jason Groves, and Ian Drury, "ISIS Plot to Use Cyber-Jihadists to Bring Down Airliners and Target UK's Nuclear Power Stations and Hospitals," *Daily Mail*, November 15, 2015, http://www. dailymail.co.uk/news/article-3321369/Cyber-jihadis-threat-UK-jets-hospitals-Ministers-issue-new-terror-alert-police-probe-600-plots-seize-one-suspect-day.html.

34. Baron Bodissey, "Who Rules Melbourne?" Gates of Vienna, July 21, 2015, http://gatesofvienna.net/2015/07/who-rules-melbourne/#more-36865.

35. "REVEALED! READ the FULL DISTURBING BLOG POSTS of Muslim Jihadi Terrorist Muhammad Youssef Abdulazeez," The Right Scoop, July 17, 2015, http://therightscoop.com/revealed-read-the-full-blog-entries-of-muslim-terrorist-muhammad-youssef-abdulazeez/.

Chapter 8: Information Wars

1. Jason Silverstein, "'American Sniper' Screening Replaced By 'Paddington,' but then Brought Back, after University Of Michigan Student Protests," *New York Daily News*, last modified April 9, 2015, http://www.nydailynews.com/news/national/american-sniper-screening-sparks-controversy-college-article-1.2178608.

2. Roger Kimball, *The Long March: How the Cultural Revolution of the 1960s Changed America* (New York: Encounter Books, 2000), 9–10.

3. Andy Coghlan, "The reasons why Gaza's population is so young," New Scientist, 1 August 2014, https://www.newscientist.com/article/dn25993-the-reasons-why-gazas-population-is-so-young/.

4. Victor Davis Hanson, "Obama and Revolutionary Romance," *National Review*, April 14, 2015, http://www.nationalreview.com/article/416870/obama-and-revolutionary-romance-victor-davis-hanson.

5. Lisa Daftari, "Islamophobia in action? 'Honor Diaries' Screening Shut Down by CAIR," Fox News, March 31, 2014, http://www.foxnews.com/opinion/2014/03/31/islamophobia-in-action-honor-diaries-screening-shut-down-by-cair.print.html.

6. Robert Spencer, "Eastern Michigan U: Muslims Disrupt 'American Sniper' Showing, Force Cancellation," Jihad Watch, April 15, 2015, https://www.jihadwatch.org/2015/04/eastern-michigan-u-muslims-disrupt-american-sniper-showing-force-cancellation.

7. Rob Crilly, "The Blasphemous Teddy Bear," *Time*, November 26, 2007, http://content.time.com/time/printout/0,8816,1687755,00.html.

8. Jason Burke, "Ayman al-Zawahiri: Al-Qaida's arrogant doctor of death," *The Guardian*, June 18, 2011, http://www.theguardian.com/theobserver/2011/jun/19/ayman-zawahiri-observer-profile.

9. Robert D. McFadden, "Army Doctor Held in Ft. Hood Rampage," *New York Times*, November 5, 2009, http://www.nytimes.com/2009/11/06/us/06forthood.html?rref=collection%2Ftimestopic%2FHasan%2C%20Nidal%20Malik&action=click&contentCollection=timestopics&region=stream&module=stream_unit&version=latest&contentPlacement=130&pgtype=collection.

10. *The Week* Staff, "The ophthalmologist dictator: Syria's Bashar al-Assad," *The Week*, May 27, 2011, http://theweek.com/articles/484476/ophthalmologist-dictator-syrias-bashar-alassad.

11. Andrew Alderson, Ben Leach and Duncan Gardham, "Bilal Abdulla: Doctor by Day, Terrorist by Night—The Secret Life of a New Breed of Terrorist," *Daily Telegraph*, December 20, 2008, http://www.telegraph.co.uk/news/uknews/law-and-order/3867334/Bilal-Abdulla-Doctor-by-day-terrorist-by-night-the-secret-life-of-a-new-breed-of-terrorist.html.

12. Matthew Taylor, "Doctors Accused of Car Bomb Terror Attacks Planned Indiscriminate and Wholesale Murder, Court Told," *The Guardian*, October 9, 2008, https://www.theguardian.com/uk/2008/oct/10/glasgowairporttrial.

13. Leslie Larson, "US Drops in State of Press Rankings: Report," Daily News, Wednesday, February 12, 2014, http://www.nydailynews.com/news/politics/u-s-drops-state-free-press-ranking-report-article-1.1611299.

14. "Four Sentenced in China over Kunming Station Attack," BBC, September 12, 2014, http://www.bbc.com/news/world-asia-china-29170238.

15. Martin Robinson, Mark Duell, and Chris Greenwood, "The Final Insult: Court Terror for Lee Rigby's Family as His Muslim Killers Are Dragged from Dock Shouting 'Allahu Akbar' While Fighting Prison Guards—before Judge Tells Them Life Will NOT Mean Life," *Daily Mail*, February 26 2014, http://www.dailymail.co.uk/news/article-2568317/Justice-Lee-Rigby-Soldiers-family-arrive-court-wearing-matching-t-shirts-act-solidarity-ahead-sentencing-two-Muslim-converts-murdered-him.html.

16. Spencer, *Arab Winter*, 15–16; and Admin, "Lee Rigby Killer Handed Blood-Stained Note to Woolwich Witness, Quotes Qur'an for His Action," *The Muslim Issue*, February 27, 2014, https://themuslimissue.wordpress.com/2014/02/27/lee-rigby-killer-handed-blood-stained-note-to-woolwich-witness/.

17. Melanie McDonagh, "Why Does David Cameron Refuse to Admit That the Terrorist Attack in Nairobi is Linked to Islam?" *The Spectator*, September 23, 2013, http://blogs.spectator.co.uk/2013/09/why-does-david-cameron-refuse-to-admit-that-the-terrorist-attack-in-nairobi-is-linked-to-islam/.

18. Pamela Geller, "Video: Kenya Mall Mass Murderers Take Breaks from Killing to Pray," *The Jewish Press,* October 18, 2012, http://www.jewishpress.com/blogs/atlas-shrugged-blogs/video-kenya-mall-mass-murderers-take-breaks-from-killing-to-pray/2013/10/18/.

19. Paul Sperry, "Could the Kenya Attack Happen Here? It Did," *New York Post*, October 12, 2013, http://nypost.com/2013/10/12/could-the-kenya-mall-attack-ever-happen-here-it-already-did/.

20. Soeren Kern, "The Islamization of France in 2013," Gatestone Institute, January 6, 2014, http://www.gatestoneinstitute.org/4120/islamization-france.

21. "100,000 British women mutilated," *Telegraph*, April 22, 2012, http://www.telegraph.co.uk/news/uknews/crime/9219217/100000-British-women-mutilated.html.

22. Daniel Greenfield, "Media Silent as Muslims Ethnically Cleanse 60,000 Christians in Philippines," *FrontPage Magazine*, September 15, 2013, http://www.frontpagemag.com/point/204227/media-silent-muslims-ethnically-cleanse-60000-daniel-greenfield.

23. Raymond Ibrahim, "U.S. 'chose to stay silent' on Muslim persecution of Christians," Gatestone Institute, February 12, 2014. http://www.gatestoneinstitute.org/4170/us-silent-muslim-persecution-christians.

24. Associated Press, "10-Year Sentence For Ohio Mall Bomb Plot," CBS News, November 27, 2007, http://www.cbsnews.com/news/10-year-sentence-for-ohio-mall-bomb-plot/.

25. David Simpson, "Kenya-Style Mall Attack: Can It Happen Here? Smaller plots have been thwarted," CNN, September 23, 2013, http://www.cnn.com/2013/09/23/us/kenya-mall-safety/.

26. "Feds Say Massachusetts Man Conspired to Help Terrorists," CNN, October 21, 2009, http://www.cnn.com/2009/CRIME/10/21/terrorism.probe/.

27. Kim Murphy, "Man Convicted In Plot to Bomb Oregon Christmas Tree Ceremony," *Los Angeles Times*, January 31, 2013, http://articles.latimes.com/2013/jan/31/nation/la-na-nn-portland-christmas-tree-bomb-20130131.

28. Rhonda Holman,"Terrorism Threat Real, Present," *The Wichita Eagle*, December 15, 2013, http://www.kansas.com/opinion/editorials/article1129692.html.

29. Robert Spencer, "California: National Guardsman, Convert to Islam, Plotted to Bomb LA Subway," Jihad Watch, March 17, 2014, https://www.jihadwatch.org/2014/03/california-national-guardsman-convert-to-islam-plotted-to-bomb-la-subway-arrested-for-trying-to-aid-al-qaeda.

30. Clare M. Lopez, "In Their Own Words," The Counter Jihad Report, February 17, 2014, https://counterjihadreport.com/2014/02/17/in-their-own-words/.

Chapter 9: Christian Enablers of Jihad

1. G. K. Chesterton, *The Flying Inn* (New York: John Lane Company, 1914), 45.

2. "Chrislam," WGCU *Religion & Ethics Newsweekly*, February 13, 2009, http://www.pbs.org/wnet/religionandethics/2009/02/13/february-13-2009-chrislam/2236/.

3. Robert Spencer, "Swedish bishop wants to remove crosses from church and mark direction of Mecca to make it more inviting for Muslims," Jihad Watch, October 4, 2015, https://www.jihadwatch.org/2015/10/swedish-bishop-wants-to-remove-crosses-from-church-and-mark-direction-of-mecca-to-make-it-more-inviting-for-muslims.

4. Oliver J. J. Lane, "World's First Lesbian Bishop Calls for Church to Remove Crosses, to Install Muslim Prayer Space," Breitbart, October 5, 2015, http://www.breitbart.com/london/2015/10/05/worlds-first-lesbian-bishop-calls-church-remove-crosses-install-muslim-prayer-space/.

5. Freddy Mayhew, "Hundreds of Muslims attend weekly prayers at iconic Christian cathedral," *The Independent*, Saturday November 15, 2014, http://www.independent.co.uk/news/world/americas/hundreds-of-muslims-attend-weekly-prayers-at-iconic-christian-cathedral-9862922.html.

6. Robert Spencer, "Church of England bishop says Qur'an should be read at Charles' coronation," Jihad Watch, November 28, 2014, https://www.jihadwatch.org/2014/11/church-of-england-bishop-says-quran-should-be-read-at-charles-coronation.

7. Thomas D. Williams, "Florida Bishop Blames Orlando Massacre on Catholic 'Contempt' for Homosexuality," Breitbart, June 14, 2016, http://www.breitbart.com/big-government/2016/06/14/florida-bishop-blames-orlando-massacre-catholic-contempt-homosexuality/.

8. Rolheiser, "Our Muslim brothers and sisters."

9. "Deborah Weiss exposes Georgetown's Orwellian "Bridges Initiative," The Counter Jihad Report, May 20, 2015, https://counterjihadreport.com/2015/05/20/deborah-weiss-exposes-georgetowns-orwellian-bridges-initiative/.

10. Caryle Murphy, "Saudi Gives $20 Million to Georgetown," *Washington Post*, December 13, 2005, http://www.washingtonpost.com/wp-dyn/content/article/2005/12/12/AR2005121200591.html.

11. Tom Gjelten, "Learning About The Quran…From a Catholic Archbishop" NPR, April 30, 2015, http://www.npr.org/sections/parallels/2015/04/30/403090790/learning-about-the-quran-from-a-catholic-archbishop.

12. Simon Caldwell, "Leader of the German Catholic Church has branded emergence of new xenophobia a 'disgrace,'" *Catholic Herald*, September 7, 2015, http://www.catholicherald.co.uk/news/2015/09/07/german-catholic-church-leader-threatens-to-punch-anyone-making-nazi-salutes-at-migrants/.

13. Yaron Steinbuch, "Pope Francis reneges on offer to take in Christian refugees," *New York Post*, April 22, 2016, http://nypost.com/2016/04/22/pope-francis-reneges-on-offer-to-take-in-christian-refugees/.

14. See, for example, "German crowds, clergy greet asylum seekers," *Washington Post*, September 5, 2015, https://www.washingtonpost.com/posttv/world/german-crowds-clergy-greet-asylum-seekers-with-claps-and-cheers/2015/09/05/d2d79c80-5402-11e5-b225-90edbd49f362_video.html; "Amid criticism, Cardinal Marx supports synod's midterm report," Catholic News Agency, October 17, 2014, http://www.catholicnewsagency.com/news/amid-criticism-cardinal-marx-supports-synods-midterm-report-26962/.

15. Elise Haris, "To welcome a migrant is to welcome God himself, Pope says," Catholic News Agency, October 1, 2015, http://www.catholicnewsagency.com/news/to-welcome-a-migrant-is-to-welcome-god-himself-pope-says-86416/.

16. Marnie Eisenstadt, "Plans to turn a church into a mosque bring pain and hope to changing neighborhood," Syracuse.com, April 6, 2014, http://www.syracuse.com/news/index.ssf/2014/04/muslim_group_can_remove_crosses_from_church_to_make_it_a_mosque.html.

17. Ibid.

18. Ibid.

19. Chesterton, *The Flying Inn*, 29.

20. Ibid., 28.

21. Peter Kreeft, *Between Allah & Jesus: What Christians Can Learn from Muslims* (Downers Grove: InterVarsity Press, 2010), 9.

22. Perry Chiaramonte, "On the brink: Christianity facing Middle East purge within decade, says group," Fox News, November 09, 2015, http://www.foxnews.com/world/2015/11/05/christianity-could-be-completely-erased-from-middle-east-in-less-than-decade.html.

23. Ibrahim Hooper, "Love for Jesus Can Bring Christians, Muslims Together," OnFaith, December 17, 2010, http://www.faithstreet.com/onfaith/2010/12/17/love-for-jesus-can-bring-christians-muslims-together/4285.

24. Pope Paul VI, *Nostra Aetate,* Declaration on the relation of the Church to non-Christian religions, Vatican website, October 28, 1965, http://www.vatican.va/archive/hist_councils/ii_vatican_council/documents/vat-ii_decl_19651028_nostra-aetate_en.html.

25. C. S. Lewis, *The Last Battle* (New York: HarperCollins, 2002), 40.

26. Ibid., 205.

27. Ibid., 202.

28. Ibid., 141.

29. Ibid., 205.

30. *The Holy Qur'an*, trans. Abdullah Yusuf Ali (Ware: Wordworth Editions Limited, 2000).

31. Pope Paul VI, *Nostra Aetate.*

32. *Catechism of the Catholic Church*, 841, http://www.vatican.va/archive/ccc_css/archive/catechism/p123a9p3.htm.

33. Ibid., 847, http://www.vatican.va/archive/ccc_css/archive/catechism/p123a9p3.htm.

34. Rolheiser, "Our Muslim brothers and sisters."

35. Benedict XVI, *Light of the World: The Pope, the Church, and the Signs of the Times: A Conversation with Peter Seewald* (San Francisco: Ignatius, 2010), 100.

36. Ibid., 100–1.

37. Ralph Sidway, "The Same God Question (Part 2)," Jihad Watch, January 31, 2016, https://www.jihadwatch.org/2016/01/the-same-god-question-part-2.

38. Ibid.
39. Joel Richardson, *The Islamic Antichrist: The Shocking Truth about the Real Nature of the Beast* (Los Angeles: WND Books, 2009), 108.
40. I. Ishaq, *The Life of Muhammad*, trans. A. Guillaume (Oxford: Oxford University Press, 2002), 464.
41. Warner, *A Self Study Course on Political Islam-Level 1-CD, Levels 2 & 3*, 41.
42. Pope Paul VI, *Nostra Aetate.*
43. Raymond Ibrahim, "Bloody Weekend: Trend of Muslim Rage against 'Infidels' Continues," The Blaze, September 25, 2013, http://www. theblaze.com/contributions/bloody-weekend-continues-trend-of-muslim-rage-against-infidels/.
44. Ibrahim, "'Are you Muslim or Christian? Death to Christians!'" Raymond Irbrahim.com, April 3, 2015, http://www.raymondibrahim. com/2015/04/03/are-you-muslim-or-christian-death-to-christians/.
45. Ibid.
46. Ibrahim, "Nigeria: Where Jihad and Christian Persecution Run Rampant," RaymondIbrahim.com, October 1, 2013, http://www. raymondibrahim.com/2013/10/01/nigeria-where-jihad-and-christian-persecution-run-rampant/.
47. Coughlin, *Catastrophic Failure*, 511–574.
48. USCCB, "Dialogue With Muslims Committee Statement," http://usccb. org/beliefs-and-teachings/ecumenical-and-interreligious/ interreligious/islam/dialogue-with-muslims-committee-statement.cfm.
49. General S. K. Malik, quoted in Coughlin, *Catastrophic Failure*, 135.

Chapter 10: Strategies for Victory

1. "How to Defeat the Jihad," *FrontPage Magazine*, May 27, 2016, http:// www.frontpagemag.com/fpm/262969/how-defeat-jihad-frontpagemag-com.
2. Jennifer Rosenberg, "Rwandan Genocide," About Education, updated February 4, 2016, http://history1900s.about.com/od/ rwandangenocide/a/Rwanda-Genocide.htm.
3. Richard Spillett, "Convert Who Protested outside Parliament over Syrian Airstrikes with Poster Saying, 'I Am a Muslim…Do You Trust Me Enough for a Hug?' Now Faces Jail for Threatening to Bomb MP's House," *Daily Mail*, December 7, 2015, http://www.dailymail.co.uk/ news/article-3349803/Muslim-convert-faces-jail-threatening-bomb-MP-s-house.html.

4.   Jennifer Rosenberg, "Rwandan Genocide."

5.   Robert Spencer, "100,000 Attend Funeral of Killer of Blasphemy Law Foe," Jihad Watch, March 1, 2016, https://www.jihadwatch.org/2016/03/pakistan-100000-attend-funeral-of-killer-of-blasphemy-laws-foe.

6.   Mubasher Bukhari, "Pakistan Religious Groups Say Law Protecting Women from Abuse 'Un-Islamic,'" Reuters, March 15, 2016, https://www.jihadwatch.org/2016/03/pakistan-100000-attend-funeral-of-killer-of-blasphemy-laws-foe.

7.   Robert Spencer, "Nigeria: Senate Rejects Gender Equality Bill, Muslim Senators Say It Violates Sharia," Jihad Watch, March 15, 2016, https://www.jihadwatch.org/2016/03/nigeria-senate-rejects-gender-equality-bill-muslim-senators-say-it-violates-sharia.

8.   Steven Erlanger, "Blaming Policy, Not Islam, for Belgium's Radicalized Youth," *New York Times*, April 7, 2016, http://mobile.nytimes.com/2016/04/08/world/europe/belgium-brussels-islam-radicalization.html?mabReward=CTM&_r=3&referer=http://www.breitbart.com/london/2016/04/11/majority-of-muslim-students-think-brussels-terrorists-are-heroes-say-teachers/.

9.   "Poll: Two-Thirds of British Muslims Wouldn't Tip Off Police on Terrorism," Haaretz, April 11, 2016, http://www.haaretz.com/world-news/europe/1.713917.

10. James V. Schall, "The Shootings in San Bernardino: Another View," *Catholic World Report*, December 6, 2015, http://www.catholicworldreport.com/Item/4421/the_shootings_in_san_bernardino_another_view.aspx.

11. Robert Spencer, "Study Claims Right-Wing Extremists Bigger Threat to US Than Jihadis," Jihad Watch, June 24, 2015, https://www.jihadwatch.org/2015/06/study-claims-right-wing-extremists-bigger-threat-to-us-than-jihadis.

12. Danios, "All Terrorists Are Muslims…Except the 94% That Aren't," Loon Watch, January 20, 2010, http://www.loonwatch.com/2010/01/not-all-terrorists-are-muslims/.

13. Spencer, "Study Claims"; Michael McGrady, "Prof DEBUNKS Study Claiming Right-Wing Extremists in U.S. More Deadly Than Islamic Terrorists," College Fix, January 18, 2016, http://www.thecollegefix.com/post/25885/; Ian Tuttle, "Are All Terrorists Muslims?" *National Review*, January 14, 2015, http://www.nationalreview.com/article/396400/are-all-terrorists-muslims-ian-tuttle; "The Myth of the

Non-Muslim Terrorist," TheReligionofPeace.com, https://www.thereligionofpeace.com/pages/articles/loonwatch-94-percent.aspx.

14. Ibid.

15. Tuttle, "Are All Terrorists Muslims?"

16. "Islamic Terrorists Have Carried Out More Than 28420 Deadly Terror Attacks since 9/11," TheReligionofPeace.com, www.religionofpeace.com.

17. Schall, "The Shootings in San Bernardino: Another View."

18. Raymond Ibrahim, *Crucified Again: Exposing Islam's New War on Christians* (Washington, D.C.: Regnery, 2013), 10.

19. Ibid., 13.

20. *FrontPage Magazine*, "How to defeat the Jihad."

21. Victor Davis Hanson, *An Autumn of War: What America Learned from September 11 and the War on Terrorism* (New York: Anchor, 2007), 158.

22. Dan Bloom, "Marched to Their Deaths: Sickening ISIS Slaughter Continues As 250 Soldiers Captured at Syrian Airbase Are Stripped Then Led to Desert for Mass Execution," *Daily Mail*, August 28, 2014, http://www.dailymail.co.uk/news/article-2736764/Marched-deaths-Sickening-ISIS-slaughter-continues-250-soldiers-captured-Syrian-airbase-stripped-led-desert-mass-execution.html.

23. Chesterton, *The Flying Inn*, 296.

24. Tom Shanker and Helene Cooper, "Pentagon plans to shrink Army to pre-World War II level," *New York Times*, February 23, 2014, http://www.nytimes.com/2014/02/24/us/politics/pentagon-plans-to-shrink-army-to-pre-world-war-ii-level.html; "Fact: Our Navy is smaller than it was in 1917," ThinkProgress, October 22, 2012, http://thinkprogress.org/lbupdate/1067951/fact-our-navy-is-smaller-than-it-was-in-1917/.

25. F. Michael Maloof, "Top Generals: Obama Is 'Purging the Military,'" WND, October 21, 2013, http://www.wnd.com/2013/10/top-generals-obama-is-purging-the-military/.

26. Sebastian Gorka, *Defeating Jihad: The Winnable War* (Washington, D.C.: Regnery, 2016), 140–44.

27. Daniel Greenfield, "Our Good Islam/Bad Islam Strategy" *FrontPage Magazine*, February 11, 2016, http://www.frontpagemag.com/fpm/261771/our-good-islambad-islam-strategy-daniel-greenfield.

28. Ibid.

29. Raymond Ibrahim, "How Nazism explains 'moderate' and 'radical' Islam," Raymond Ibrahim.com, August 16, 2015, http://www.raymondibrahim.com/2015/08/16/how-nazism-explains-moderate-and-radical-islam/.

30. Greenfield, "Our Good Islam/Bad Islam Strategy."

31. Moorthy S. Muthuswamy, *Defeating Political Islam: The New Cold War* (Amherst: Prometheus Books, 2009), 205.

32. Greenfield, "Our Good Islam/Bad Islam Strategy."

33. Amir Handjani, "To Save Iraq, the U.S. Military Must Work with Iran's Revolutionary Guard," Reuters, June 5, 2015, http://blogs.reuters.com/great-debate/2015/06/05/to-save-iraq-the-u-s-military-must-work-with-irans-revolutionary-guard/.

34. Robert Spencer, *The Complete Infidel's Guide to Iran* (Washington, D.C.: Regnery, 2016), 104.

35. Anthony H. Cordesman, "Iran, Missiles, and Nuclear Weapons," Center for Strategic and International Studies, December 9, 2015, https://www.csis.org/analysis/iran-missiles-and-nuclear-weapons.

36. Spencer, *The Complete Infidel's Guide to Iran*, 131.

37. Van Hipp, *The New Terrorism: How to Fight and Defeat it* (Bloomfield Hills: Countinghouse Press, 2015), 160, 162.

38. Spencer, *The Complete Infidel's Guide to Iran*, 218, 229–31.

39. Denis MacEoin, "What the White House Might Not See about Iran," Gatestone Institute, March 10, 2015, http://www.gatestoneinstitute.org/5359/iran-nuclear-theology.

40. Joe Cirincione, "The Risk of a Nuclear ISIS Grows," Huffington Post, October 7, 2015, http://www.huffingtonpost.com/joe-cirincione/the-risk-of-a-nuclear-isi_b_8259978.html.

41. "Obama: According to Iran's Supreme Leader, 'It Would Be Contrary to Their Faith to Obtain a Nuclear Weapon,'" Townhall, Feburary 9, 2015, http://townhall.com/news/around-the-web/2015/02/09/obama-according-to-irans-supreme-leader-it-would-be-contrary-to-their-faith-to-obtain-a-nuclear-weapon-n1955031.

42. Yousaf Butt, "How Saudi Wahhabism Is the Fountainhead of Islamic Terrorism," Huffington Post, March 22, 2015, http://www.huffingtonpost.com/dr-yousaf-butt-/saudi-wahhabism-islam-terrorism_b_6501916.html.

43. Hipp, *The New Terrorism*, 74.

44. Muthuswamy, *Defeating Political Islam*, 195.

45. Spencer, *The Complete Infidel's Guide to Iran*, 24–26; Saeed Kamali Dehghan, "Iran Capitalises on Sanctions Removal with Slew of Deals with Western Businesses," The *Guardian*, January 18, 2016, http://www.theguardian.com/world/2016/jan/18/iran-capitalises-on-sanctions-removal-with-slew-of-deals-with-western-businesses.

46. Christine Williams, "Warning to the West: Jihad groups acquiring Cyber capability to bring major cities to standstill," Jihad Watch, June 9, 2016, https://www.jihadwatch.org/2016/06/warning-to-the-west-jihad-groups-acquiring-cyber-capability-to-bring-major-cities-to-a-standstill.

47. Spencer, *The Complete Infidel's Guide to Iran*, 129–30.

48. Spencer, *The Complete Infidel's Guide to ISIS*, 69–71.

49. See Robert Spencer, "Facebook Removes SIOA Page, Reddit Bans Users Who Say Orlando Jihad Was Muslim," June 12, 2016, https://www.jihadwatch.org/2016/06/facebook-removes-sioa-page.

50. Oliver Darcy, "This Is Why Most Military Personnel Aren't Armed on Military Bases—and It's Not Clinton's Fault," The Blaze, September 17, 2013, http://www.theblaze.com/stories/2013/09/17/this-is-why-most-military-personnel-are-disarmed-on-military-bases-and-its-not-clintons-fault/.

51. Hipp, *The New Terrorism*, 59.

52. Geert Wilders, "Muslims, free yourself and leave Islam!" Gates of Vienna, June 4, 2016, http://gatesofvienna.net/2016/06/geert-wilders-muslims-free-yourselves-and-leave-islam/.

53. Raymond Ibrahim, "Lessons on the Long Road to Hijab," RaymondIbrahim.com, December 28, 2011, http://www.raymondibrahim.com/2011/12/28/lessons-on-the-long-road-to-hijab/.

54. Ibrahim, *Crucified Again*, 10; and Ali A. Allawi, "Islamic Civilization in Peril," *Chronicle of Higher Education*, June 29, 2009, http://chronicle.com/article/Islamic-Civilization-in-Peril/46964/.

Chapter 11: Psychological, Spiritual, and Ideological Warfare

1. John O'Sullivan, *The President, the Pope, And the Prime Minister: Three Who Changed the World* (Washington, D.C.: Regnery, 2006), 1–32.

2. Graeme Wood, "What ISIS really wants," *The Atlantic*, March 2015 issue, http://www.theatlantic.com/magazine/archive/2015/03/what-isis-really-wants/384980/.

3. Gorka, *Defeating Jihad: The Winnable War*, 140–44.

4. Kilpatrick, *Christianity, Islam, and Atheism*, 211.

5. Kerry Picket, "Did FBI training material purge cause agency to drop the ball on Orlando shooter?" The Daily Caller, June 12, 2016, http://dailycaller.com/2016/06/12/did-fbi-training-material-purge-cause-agency-to-drop-the-ball-on-orlando-shooter/.

6. Mark Steyn, "This Youth Movement Has Women Covered," *Orange County Register*, August 21, 2013, http://www.ocregister.com/articles/young-363612-muslim-world.html; see also "Iran in the 1970s before the Islamic Revolution," *Orange County Register*, April 15, 2009, F30; and Andrew Bolt, "The Veil Falls on Cairo," *Herald Sun* (Melbourne), February 16, 2011, http://blogs.news.com.au/heraldsun/andrewbolt/index.php/heraldsun/comments/the_veil_falls_on_cairo.

7. Ibrahim, *Crucified Again: Exposing Islam's New War on Christians*, 10.

8. See for example, Gorka, *Defeating Jihad*; see also, Walid Phares, *The War of Ideas: Jihadism against Democracy* (New York: Palgrave MacMillan, 2007).

9. Bill Warner, *A Self-Study Course on Political Islam, Level 2* (CSPI Publishing, 2011), 40–41.

10. "Mohammed and Mohammedanism," *New Advent Encyclopedia*, http://www.newadvent.org/cathen/10424a.htm.

11. "FBI 'never guessed' gay club would be target of jihad attacks," Jihad Watch, June 13, 2016, https://www.jihadwatch.org/2016/06/fbi-never-guessed-gay-club-would-be-target-of-jihad-attack.

12. Robert Spencer, "Did Muhammad Exist?" *Crisis Magazine*, April 26, 2012, http://www.crisismagazine.com/2012/did-muhammad-exist.

13. "A New Koran," *FrontPage Magazine*, April 18, 2008, http://archive.frontpagemag.com/readArticle.aspx?ARTID=30658.

14. See, for example, Joseph Fadelle, *The Price to Pay: A Muslim Risks All to Follow Christ* (San Francisco: Ignatius, 2012), 33–36; see also, "Rising number of Muslims reporting dreams about Jesus," WND, November 1, 2014, http://www.wnd.com/2014/11/rising-number-of-muslims-reporting-dreams-about-jesus/#!.

15. Spencer, *The Complete Infidel's Guide to the Koran*, 149–150.

16. Mark Gollom and Tracey Lindeman, "Who is Martin Couture-Rouleau?" *CBC News*, October 21, 2014, http://www.cbc.ca/news/canada/who-is-martin-couture-rouleau-1.2807285.

17. Robert Spencer, "Facebook page of Canadian Muslim who ran down soldiers full of Qur'an quotes, support for jihad," Jihad Watch, October 20, 2014, https://www.jihadwatch.org/2014/10/facebook-page-of-canadian-muslim-who-ran-down-soldiers-full-of-quran-quotes-support-for-jihad.

18. Ibid.

19. Robert Spencer, "Chattanooga Jihad Murderer Wrote in Diary about 'Becoming a martyr,'" Jihad Watch, July 20, 2015, https://www.jihadwatch.org/2015/07/chattanooga-jihad-murderer-wrote-in-diary-about-becoming-a-martyr.

20. Ibid.

21. Fr.John,"More Imams Convert To Christ," *Journey to Orthodoxy*, April 13, 2013, http://journeytoorthodoxy.com/2013/04/more-imams-convert-to-christ/.

22. Raymond Ibrahim, "Father Zakaria Botros on 'The perverse sexual habits of the Prophet,'" Jihad Watch, January 12, 2009, https://www.jihadwatch.org/2009/01/father-zakaria-botros-on-the-perverse-sexual-habits-of-the-prophet.

23. Raymond Ibrahim, "Islam's 'Public Enemy #1,'" *National Review*, March 25, 2008, http://www.nationalreview.com/article/223965/islams-public-enemy-1-raymond-ibrahim.

24. David Wood, "Answering Muslims," http://www.answeringmuslims.com/.

25. Emmett Scott, *Mohammed and Charlemagne Revisited: The History of a Controversy* (London: New English Review, 2012), 68–85. See also Dario Fernandez-Morera, *The Myth of the Andalusian Paradise* (Wilmington: ISI Books, 2016).

26. See Fred Fleitz, "Shutdown of Anti-Jihadist Network Sun News a Big Loss for Canada and the World,"Breitbart, March 12, 2015, http://www.breitbart.com/national-security/2015/03/12/shutdown-of-anti-jihadist-network-sun-news-a-big-loss-for-canada-and-the-world/.

27. See "Bill O'Reilly: Is Islam a Destructive Force in the World?," Fox News, October 6, 2014, http://www.foxnews.com/transcript/2014/10/07/bill-oreilly-islam-destructive-force-world/.

28. See "Hannity: Radical Islam in America: Is Islam Truly a Religion of Peace?," Fox News, October 13, 2014, http://www.foxnews.com/transcript/2014/10/13/radical-islam-america-islam-truly-religion-peace/.

29. See "CAIR Rep Debates Fox's Megyn Kelly on Separating ISIS Violence from Islam," YouTube video, posted by "I Hooper," September 11, 2014, https://www.youtube.com/watch?v=wn2BmiXUVKY.

30. "Judge Jeanine Pirro: We Need to Kill Them! Jan 10, 2015," YouTube video, posted by "WesternFreePress," January 10, 2015, https://www.youtube.com/watch?v=0w2ZS231BAQ.

31. Wilders, "Muslims, Free Yourself and Leave Islam!"
32. Muthuswamy, *Defeating Political Islam*, 195.
33. Steyn, *America Alone: The End of the World as We Know It*, 96.

Index

A

Abdeslam, Salah, 93
Abdulazeez, Muhammad Youssuf, 154, 157, 244
Abdulmutallab, Umar Farouk, 15
Abedin, Huma, 107
Abraham, Abrahamic, 52, 177, 185, 192, 197, 201
Adebolajo, Michael, 31, 170
adolescence, 160, 163
Afghanistan, 29, 70, 77, 82, 89, 105, 111, 142, 205, 214
Ahmad, Omar, 85
Ahmadiyya community, 46
al-Awlaki, Anwar, 34, 105–6
al-Baghdadi, Abu Bakr, 31–34, 108
al-Husseini, Haj Amin, 129
Allah, 2, 6, 15–16, 24, 30, 32–33, 41–45, 47, 50, 53, 55–56, 71, 78, 142, 147, 165, 173, 188–89, 191–92, 196, 198, 210–11, 221, 226, 234, 237, 243–45
"Allahu akbar," 4, 22, 31, 124, 171

Allawi, Ali A., 58, 227
al-Qaradawi, Sheik Yusuf, 54, 127
Al-Shabaab, 1, 142
Alwaleed bin Talal Center, 179
al-Wazzan, Raied, 143
American-Muslim Task Force, 85
American Sniper, 159, 164
Angelus, 23
Answering Muslims, 245
anti-Semitism, 29, 124, 126–27, 129–30
appeasement, 3, 21, 139, 143, 154, 181, 201, 212, 230, 235
Arab Spring, 16, 214
Army, 22–23, 104–6, 108, 112, 153–54, 205, 217, 224, 226
Atta, Mohamed, 64–65
Azzam, Abdullah, 34

B

"baby jihad," 8, 115, 130, 132, 139
Banu Qurayza tribe, 40

barbarism, 13–14

Basseley, Nakoula, 151

Battle of Vienna, 58

"beating etiquette," 11

beheadings, 2–3, 14, 27, 37, 40, 91, 133, 141, 198, 215, 220, 226

Benedict XVI, 194

Beres, Louis René, 64

Bhatti, Shabaz, 67

bin Laden, Osama, 27, 31–34, 58, 63, 195, 215, 219–20

Birmingham, England, 7, 89, 122, 124–25, 132, 134

Black Flags from Rome, 6

Blair, Tony, 27–28, 89

Boko Haram, 1, 3, 13, 25, 40, 54, 130, 142, 229

Bostom, Andrew, 72

Boston Marathon, 13, 15, 24, 31, 35, 61–62, 101, 106, 170

Botros, Zakaria, 245–46

Boubakeur, Dali, 77

Boumedienne, Houari, 116, 130

Brennan, John, 107, 111

Brown, Molly, 69

Brunne, Eva, 178

Brussels, 13, 17, 62, 74, 93, 100, 120, 134–36, 210, 213

Bukhari, 40–41, 65

Bush, George W., 3, 30, 85

C

caliphate, 142, 209, 211, 227

caliphs, 32, 34, 73, 126, 138, 213

Cameron, David, 31, 35, 153, 155, 170

Camerota, Alisyn, 66

Carlyle, Thomas, 49

Catastrophic Failure, 109, 201

Catholics, 36, 66, 74, 77, 80–81, 86, 113, 166, 179, 182–84, 193, 211

Center for American Progress, 21, 168

Center for the Study of Political Islam, 46, 239

Central Intelligence Agency (CIA), 106–9, 111

Charlie Hebdo, 24, 66, 92, 97, 124, 163, 246

Chattanooga, TN, 15, 154, 157, 244

Chesterton, G. K., 137, 139, 146–47, 177, 185, 217

Choudary, Anjem, 56

"Chrislam," 177–79, 181, 190

Christianity, Islam, and Atheism, 50, 64, 149, 230

Christians, 2, 6, 13, 15, 24–25, 35, 42, 48, 50, 54, 57, 64–65, 67, 70, 72–74, 76–78, 80, 86, 93, 99, 115, 119, 130, 132, 143–45, 147–48, 158, 167, 171–72, 177–78, 180–94, 197–201, 214, 219, 221–22, 225, 240–42, 244

"Cleaver of Vertebrae," 42

Clinton, Hillary, 107, 151–52

"Clock Boy, the," 89, 101–2

Cold War, 28, 229, 235, 246

Cologne, Germany, 24, 75, 120, 148–50

communism, 28, 180, 194, 229–30, 235–36, 246–47

Communist Party U.S.A., 81

Condell, Pat, 121, 134
Congress, 103, 107–9, 222
Cook, M., 49
Coughlin, Stephen, 105–6, 109–13, 201
Coulibaly, Amed, 92
Council on American-Islamic Relations (CAIR), 3, 61, 85, 93–95, 100, 102–4, 110, 153, 186, 218
Couture-Rouleau, Martin, 241, 242–43
Crone, P., 49
Cruel and Usual Punishment, 81
culture, 2, 5, 7, 23, 76, 79–80, 83–85, 90, 92, 96, 111, 113, 115–16, 125, 127–28, 131, 133–41, 146–49, 153–55, 158–65, 180–81, 185, 201, 208–9, 231, 243–45, 248

D

Daily Mail, 90, 207
dar al-harb, 54, 119
dar al-Islam, 54
Darwish, Nonie, 61, 81, 83–84, 133–34
Dearborn, MI, 164, 166–67
Defenders of Islam Inc., 67
Defense Department, 23
Department of Justice, 108, 111
dhimmi, dhimmitude, 7–8, 72–73, 75, 78–79, 85, 214
dialogue, 6, 19, 48, 67, 98, 113, 177, 186, 189, 201–2, 230
Dolan, Timothy, 80
D'Souza, Dinesh, 81

E

Eastern Michigan University, 165
education, 61, 63–64, 70, 84, 90, 111, 129, 137, 153, 159, 183
Egypt, Egyptians, 36–37, 57–58, 61, 67, 83, 93, 108, 122, 152–53, 163, 180, 206, 214, 216, 223–24, 227, 232
Egyptian TV, 11,
el-Sisi, Abdel Fatah, 224
Emerson, Steve, 122–24
Erdogan, Recep Tayyip, 100, 147, 163, 168
Europe, Europeans, 7, 15, 17–19, 24–25, 29, 53, 62, 68, 70, 75–76, 78–79, 84, 89–90, 92–94, 96, 115–28, 130–38, 145, 147–48, 150, 158, 160, 174, 180–81, 194, 200, 206, 208, 214, 229–30, 247–48
extremists, 3, 5–6, 27, 39, 71, 98, 150, 210–11, 219–20, 223

F

Facebook, 144, 241–44
faith, 3–6, 20, 36–38, 43, 45, 52–53, 57–59, 62, 74, 77–78, 81, 86, 112–13, 125, 131, 136–37, 140, 174, 177–79, 182, 185–86, 191–97, 200–2, 206, 209, 213, 219, 223, 226–27, 229, 232, 235, 237, 242, 247–48
Faith Matters, 20
Fallaci, Oriana, 17
family, 8, 24–25, 38, 58, 81, 91, 102–3, 122, 134–35, 145, 157, 162–63, 180, 183, 192, 194

Fear Inc. The Roots of the Islamophobia Network in America, 21
Federal Bureau of Investigation (FBI), 20, 23, 106, 108, 111, 153, 171, 173, 218, 223, 232, 236
Fiqh Council of North America, 94
First Things, 80
Fitzgerald, Michael, 179
"Five Pillars of Islam," 4, 39, 54, 236
"flying imams," 102–3
Flying Inn, The, 146, 177, 185
Force of Reason, The, 17
foreign aid, 142, 223–24
Fort Dix Army Base, 22
Fort Hood, 15, 22, 24, 31, 167, 170, 173, 226
France, 18, 77–78, 120, 122–24, 131–32, 155, 171–72, 220
FrontPage Magazine, 218
fundamentalists, 6, 214

G

Gaddafi, Muammar, 57
Gardzinski, Matthew, 120–21
"gates of *ijtihad*," 46
Gatestone Institute, 64, 119, 123
Gaubatz, David, 93–94
Geller, Pamela, 22, 66–69, 71
George, Robert, 80–81, 83–85, 184
Georgetown University, 65, 168, 179
Germany, 18, 29, 121–22, 126, 128–30, 150, 206, 215
Gibbons, Gillian, 165–66

Gorka, Sebastian, 218, 231
Gramsci, Antoni, 90
Greenfield, Daniel, 218–20, 226

H

hadith, 28, 44, 54, 62, 65, 195, 237
Hagarism: The Making of the Muslim World, 49
Hamas, 156, 225
Hamza, Mujaahid Abu, 31, 47, 170
Hanson, Victor Davis, 163, 215
Hasan, Nidal, 22, 24, 106, 154, 167, 173
Hedegaard, Lars, 18
Hemingway, Ernest, 7
Hezbollah, 63, 225
hijra, 116, 122, 130, 139, 180
Hirsi Ali, Ayaan, 69, 83, 133
Hitchens, Peter, 118, 125, 200
Hollobone, Philip, 76
Holy Land Foundation Trial, 94
Holy Trinity Catholic Church, 181–83
honor killings, 141, 200
Hooper, Ibrahim, 186–87
Hope Not Hate, 20
Human Rights Commission, 144, 148
Hussein, 57

I

ibn al-Rabi, Kinana, 40
ibn al-Rabi, Safiya, 41
Ibn Ishaq, 40–41, 47, 226
Ibn Kathir, 65

Ibn Majah, 65

Ibn Warraq, 52

Ibrahim, Raymond, 130, 132, 198–99, 214, 219, 227, 233

ideology, 27–28, 53, 69, 81, 96, 98, 109, 126, 140, 161, 205, 213, 215, 219, 223–24, 226, 229–31, 235–36

imams, 4, 15, 67, 99, 102–3, 105–6, 178, 210, 222, 227, 237

immigration, 7, 22, 24, 115–20, 125–26, 130–31, 134, 150, 158, 181, 225

Iran, Iranians, 15, 34, 57–58, 71, 73, 75, 77, 82, 84, 86, 140, 152, 163, 214, 220–24, 232

Iranian Parliament, 84,

Iranian Revolution, 16, 34, 161,

Iraq, 2, 14, 57–58, 73, 77, 108, 119, 130, 180, 201, 205, 214, 220–21

Iraqi War, 29

Isa, 240–41

Isfenani, Mohammad Ali, 84

ISIS, 1–4, 6, 12–15, 25, 32, 34–35, 37–38, 40–41, 54, 56, 58, 63, 65, 77, 93, 95, 99, 108, 119, 133, 180, 209, 211, 213–16, 220–23, 225, 229

Islam, 1–6, 8, 16–18, 20–23, 27–40, 42–48, 50, 52–59, 61–62, 64–69, 71–74, 76–81, 84–86, 89, 92–95, 97, 99–100, 102, 104–14, 116, 128, 131, 135–40, 142–49, 151–53, 157, 159, 161–65, 168–70, 172–75, 177–87, 189–90, 192–201, 207–9, 211–14, 217–27, 229–42, 244–48

Islamic Circle of North America (ICNA), 94

Islamic Society of North America (ISNA), 3, 94, 105, 110, 153, 201

Islamophobia, 2, 5–6, 19, 20–23, 77, 97, 101–3, 106, 108, 117, 121, 137, 149, 156, 168, 179, 201

"Islamophobia-phobia," 19–20, 23

J

Jack Ryan: Shadow Recruit, 166

Japan, Japanese, 15, 205–6, 215, 233

Jesus Christ, 39, 42, 177, 181–83, 185–93, 195–98, 209, 219, 222, 237, 239–43, 245

Jewish Foundation of Islam, The, 48

Jews, 40, 48, 74, 77–78, 116, 118, 122, 124, 127–28, 130, 135, 197, 219, 225, 240

jihad, jihadists, 1–8, 11, 13–15, 17–25, 28–33, 35–37, 39–40, 44–47, 54–59, 61–66, 68, 71, 80, 89–109, 112, 114–15, 122, 130, 132, 138–39, 142–43, 148, 150, 154–57, 159, 165, 169–75, 178–81, 184–86, 201–2, 205–6, 209, 213, 215–18, 220–26, 229, 232–34, 237–38, 241, 244–45, 248

Jihad Watch, 68

jizya tax, 55, 59, 71–73, 75, 214

John Paul II, 194, 229–30

Jones, E. Michael, 80–81

K

Kahn, Majid, 76

Kern, Soeren, 119, 123–24

Kerry, John, 155, 163

Khomeini, Ayatollah Ruhollah, 34, 58, 84

Koran, 4, 28, 30, 33, 39–55, 59, 62, 64–65, 71–73, 85–86, 93, 102, 113, 170–71, 173–74, 177, 179, 182, 185,

187–96, 216, 226, 233–35, 237–41, 245

Kouachi, Cherif, 92

Kramer, Jane, 82

Kreeft, Peter, 80–81, 185

Krueger, Alan, 63

L

Last Battle, The, 190

Legal Affairs Committee, 84

Lewis, C. S., 190

Loewen, Terry Lee, 44, 173–74

Londonistan, 153

L'Osservatore Romano, 66

M

MacEoin, Denis, 222–23

Mahdi, 215, 222

Malechova, Jitka, 63

marriage, 40–41, 48, 78, 84, 133–35, 157–58, 164, 200

Massignon, Louis, 52

Mateen, Omar, 232, 244

McClatchy DC, 70

McConnell, James, 143–45

Mecca, 45, 102, 116, 178, 183

media, 2–5, 16, 18, 38, 61, 63, 68, 78, 90, 93, 98, 100–2, 104, 117, 119, 123–24, 154, 157–59, 169–70, 172–75, 225, 234, 240

Medical News Today, 64

Medina, 45–46, 116

Mehsud, Baitullah, 45

Meotti, Giulio, 78

Middle East and North Africa (MENA), 127–28

military, 8, 15, 89, 95, 104–5, 109, 111–13, 158, 207, 212–15, 217, 224–26, 229

Miniter, Rich, 206, 215

Mohamed, Ahmed, 101–4

"Mohammedanism," 43

Mosque of Jesus, Son of Mary, 181–83

Mosul, 12, 144

Muhammad, 3–4, 7, 15, 28, 39–44, 46–47, 51, 54–57, 59, 65–67, 69–71, 85, 115–16, 147, 151, 154, 157, 165, 178, 183, 187–90, 192, 195–98, 207, 209, 213, 226, 229, 233–34, 236–39, 242, 245–46

Muhammad Art Exhibit, 66, 70–71

multiculturism, 2, 20, 96, 130, 140–41, 154, 161, 184

Muslim American Society (MAS), 3, 110

Muslim Brotherhood, 3–4, 11, 16, 21, 58, 86, 93–94, 98, 105, 107–13, 152–53, 156, 163, 177, 201, 223, 227, 232

Muslim Mafia, 93–94

Muslims, 3, 6, 15, 18, 21–25, 27, 30, 35–42, 44–48, 50, 52–58, 61–63, 65–67, 69–74, 77, 79–81, 84–86, 89, 92, 94–97, 99, 102, 105, 111, 113, 115–17, 119, 122–24, 126–33, 136–37, 139, 143, 146–50, 153, 155, 161, 166–70, 172, 174, 177, 179–80, 182–87, 189–90, 192–93, 195, 198–201, 205–6, 209–16, 218–22, 225–27, 229, 232–34, 238, 240, 245–47

Muslim Student Association, 34, 94, 107

Muthuswamy, Moorthy, 220, 223, 248

mutilation, 135, 141, 164, 171, 200

N

Nairobi Mall, 170

Nasser, 57, 227

National Bureau of Economics, 63

NATO, 137, 217

Navy, 73, 105, 140, 205, 217

Nazis, Nazism, 11, 15, 18, 28–29, 126, 128, 150, 166, 194, 206, 215, 219, 225, 233, 236

New York Police Department, 21

New York Times, 135, 210

19th Arrondissement Network, 92

niqab, 83

"no-go" zones, 17, 122–24, 129

Noldeke, Theodor, 49

Non-Stop, 167–68

Norris, Molly, 69

Nostra Aetate, 189, 192, 198

Nouri, Sheikh Fazlollah, 58

nuclear weapons, 8, 15, 220–21

O

Obama, Barack, 3, 35–36, 42, 85, 108, 151–53, 158, 163, 217, 223

Occam's razor, 33, 64

"occultation," 222

oil, 12, 161, 223

Omar, Mullah Mohammed, 34

Organization of Islamic Cooperation (OIC), 151, 168

Orlando, FL, 20, 179, 236, 244

Orwell, George, 20

P

Pact of Omar, 73

Paddington, 159, 163, 164–66

Paris, France, 13, 17, 24, 77, 82, 92–93, 100, 123–24, 134

Parolin, Pietro, 63, 65

Pearl Harbor, 11, 15

PEGIDA, 150

Pentagon, 5, 105, 109, 112

Pervez, Mohammed, 76

Phillips, Melanie, 153

pilgrims, pilgrimage, 39, 62, 183

Pilot's Wife, The, 166

police, 11–12, 14, 19, 21, 27, 30, 37, 92, 100–1, 103, 107–8, 119, 123–24, 133, 139, 145, 147–50, 154, 171, 205, 209–10, 241

political correctness, 2–3, 5, 20, 94–96, 99, 104–6, 117, 140, 150, 166, 185, 196, 224–25, 248

polygamy, 129, 133, 135, 141, 147

"pronouncing *takfir*," 56

Q

Qutb, Sayyid, 58

R

racism, 5, 19–20, 22, 97, 117, 126, 147, 154, 161

Rahman, Omar Abdel, 34

rape, 2, 17, 19–20, 24, 40, 75, 82, 118–21, 133–34, 141, 148, 178, 193, 238

Reclaim Australia, 156

refugees, 7, 116–22, 125–28, 158, 178, 180–81, 212

Reid, Richard, 15

relativism, 79, 140–41, 161, 184

Reliance of the Traveller, 36, 43, 45, 84

Ribadeau-Dumas, Monseigneur, 77

Rigby, Drummer Lee, 31, 35, 159, 170

Rolheiser, Ronald, 23–24, 179, 193

Rome, 6–7, 15, 18, 31, 72, 180

Rotherham, 19–20, 24, 120, 132–33

Rwanda genocide, 207

S

Said, Edward, 111, 113

San Bernardino, 15, 23, 31, 35

Saudi Arabia, 37, 63, 70, 73, 84, 95, 121, 145, 220, 223, 240

Schall, James, 65, 211

Seamen's Church, 178

Seattle Weekly, 69

secularism, 28, 58, 78, 80, 86, 184–85, 194

Seewald, Peter, 194–95

sensitivity, 52, 139, 162, 164

Shah, the, 57–59, 214

shahada, 4, 206

sharia, 12, 18, 36–37, 44, 59, 71–72, 79, 84–85, 90–91, 93, 129, 141–42, 195, 199–201, 207, 209, 214

shirk, 197

sira, 3, 44, 46, 62, 195

Somalia, 12, 83, 142, 206

Soros, George, 21

Southern Poverty Law Center, 5, 21, 68, 98

Sparta, Spartans, 208–9

Spencer, Robert, 20, 22, 30, 40, 45, 68, 71, 154, 221, 238, 244

Sperry, Paul, 93–94

"Stand With the Prophet," 66

Steyn, Mark, 6, 17–18, 104, 115, 117, 132, 144, 248

submission, 25, 27, 30, 71–74, 89, 92, 139, 180, 200,

Submission, 119–20

Sudan, 102, 165–66

Sultan, Wafa, 83, 133

Sum of All Fears, The, 159, 166

Sweden, 2, 17–18, 24, 54, 118, 120, 177–78, 208

Syracuse, NY, 181–82

Syria, Syrians, 2, 14, 73, 77, 83–84, 118–19, 121, 130, 167, 180, 201, 205, 207, 214, 216, 220–21

T

Talovic, Sulejmen, 171

"Tashlan," 190

Teausant, Nicholas, 174

teenagers, 131

Tell Mama, 20

tolerance, 28, 99, 139, 141, 154, 162, 178

Torrey, C. C., 48

Trifkovic, Serge, 82

Tsarnaev, Dzhokhar, 61, 154

Tsarnaev, Tamerlan, 61, 106, 154

Turkey, 11, 16, 119, 129, 147, 163, 217, 227

Turkish-Islamic Union for
Religious Affairs (DITIB), 129

U

umma, 59, 122, 155, 157, 162
United Arab Emirates, 94
University of Michigan, 159, 164,
166
University of Michigan at
Dearborn, 164
UN Security Council, 63
USCCB, 201
USS *Cole*, 29

V

Valls, Manuel, 80
"violent extremism," 1, 137, 230
virgins, 161, 187, 193, 213, 226, 235

W

Wallace, Craig, 207
war, 2, 20, 28–29, 45–47, 53–56,
61–62, 68, 71–72, 75–76, 79–80,
93, 96, 111–13, 119, 130, 137, 151,
165, 174–75, 184–85, 193–94, 199,
202, 205–6, 208–9, 213, 215–18,
224–25, 229–31, 233–36, 241, 248
Washington Post, 106–7
Watt, Montgomery, 52
Wenzel Strategies, 85
Wilders, Geert, 18, 68–69, 145, 227,
247
Wood, David, 245
World Hijab Day, 80
World Population Conference, 86

World Trade Center, 16, 29, 34, 167,
214, 224
World War II, 15, 28, 75, 128, 205–6,
217

X

xenophobia, 126

Z

Zakaria, Fareed, 35
Zakarneh, Ahmad, 30–31
Zaynab, 41